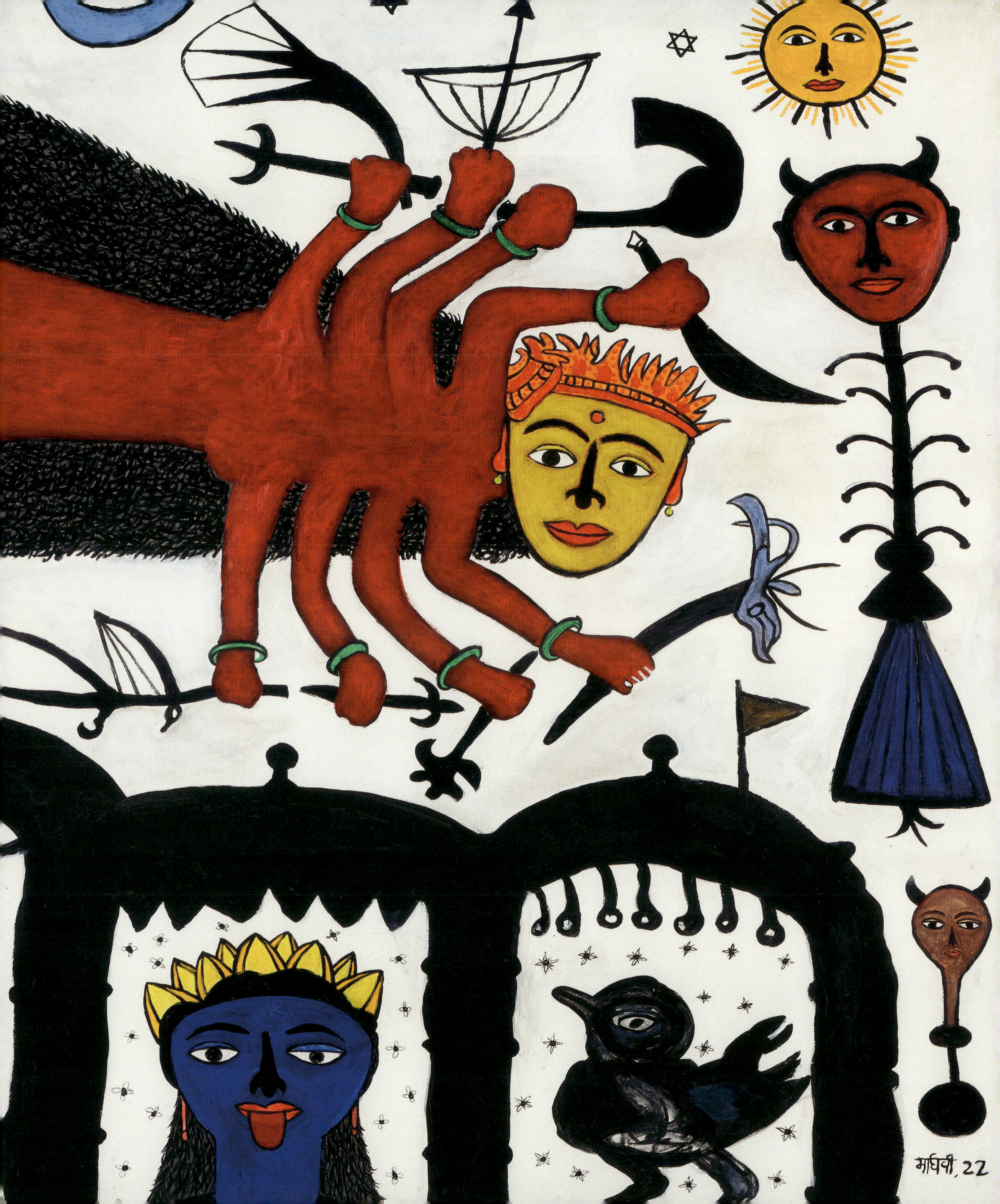
माधवी, 22

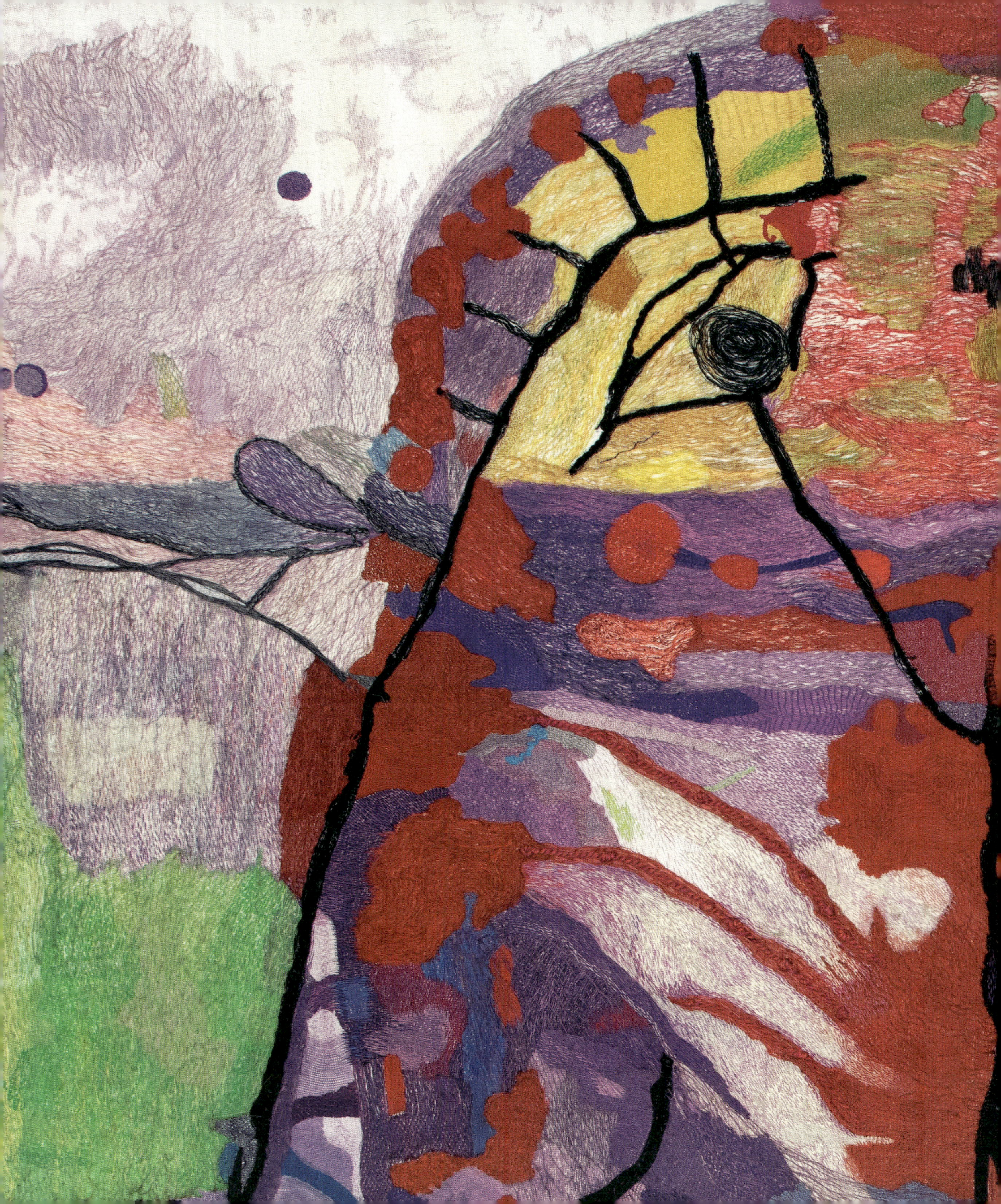

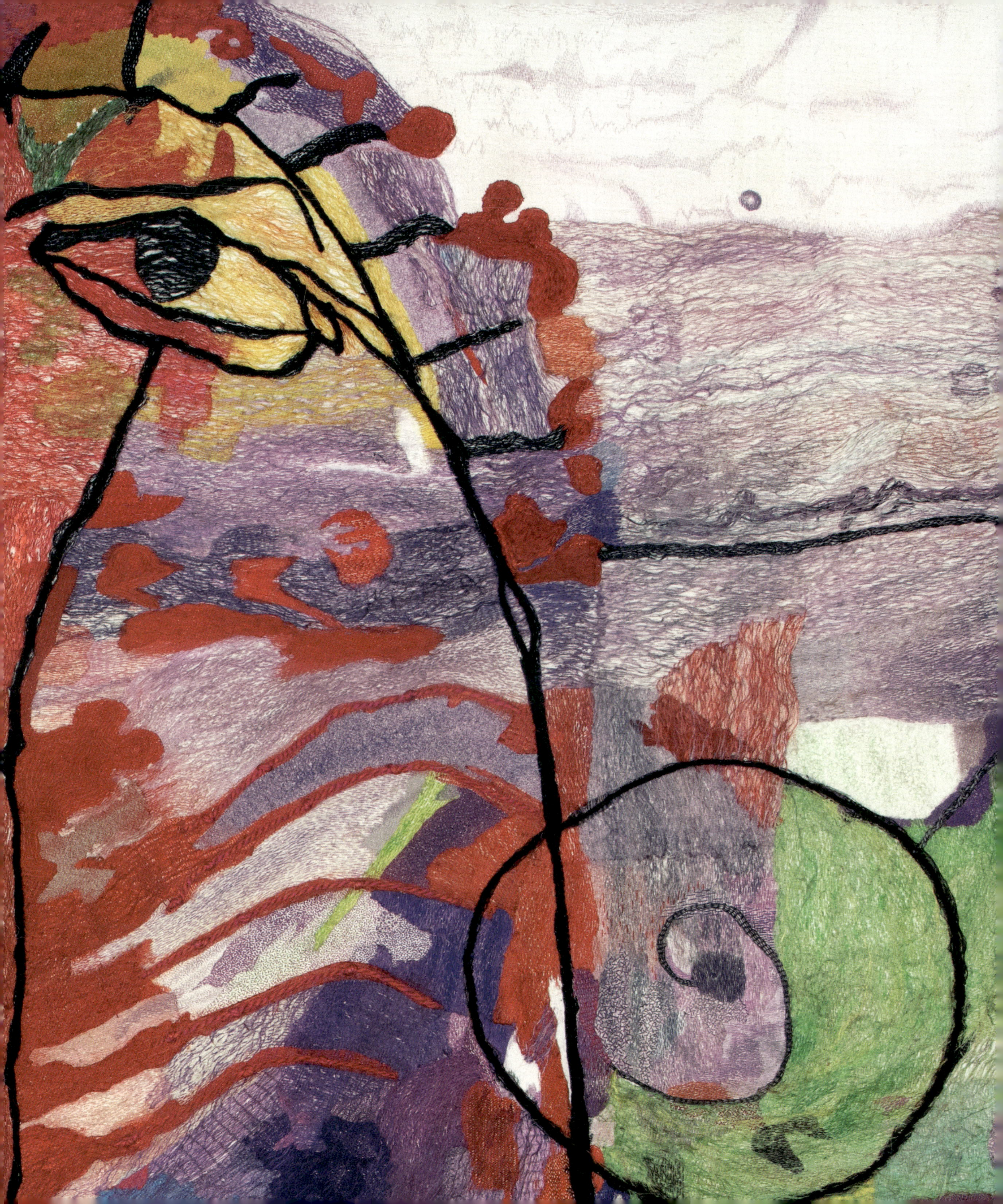

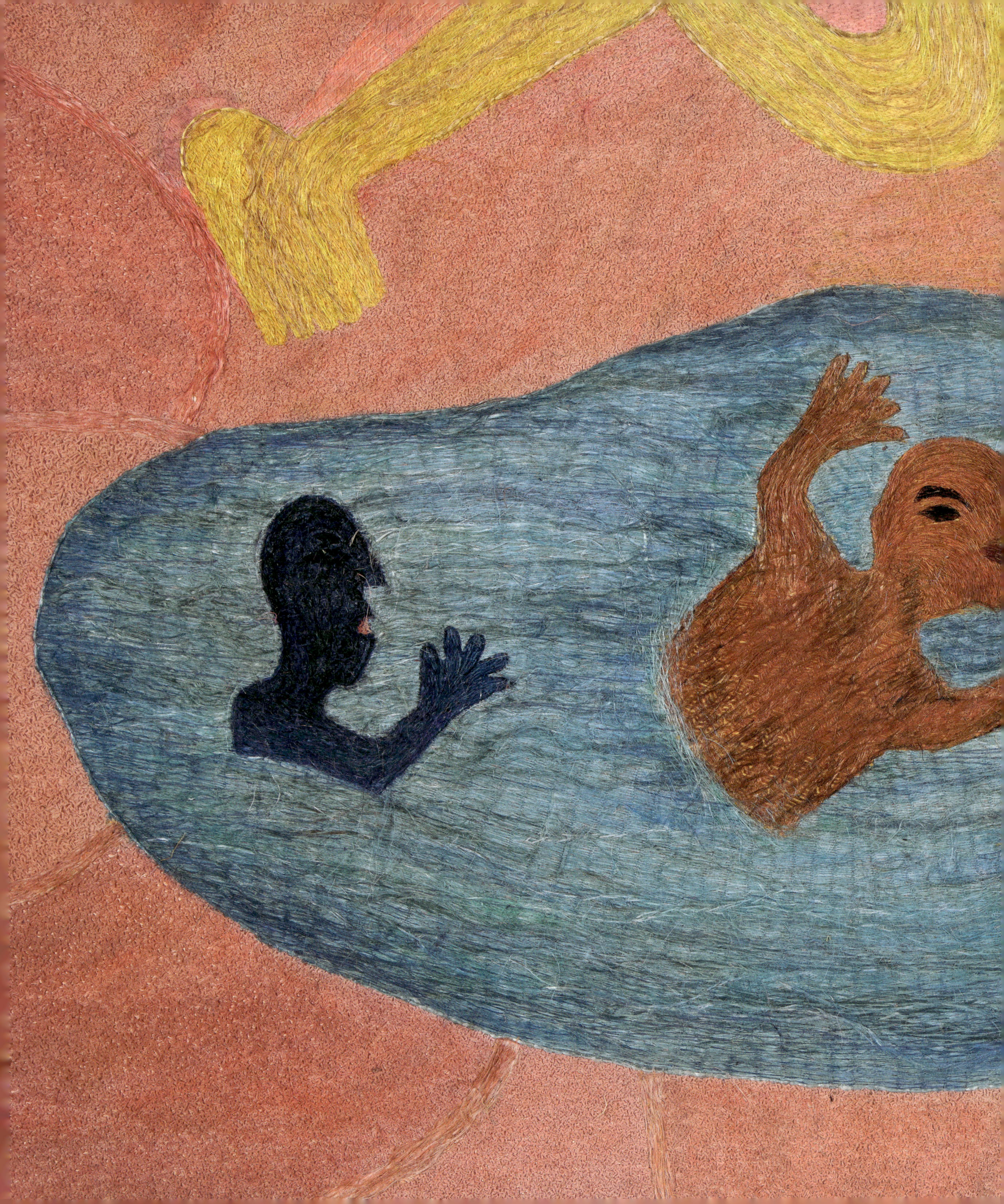

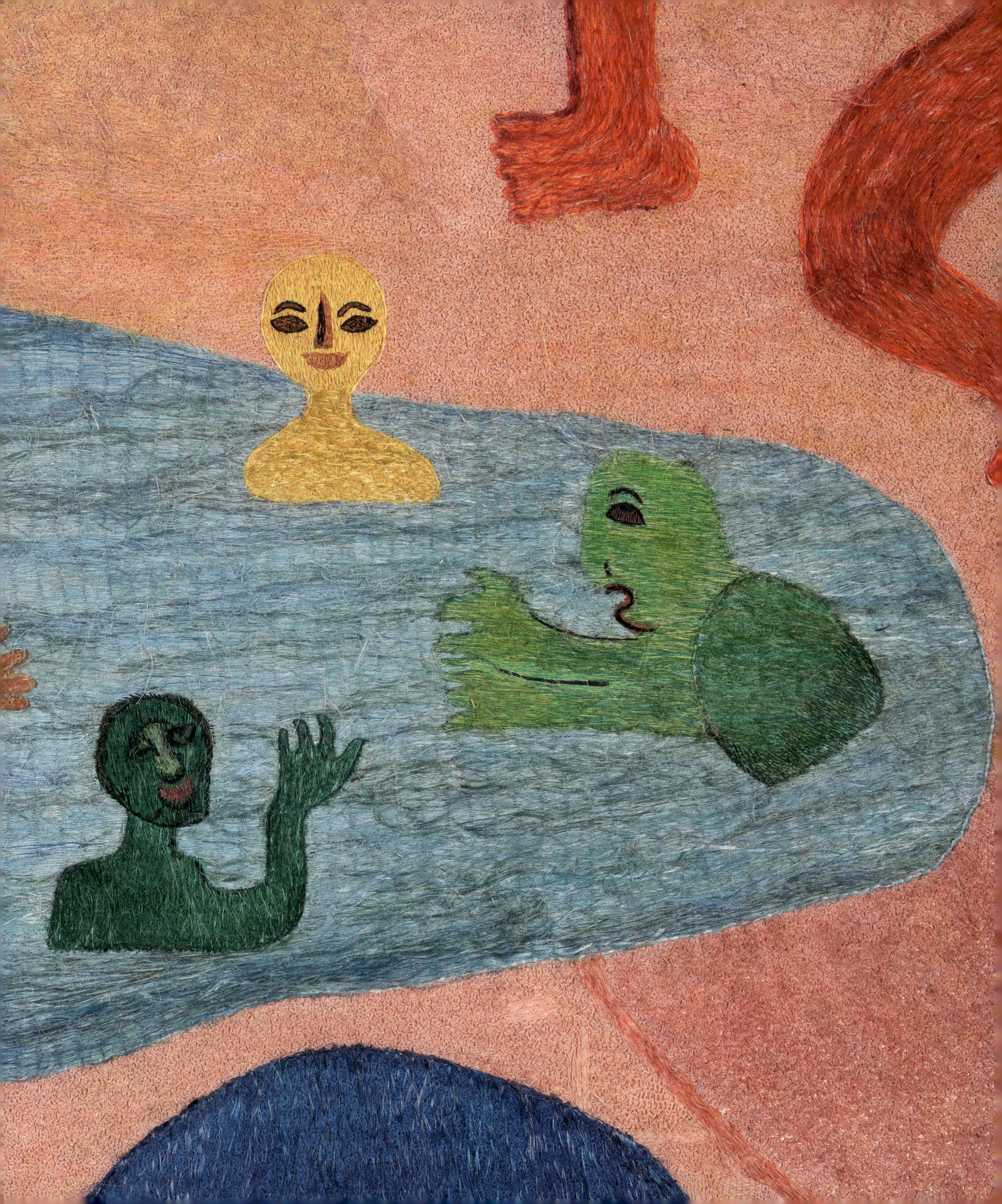

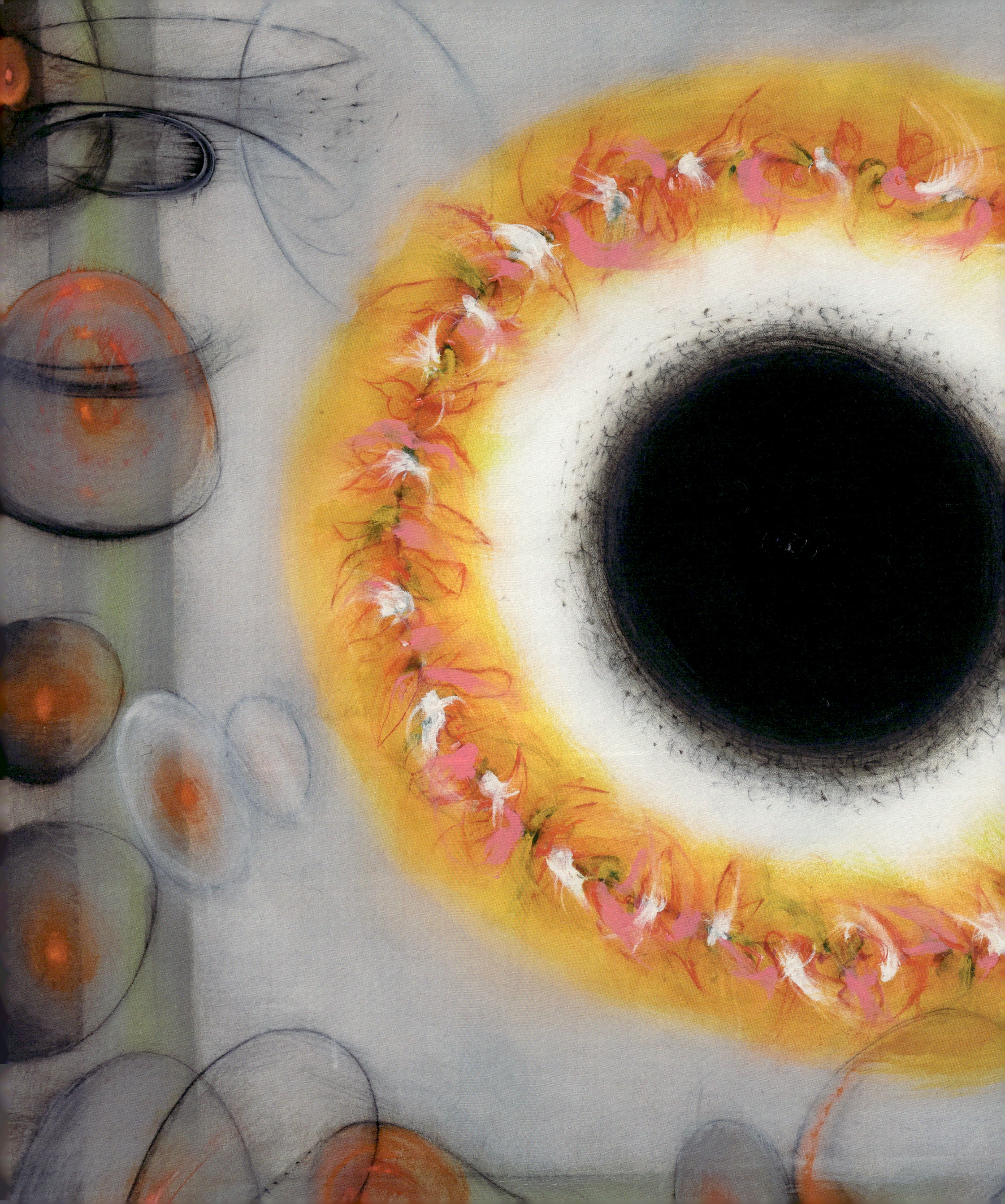

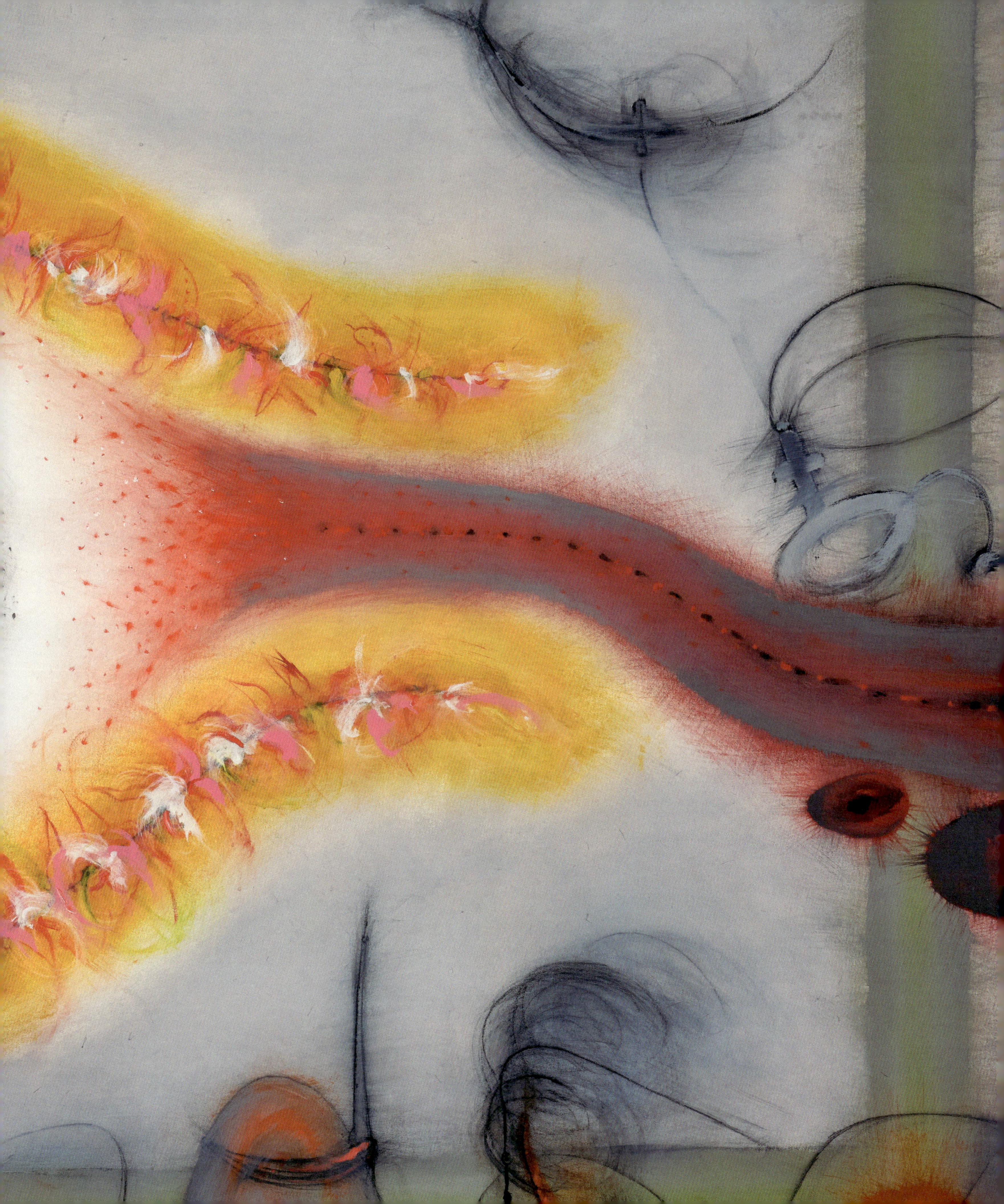

कॉस्मिक गार्डन

Madhvi Parekh and Manu Parekh
Karishma Swali and Chanakya School of Craft

COSMIC GARDEN

5 Continents Editions

Editor-in-Chief
Aldo Carioli

Art Direction and Layout
Oliver Barstow

Editor
Lucia Moretti

Proofreading
Charles Gute

Pre-press
Maurizio Brivio, Milan, Italy

Printed and bound in Italy in December 2025
by Tecnostampa – Pigini Group Printing Division Loreto – Trevi, Italy
for 5 Continents Editions, Milan

www.fivecontinentseditions.com

ISBN 979-12-5460-097-9

Distributed by ACC Art Books throughout the world,
excluding Italy and France. Distributed in France
by BELLES LETTRES / Diffusion L'entreLivres.
Distributed in Italy and Canton Ticino (Switzerland)
by Messaggerie Libri S.p.A.

Cover: Madhvi Parekh, Karishma Swali,
and the Chanakya School of Craft,
Devi and Asura, 2023 (detail)
Photo by Ryan Martis. Courtesy of the Chanakya Foundation

Contents

Preface

Cosmic Garden unfolds from a confluence of intergenerational knowledge, artistic methodologies, and material epistemologies. It brings into conversation the distinct oeuvres of Madhvi Parekh and Manu Parekh, two foundational voices in Indian contemporary art, and the evolving pedagogies nurtured within the Chanakya School of Craft. Through this project, we have sought to shape a framework in which embodied knowledge, contemporary visual idioms, and collaborative authorship intersect to yield a space of mutual transformation. This exhibition is a living testament to our institutional conviction that material practices are not only vessels of memory, but also critical tools through which culture, history, and identity are continually re-inscribed.

Founded in 2016, the Chanakya School of Craft was envisioned as a site for recuperating and rearticulating craft knowledge that has historically been excluded from dominant narratives transmitted orally, practiced domestically, and too often consigned to the margins. Drawing from the four-decade legacy of Chanakya International, the School provides women with access to structured, contextually rich training in over 300 embroidery techniques, each rooted in ancestral wisdom, yet oriented toward contemporary application. To date, over 1,300 women, many of them first-generation learners, have passed through our doors, forming an interdependent and ever-expanding community of skilled artisans, cultural agents, and artistic collaborators.

Presented as a Collateral Event of the 60th International Art Exhibition – La Biennale di Venezia, *Cosmic Garden* extends this ethos into the public realm. In dialogue with the spiritual and narrative-driven practice of Madhvi Parekh and the expressive abstraction of Manu Parekh, the works developed at the School introduce a third modality that privileges the hand, the collective, and the ritual of making as critical sites of meaning. If the exhibition appears interdisciplinary, it is because it resists containment. It is an attempt not only to question the distinction between art and craft, but to trace its origins and explore how it might be reimagined for the future.

The Chanakya Foundation was established in response to the intersecting challenges of social equity, environmental responsibility, and cultural preservation. Committed to cultural stewardship, it advances sustainability through education, skill development, and the preservation of India's artisanal knowledge systems. *Cosmic Garden* is an articulation of these values: a considered effort to reflect on how we honour process, whose narratives we amplify, and what forms of expression we make visible.

In a cultural landscape still governed by exclusionary histories, often of gender, geography, and form, this exhibition raises a set of questions: Can authorship be shared? Can institutions centre the hands of the maker as a site of knowledge? Can we begin to imagine craft not as a static tradition, but as a vital, evolving language of contemporary expression?

It is with these provocations that we offer *Cosmic Garden* — a project rooted in India's pluralist traditions, and reaching toward new forms, new vocabularies, and new possibilities.

> Artisans working on *Resting Near the Pond*
Photo by Hashim Badani. Courtesy of the Chanakya Foundation

Karishma Swali
Chairperson, Chanakya Foundation and Creative Director,
Chanakya School of Craft

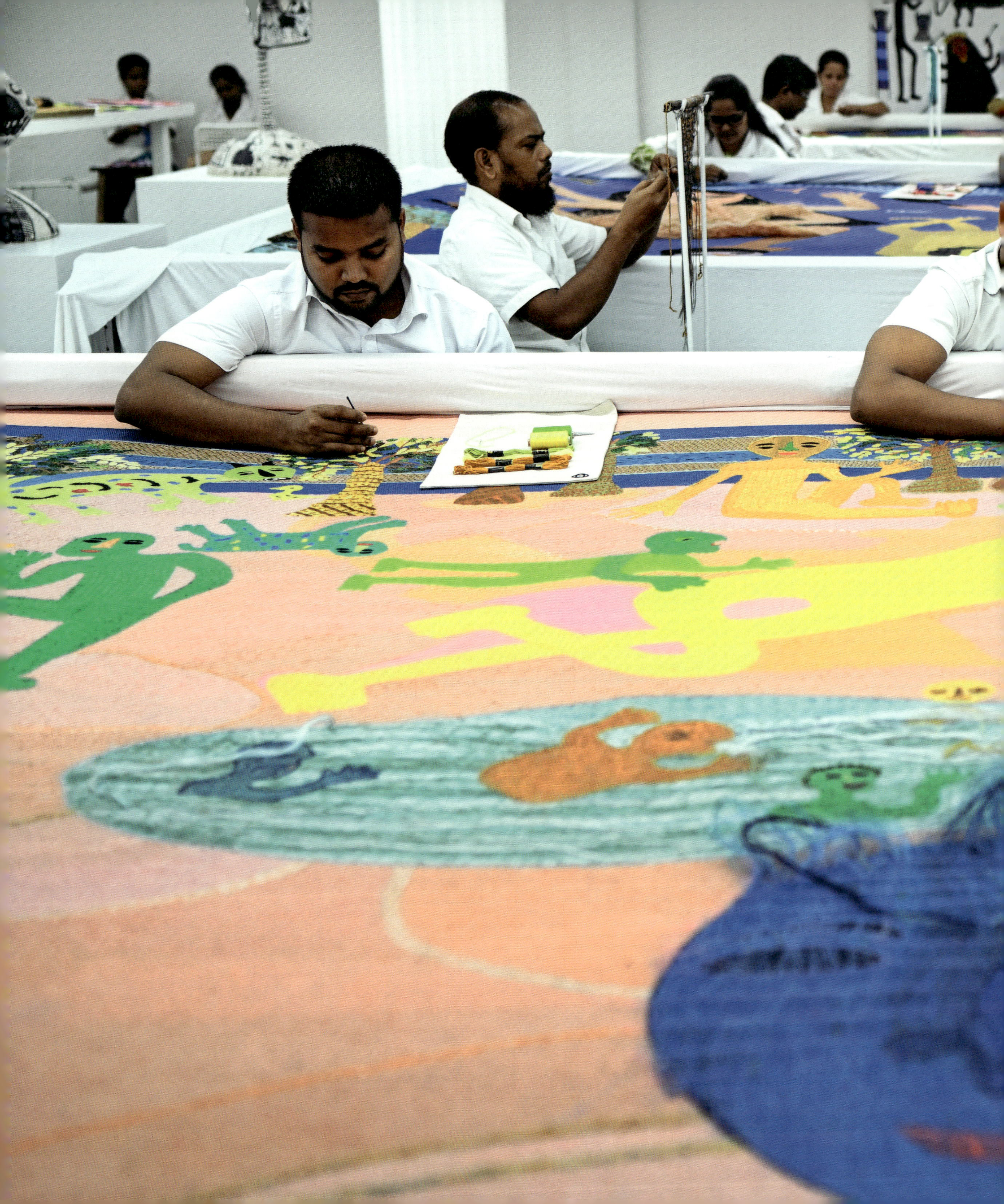

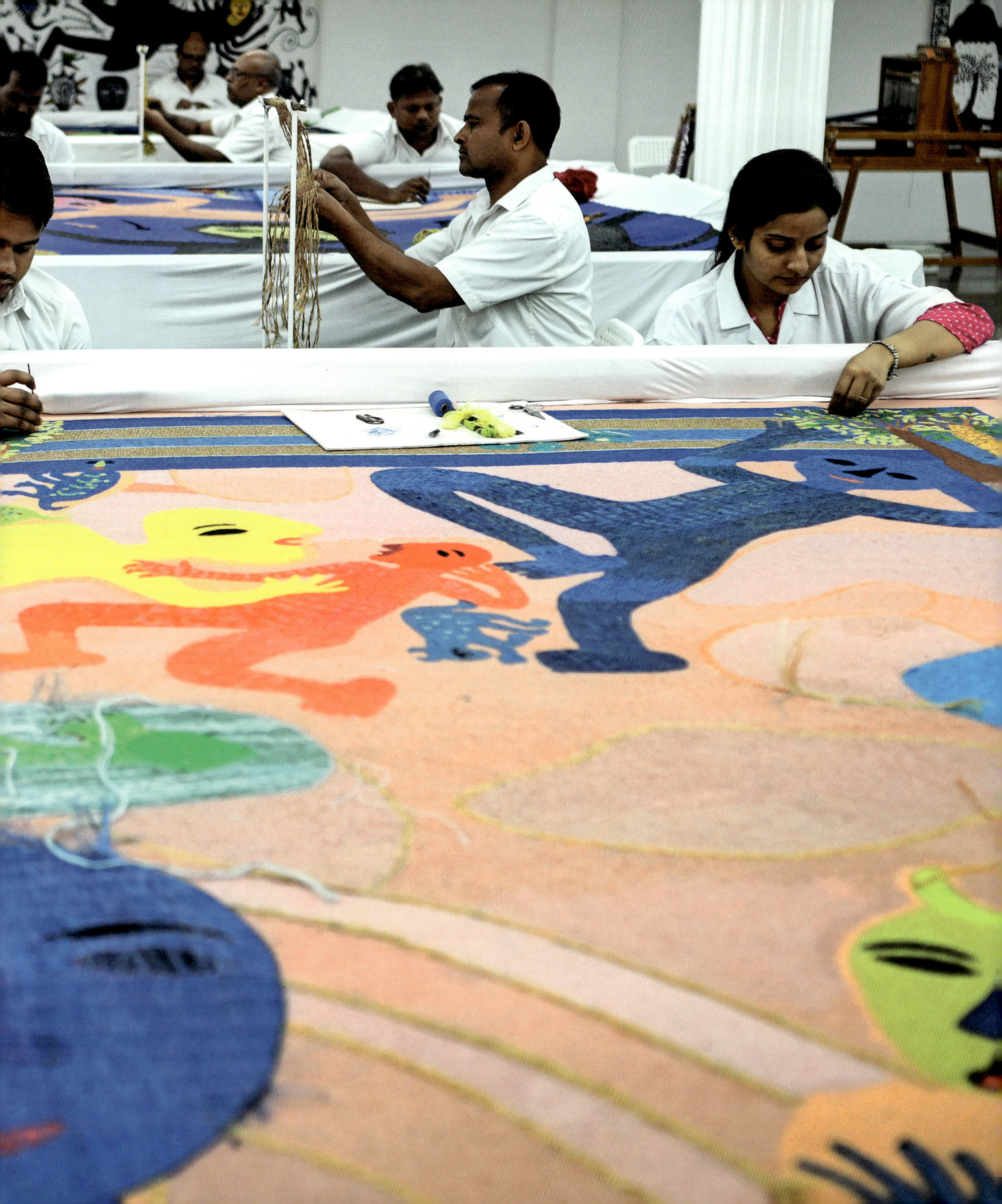

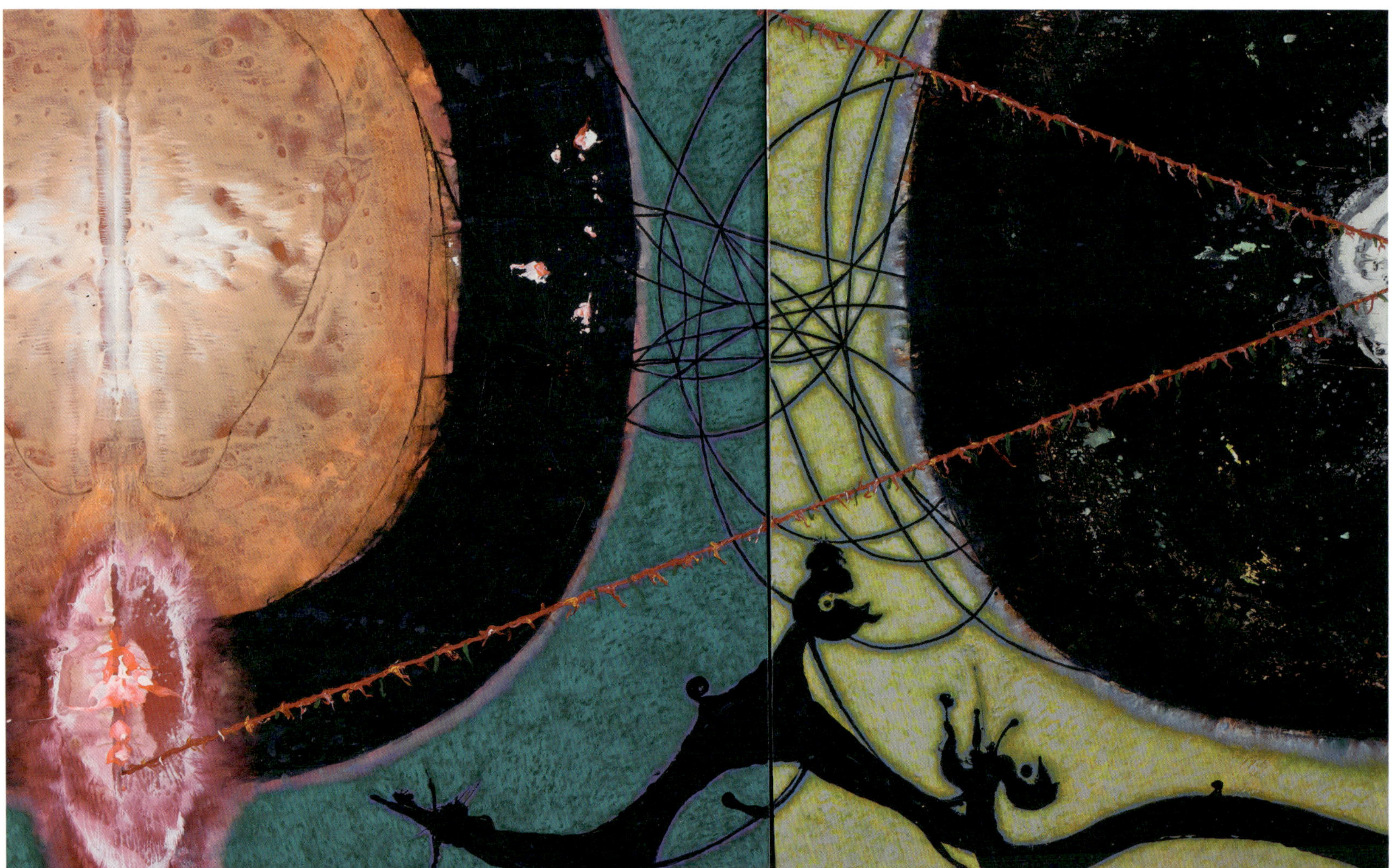

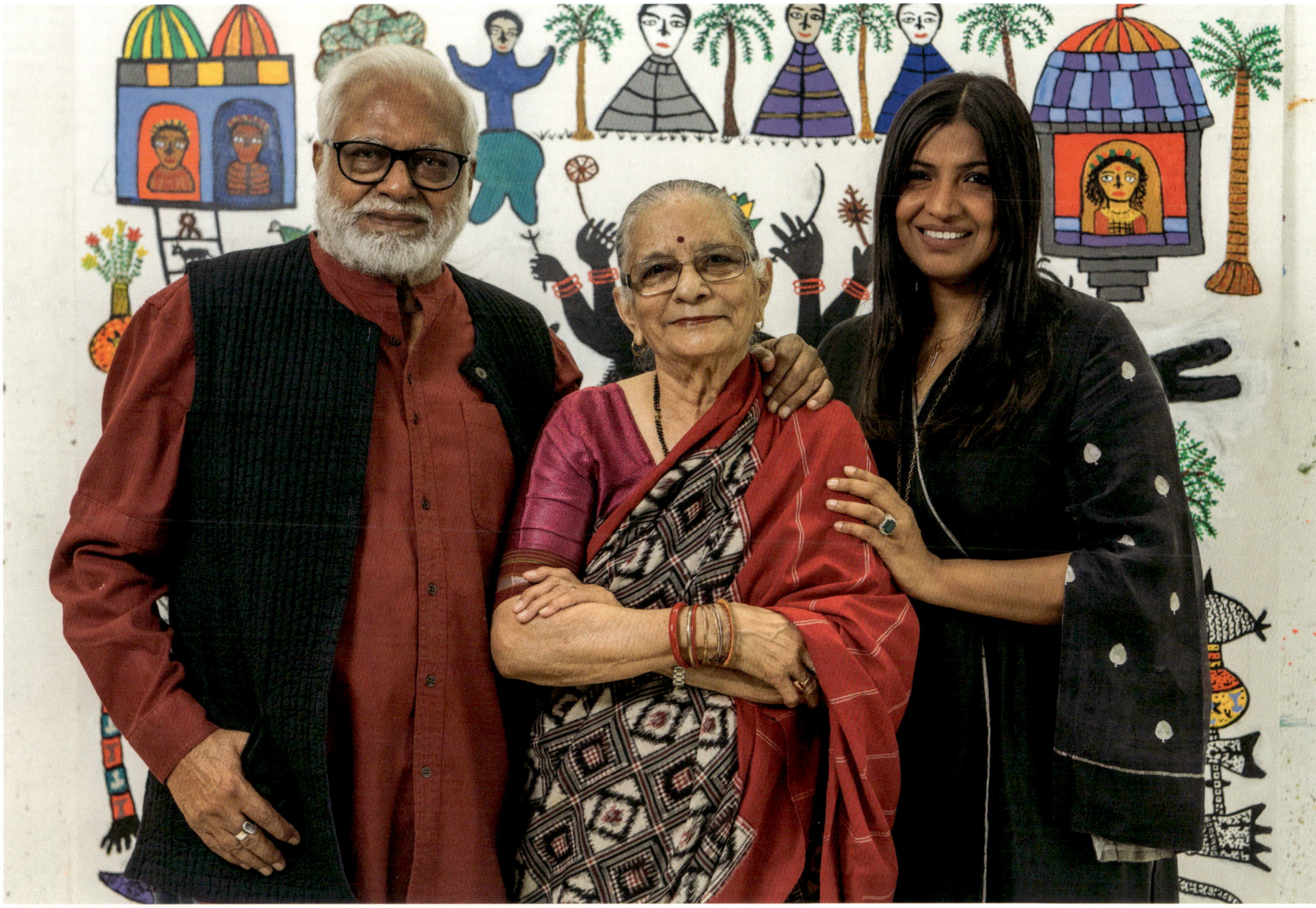

< Manu Parekh
Shiva's Tandav (*Fury of Shiva*), 2023 (detail)
Photo by Hashim Badani. Courtesy of the Chanakya Foundation

Karishma Swali, Manu Parekh and Madhvi Parekh
at the artist's studio in Delhi, 2023
Photo by Sahiba Sawhney. Courtesy of the Chanakya Foundation

Introduction

Building Bridges through Craft and Art

Cosmic Garden pays homage to the enduring legacy of Indian embroidery, a cultural inheritance that the Chanakya Foundation seeks not only to safeguard but to recontextualise within the evolving currents of contemporary cultural discourse.

We had the privilege and pleasure of curating this exhibition as a Collateral Event of the 60th International Art Exhibition – La Biennale di Venezia, featuring the work of two celebrated Indian contemporary artists: Madhvi Parekh and Manu Parekh. Their paintings and sculptures are brought into a layered visual and conceptual dialogue with interdisciplinary responses crafted by the female graduates of the Chanakya School of Craft, under the guidance of Creative Director Karishma Swali.

Karishma Swali has devoted her practice to the preservation and elevation of India's cultural heritage through a sustained commitment to craft excellence. In 2015, in response to the intersecting socio-economic and environmental challenges confronting India's craft communities, she founded the Chanakya Foundation. Anchored in a vision of cultural sustainability, the Foundation advances education, skill development, and the safeguarding of India's vast artisanal legacy. This vision took further institutional form in 2016 with the establishment of the Chanakya School of Craft: a non-profit institute that repositions craft as a space for learning, liberation, and new authorship for women. Positioned at the intersection of craft and social transformation, the school has so far trained more than 1,300 women across generations and backgrounds, cultivating a vibrant community of skilled, self-determined practitioners.

Our objective was not merely to celebrate this rich textile and craft heritage, but more crucially to construct a conceptual bridge across disciplines that connect art and craft, individual authorship and collective making, and traditional and contemporary research. The works assembled here adopt a multidisciplinary approach, challenging the ideological hierarchies between 'major' and 'minor' art forms. In doing so, they illuminate contemporary practices that re-engage traditional techniques as a means of articulating new artistic languages rooted in the sedimented textures of cultural memory.

We wished to emphasise the fruitful dialogue between the Indian craft traditions and the artworks of Madhvi and Manu Parekh. This synergy seeks to construct a new narrative that blurs the boundaries between art and artisanry, honoring the pluralistic beauty of India's artisanal legacies. Our essays also underscore the socio-political significance of enabling women to access income-generating practices and engage with markets capable of transforming not only their individual life trajectories but those of their families and communities. In order to reflect a multiplicity of perspectives and to highlight the cultural significance of India's craft traditions, we invited contributions from distinguished voices engaged in the study and preservation of Indian culture. Dr. Sethi, founder-trustee of the Craft Revival Trust and editor of Global InCH, the online international journal of intangible cultural heritage, offers an illuminating essay that traces the millennia-spanning history of this artistic lineage, guiding readers through its evolving forms and enduring relevance.

Sumesh Sharma, a curator who has consistently engaged with alternative art histories and cultural perspectives influenced by socio-economic and political contexts, provides a critical analysis of the works of Madhvi and Manu

Parekh. His essay explores their profound engagement with the esoteric and philosophical traditions of India, while also situating their practices within the vernacular visual languages of rural life.

With this book we want to celebrate *Cosmic Garden* in all its complexity, without being forced to choose between a binary either/or (art or craft). This multivalent, interdisciplinary practice on embracing simultaneities: art and craft, major and minor, visual and functional, serious and beautiful. Such openness is part of what renders completely alive this form of art, with its ability to sustain multiple – at times, contradictory – reinterpretations, repositioning, and readings. And, as we wrote in our essay, this is also the hallmark of all great works of art, both fine and applied.

Maria Alicata and Paola Ugolini

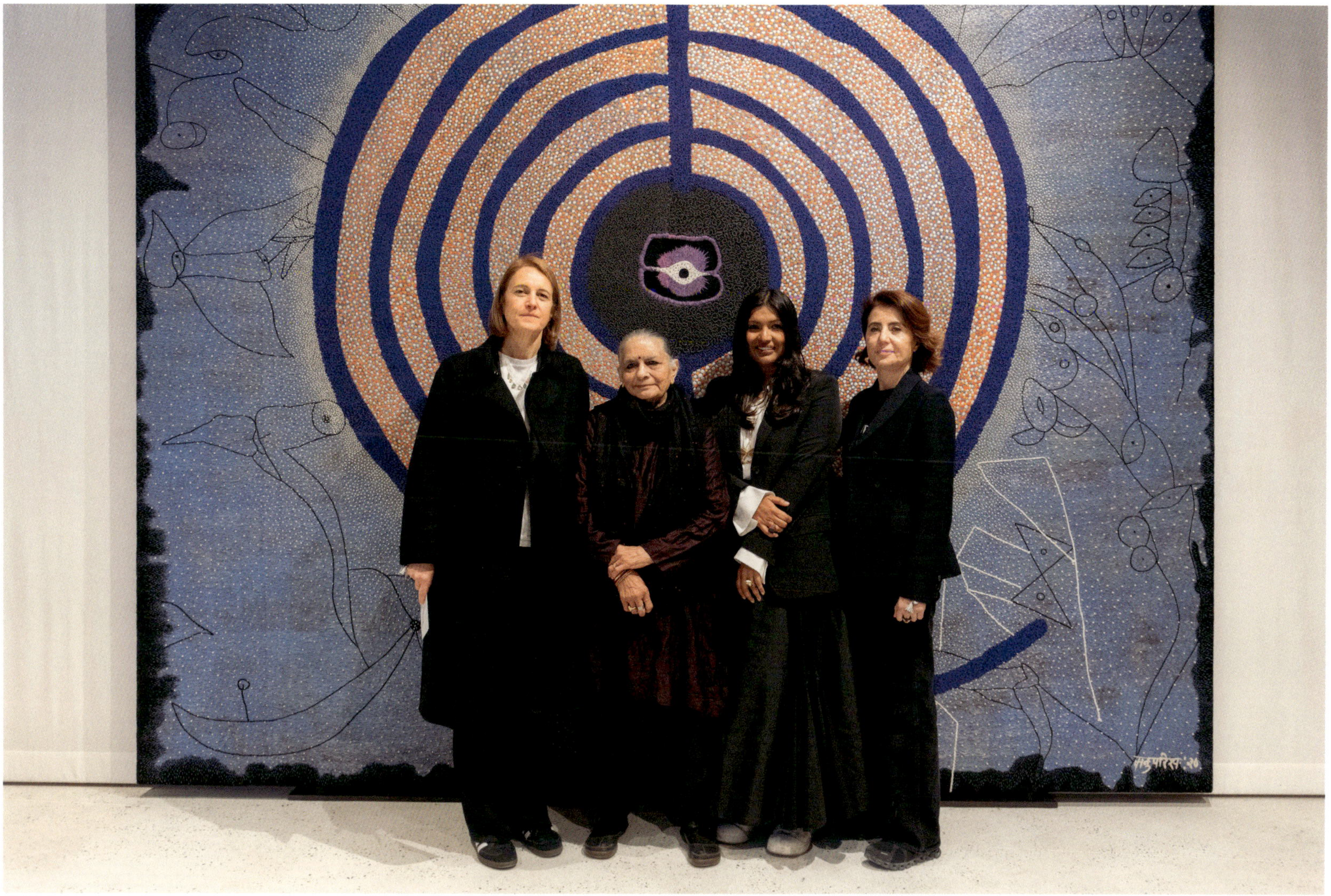

Maria Alicata, Madhvi Parekh, Karishma Swali, and Paola Ugolini
at the *Cosmic Garden* exhibition
Photo by Daniele Zoico. Courtesy of the Chanakya Foundation

Embroidery as Empowerment

Maria Alicata and Paola Ugolini

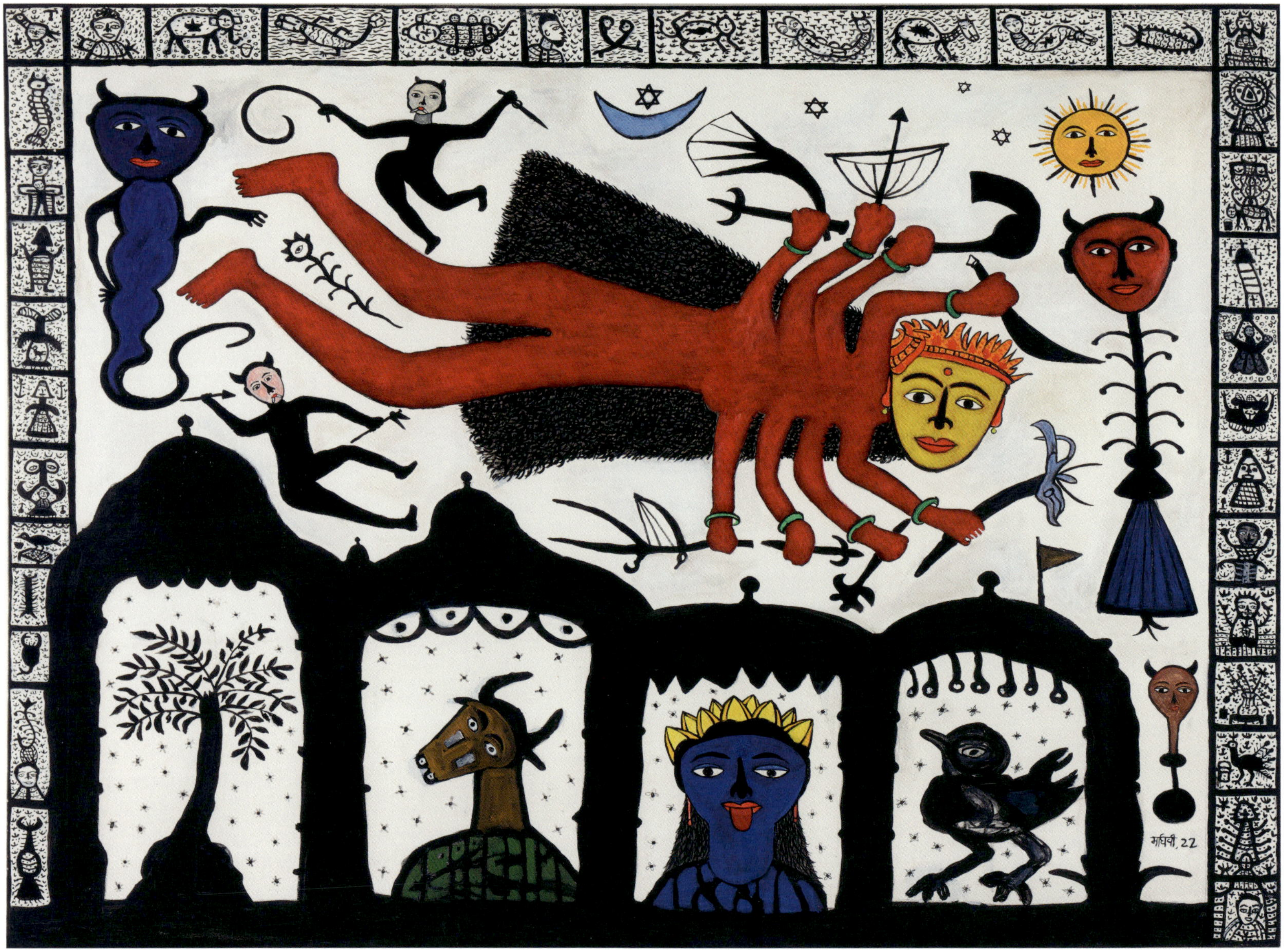

Madhvi Parekh
Flying Goddess, 2022
Acrylic on canvas, 183 × 152 cm
Photo by Abner Fernandes. Courtesy of the Chanakya Foundation

Today, as the exclusionary character of our received art histories becomes ever more apparent, we believe that *Cosmic Garden* — here intended as a collective project by Madhvi Parekh and Manu Parekh, alongside Karishma Swali's multifaceted oeuvre, which is as consistent in its technical and stylistic precision as it is materially diverse — has heightened relevance.

On the one hand, it makes us think about the history of modern art in a more open-ended and generative way, by challenging distinctions between fine art and craft, major and minor, painting and decoration, precise planning and creativity. On the other, it offers a vibrant model of what might best be described as a form of art that relates to the body, to the applied arts, to the environment and the political, social, and cultural situation in which it is made, while extending this practice in terms that are relevant to the times we live in, crossing borders both geographical and cultural.

Historically, from a Western perspective, the ideas of the British Arts and Crafts theorist William Morris[1] — who was convinced that the applied arts could bring about social, cultural, and moral change — were hugely influential throughout late nineteenth and early twentieth century Europe; moreover, they also had a profound impact on later avant-garde movements such as Dada and Surrealism.

As feminist art historian Rozsika Parker writes: "The artists involved in Dada, Surrealism and Russian Constructivism believed that an end to distinctions between the fine and the applied arts would create an art relevant to the lives of the masses of the people — and infinitely richer in itself. Although all three movements manifestly failed to achieve their ideals, for different historical reasons, they nevertheless opened up a space for women artists. Women's particular skills and traditional areas of activity in the domestic sphere, previously thought to be beneath the concern of the fine artist, were accorded a new importance."[2]

In the Western world, embroidery was one of the ways through which to educate women about the ideal of femininity and, at the same time, it also served as an unintended weapon of resistance against the constrictions of that ideal.

Femininity, which it would be superficial to identify purely with grace and beauty, is a complex code of limitations that embodies a culture of obedience and insubstantiality; one that has elevated vulnerability, weakness, and inability to the status of values. Sitting at home, "needle in hand," is, then, the quintessence of what, until not too many decades ago, a woman from an aristocratic or middle-class family was expected to do with herself to comply with her gender role, which was identified with immobility and submission, together with a lack of intellectual prowess.

Over the course of the centuries, the art of embroidery, as theorised by Parker, "[...] provided a weapon of resistance to the constraints of femininity [...] Eyes lowered, head bent, shoulders hunched — the position signifies repression and subjugation, yet the embroiderer's silence, her concentration also suggests a self-containment, a kind of autonomy."[3] By enhancing our capacity to develop complex thinking, manual artistic work is a means for connecting our spiritual and imaginative sides. To this end, it is interesting to consider how the French writer Colette described the observation of this intimately creative process as carried out by her daughter "[...] she is silent when she sews, silent for hours on end... she is silent, and she — why not write it down, the word that frightens me — she is thinking."[4] Modern psychoanalytical theories, too, have underlined the importance of creativity as an aid to thinking.

In particular, Margot Waddell has posited how the theory of "containment" formulated by W.R. Bion can be applied to the experience of the artist with her work.[5] In this regard, she writes, "The art object promotes and expands mental capacities by offering a shape and containing structure for the transformation of emotional experience into recognisable form."[6] Those who embroider maintain that it helps their ability to think, and indeed, the embroidered item often reflects the presence of a rich, profound inner world. It is interesting to note that, in the hands of the British Suffragette movement,[7] embroidery became a political weapon to overcome the patriarchal concept of femininity, and went from being a passive, bourgeois practice to being a method through which to evoke visually a strong, combative femininity, with the production of banners to march with during their protests demanding the right to vote.

These introductory remarks serve to highlight the socio-cultural difference that infuses what is a very ancient technique in this part of the world, in contrast to other geographical areas in which it has had the opposite connotation in terms of gender roles, such as in India, where embroidery is a typically male art form. In India, embroidery is widely regarded as a prestigious art form; however, it is important to differentiate between applied art and embroidery. Applied art typically encompasses artistic disciplines focused on functional design, including textiles, jewellery, and architecture, while embroidery is considered a specialised craft within the broader domain of textile arts. Despite this distinction, traditional embroidery styles such as *zardozi*, *chikankari*, *kantha*, and *phulkari* transcend mere decoration. They are deeply symbolic, encapsulating regional histories, spiritual motifs, and narrative elements. In numerous contexts, embroidery is perceived as both a craft and an art, with master artisans celebrated for their exceptional skill and creativity.

We should point out that the appeal by Mohandas K. Gandhi (1869-1948) to women to spin yarn was aimed at every household in every corner of the country, so that women from all walks of life could find purpose and meaning in their domestic industry, not only as an option for their livelihood or for supplementary income, but also as a moral duty and a code of conduct in the creation of a national sisterhood.[8]

Anti-colonial cultural and political voices, such as Gandhi and Rabindranath Tagore (1861–1941), referenced both the colonial nostalgia for a pre-industrial past and the salience of Indian crafts in modernity to critique the material and moral estrangement of factory production under capitalism. For them, craft offered a civilisational alternative to the telos of progress underlying colonialism. The educationalists who were part of Tagore's intellectual circle included Sister Nivedita (Margaret Noble, 1867–1911), an Irish teacher who met Swami Vivekananda in 1895 in London and joined the Indian nationalist cause to work in Calcutta. She was concerned about the uplift of Indian women. With the freedom struggle underway, women came to be viewed as sites of resistance from the interior spaces of their homes.[9]

In India, permitting women — of any age, religion or social class — to learn how to embroider was a revolutionary undertaking, given that the various techniques used by the artisans were handed down within families exclusively through the male line, from father to son, whereas women were given the far more wretched task of darning. Teaching women a noble art was akin to emancipating them, allowing them to leave the confines of the home and to engage with the contemporary world and its challenges.

Women who access practices to generate income and reach markets can change their own personal life trajectories and those of their families. Incomes provide opportunities of choice to women and allow them to have a voice in their futures, affording them dignity in making an income that can move them away from poverty and its attendant traps. Women craft makers should be seen not as passive recipients of policy initiatives that aim to shape their futures, but as key stakeholders in policy making, in a collaborative manner.[10]

As Clare Hunter writes in her book *Threads of Life*, "Embroidery is the interweaving of relationships." Embroidery helps to strengthen relationships, with our past, our family, and our history. Embroidery is sharing, when many hands are involved in a piece of work. It is a community practice and a self-inclusive process.

Of late, this undertaking has been carried out by a woman, Karishma Swali, who in 2016, in Mumbai, founded the Chanakya School of Craft, a nonprofit institution that aims to make available craft knowledge and techniques to help women, of every age and class, to become economically independent and autonomous. Every artistic collaboration undertaken by Karishma and the school is a collective project in which pictorial visions are materialised as embroidery thanks to a long, shared, fertile, creative process in which Karishma determines the techniques, colours, and needlepoint techniques that are to be used to recast the painting in textile form. This is, then, embroidery as a tool for both intellectual and financial emancipation, to enable women to become an active part of a creative adventure, with which to give shape and visual structure to their imaginations.

Getting painting, sculpture, and embroidery to engage with each other is the challenge faced by *Cosmic Garden*, an exhibition that aims to cross-pollinate Vedic philosophy with the legends and goddesses of India's rural and craft heritage, so as to create an original conceptual and visual fresco of a subcontinent in which tradition, modernity, spirituality, and creativity have always been intimately connected.

Entering into a dialogue with Karishma Swali and the female graduates of the Chanakya School of Craft, the artists Madhvi Parekh (b. 1942) and Manu Parekh (b. 1939) have transformed some of their works into complex textile masterpieces.

Karishma Swali, in collaboration with the female graduates of the Chanakya School of Craft and the master artisans of the Chanakya ateliers, has cultivated a quietly transformative artistic language — one in which embroidery is reimagined not as merely decorative or domestic, but as a vital medium within the realm of contemporary art. Rooted in a model of collective authorship and informed by a feminist pedagogy, the School serves as both a sanctuary and a site of innovation for some of India's most intricate and endangered craft traditions. Here, these practices are not only preserved, but thoughtfully engage in conversation with modernist aesthetics, sculptural form, and philosophical inquiry.

By extending this historically gated knowledge to hundreds of women from varied social and economic contexts, Swali has fostered a practice that is at once expansive and deeply grounded. Her work invites us to reconsider long-standing hierarchies — particularly the inherited divisions between craft and fine art — and to recognise Indian artisanship as being not on the margins, but at the very centre of contemporary cultural discourse.

The work of these two artists differs in formal terms — figurative for Madhvi and abstract for her husband, Manu — but is conceptually similar, given their shared cultural roots, which are embedded in the ancient figurative and philosophical tradition of their homeland.

In the works of self-taught artist Madhvi, moments of daily life in the villages of Gujarat alternate with fantastical animals and figures of divinities, especially Durga, Kali, and Ganesha, taken from the Hindu pantheon,[11] who come thick and fast on the white surface of the canvas, one after the other, creating powerful mythologies that are visually similar to the coloured figurations of animals and deities typically seen across rural India. Together with memories of her childhood, spent in a village in that region, also appearing in her works is the triumphal image of Durga, the warrior goddess. In Sanskrit, Durga means "strength" or "impassable, invincible or unassailable." This goddess is, then, a symbol of power, force, and protection, above all for women. The spirit of this fearless goddess is fundamental in enacting the necessary changes with which to take on the difficulties and challenges of life, because she embodies the power of transformation to overcome dependence, obstacles, and illusions. Legend has it that Durga was created as a warrior goddess to fight and destroy the demon Mahishasura, who could not be defeated by any man or any male celestial being. Since only a woman could vanquish the demon, who had established a kingdom of terror on Earth, the gods created a dazzling energy ray that gave birth to Durga, the beautiful goddess with ten arms. Durga helps us to bring light to our dark areas, and, appropriately enough, the demons that she fights are the representation of dark forces such as jealousy, dependence, attachment, and envy, which impede our spiritual journey. Durga's presence in Madhvi's works is, therefore, no accident, since it serves to underline the importance of the inner work required for our personal development.

In all of Madhvi's pictorial works, the figures of goddesses are a constant presence; one that has nothing to do with the simple quoting of the local folklore and everything to do, on the symbolic level, with the transformative, female, spiritual power that they embody. In many of these canvases we find the goddess Kali, recognisable for her blue and black appearance. She is perhaps the most well-known of the Hindu pantheon: the goddess of volatile and untamed feminine energy, she wields unstoppable power as the heir to the ancient deity of death and transformation.

In contrast to our Western cultural models, which have always attributed passivity to the female archetype and active energy to its male counterpart, in Hindu philosophical and religious thinking, passivity belongs to the male, whereas the active, expression function is the prerogative of the goddess.

Kali is a Hindu goddess associated with time, destruction, and transformation. She is often depicted with black or dark blue skin, symbolising the infinite and the transcendence of form. Her fierce form, with a garland of skulls and a lolling tongue, represents her role as the destroyer of evil and ignorance.

She is a goddess who destroys in order to transform and purify. According to the tantric tradition, Kali, as the supreme female energy, is the prime motor of the creation of the universe. This goddess also presides over the unconventional routes to spiritual elevation that are activated through sex and the breaking of rules and taboos.

Madhvi's artistic career got under way in the mid-1960s, when she began to draw under the guidance of her husband, Manu Parekh, who taught her the techniques of drawing and composition, above all in a Western, modernist key, since he was an admirer of the subtle and linear abstraction of Paul Klee. Despite this early, non-academic training, from the 1970s onwards Madhvi began to develop her own, entirely original formal idiom. In some small, valuable works of that period, such as *Snake in the Sea* (1975), she provided proof of her great expressive creativity and freedom. Using a flattened perspective, the artist incorporates into the field of the canvas a series of geometric shapes, such as triangles, circles, and rectangles, while the body of the central figure is filled with stitches, broken lines, and dashes that recall *kantha* and *sujani* needlework.[12] At the centre of the canvas, a vertically elongated animal figure, a sort of fantastical hybrid between a snake and a cat, is surrounded by beings of an uncertain, metamorphic nature, which render the composition a captivating one-off in stylistic terms.

Red Fighter (1998) features another imaginary figure that occupies the small canvas. The image of its rounded, enveloping body is as far away as possible from the traditional idea of a warrior. This fanciful figure, too, is a hybrid, but rather than between animals of various species as in the previous work, here the artist seems to have had fun creating a being half-way between a puppet and a human. The colouring is entirely based on warm shades — the red figure, standing sturdily on squat legs with arms open, contrasts with the light-pink background. The inside of the body of this unlikely warrior is inhabited by strange animal beings, all rigorously black and white, which decorate it as if they were tattoos. Twirling on the base of the canvas, minutely embellished by a continuous weave of lines and stitches, are a series of animals and anthropomorphic figures in delicate pastel colours.

A stylistic change in Madhvi's compositions got under way in the new millennium, and has come to fruition in the large paintings of recent years, which feature a strong sense of rhythm that has been further accentuated by the paratactic repetition of the figures, inspired by the paintings of *kalamkari* and *pichwai*.[13] For more than twenty years, Kali and Durga have been the main figures in these late works, in which Madhvi depicts the perennial cycle of life and its transformations.

In *Flying Goddess* (2022), Durga, depicted in the centre of the canvas, flies over the roofs of a series of little temples that are outlined in black. Inside them, a tree, an animal figure (half-bull and half-donkey), the goddess Kali — whose face occupies almost all of the space — and a small bird all seem to stare at the viewers, who themselves are looking back as if through virtual windows that open onto a fantasy world in which humans and animals live in harmony. A frame formed by small rectangles that contain figures and geometric symbols in

> Madhvi Parekh
Red Figure, 1998
Oil on canvas, 90 × 69 cm
Photo by Daniele Zoico. Courtesy of the Chanakya Foundation

>> Madhvi Parekh
Snake in the Sea, 1975
Oil on canvas, 69 × 123 cm
Photo by Daniele Zoico. Courtesy of the Chanakya Foundation

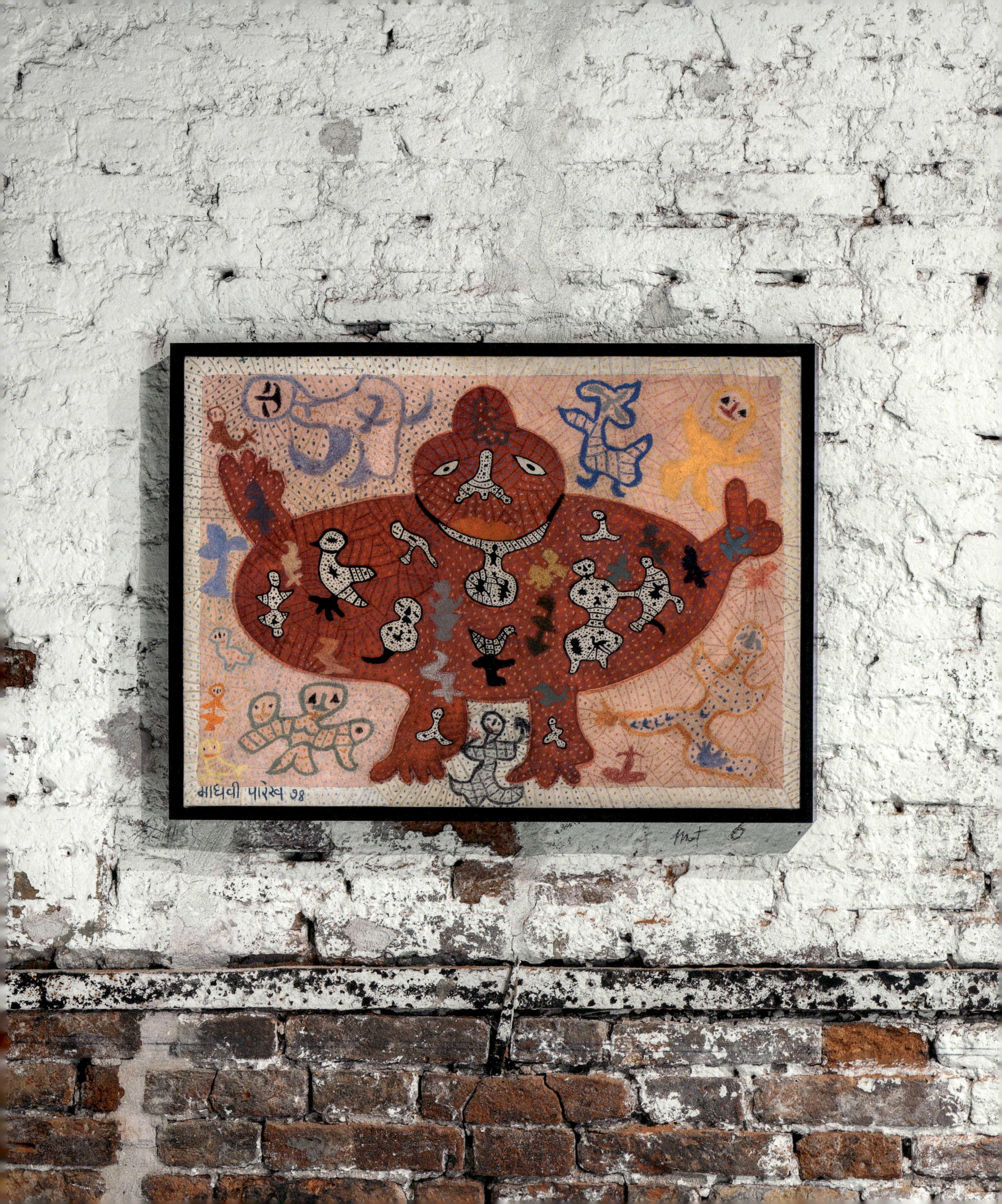
माधवी पारेख ७८

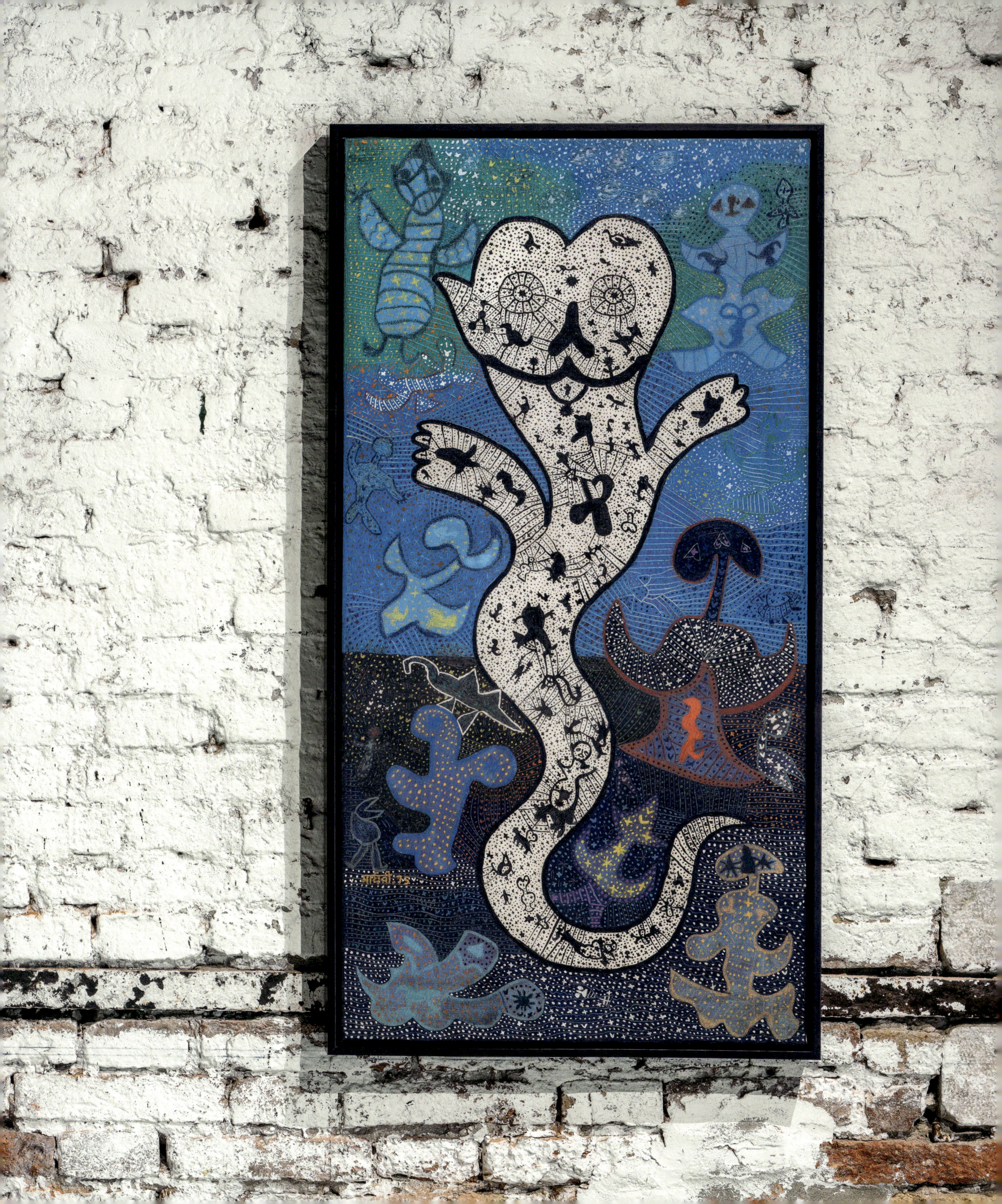

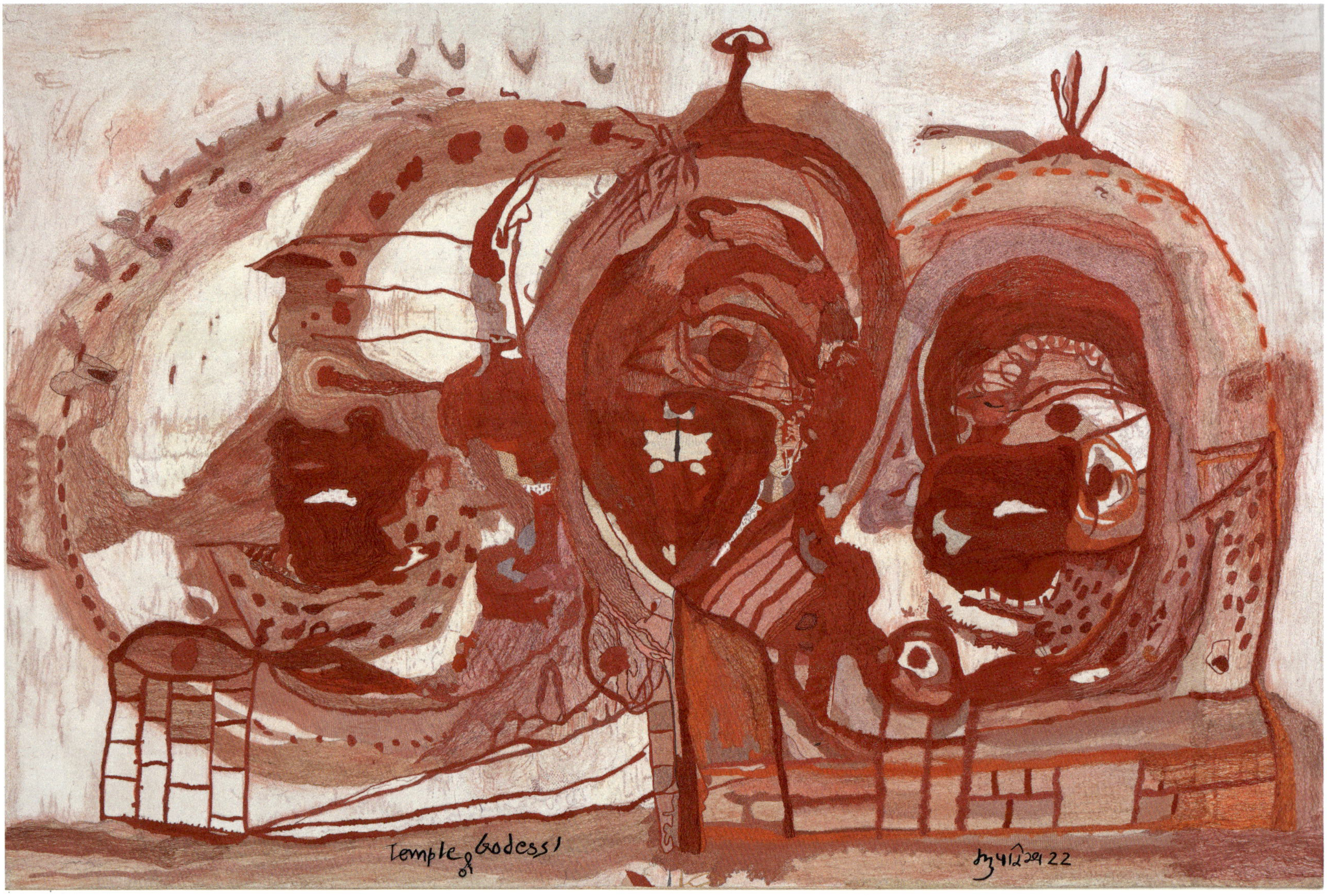

Manu Parekh, Karishma Swali, and the Chanakya School of Craft
Temple of Goddess, 2023
Organic jute, cotton, linen, and raw silk thread
on cotton textile, 282 × 412 cm
Photo by Ryan Martis. Courtesy of the Chanakya Foundation

black and white runs along and embellishes three sides of the canvas, as numerous other figures of supernatural beings seem to spin around the many-armed goddess, filling up the background. Every work by Madhvi is a visual journey into a make-believe world in which reality and imagination live together.

Village Opera (2022), a masterwork of her late period, is a joyous representation of the gods, surrounded by a myriad of semi-human and animal figures that flutter around in the background of the canvas. In the centre is Ganesha,[14] the child-God with the elephant's head, represented as sitting on a figure of which we can see only the face, probably an anthropomorphised mouse, within a container that is reminiscent of a small boat. Durga is shown standing on her vehicle, while a tiger with a half-human face closes off the composition on the left-hand side, and Kali, who rests her foot on the prostrate body of Shiva, is located on the other side of the canvas. Ganesha, like Durga and Kali, represents change, in that he is the one who was able to discover the divine spark — the emanation of everything — within himself, and he is also worshipped as the one who removes obstacles, both spiritual and material, defends good actions, and scatters difficulties along the path of evildoers. This god embodies perfect harmony between the male energies, represented by Shiva, and the female energies embodied by Shiva's consort Parvati, a manifestation of the goddess Shakti. This is the fluid integration between strength and delicacy, between power and grace, which also expresses the predisposition to know how to distinguish truth from what is illusory, and reality from what is imaginary. The figures outlined in black stand out clearly against the white background of the canvas and, as in all of her late-period works, the main figures are depicted front-on, with the colour scheme limited to the primary colours.

On display is the series called *Kalpavriksha* (I, II, III, IV), made up of paper-mache sculptures, created by assembling everyday objects and tools such as broom handles, baskets for fruit and vegetables, and brushes. The surface of her three-dimensional works is also entirely painted white, against which stand out in black the depictions of abstract decorative elements, such as run stitches, broken lines, and crosses that seem to form a continuous frill surrounding the stylised figures of animals, human beings, or elements of the cosmos such as stars and suns, or even architectural and natural elements. With her works, Madhvi transports us into her magical world of memories, cultural evocations, folklore, and philosophy.

Manu Parekh, born in Ahmedabad in 1939, had his initiation in drawing and painting under Mukund Shroff before applying to the local Seth C.N. School of Fine Arts to study for a diploma that would make him eligible to become an art teacher. In 1963, just after he got his diploma in Drawing and Painting from Mumbai's J.J. School of Art, Parekh joined the Weavers' Service Centre, an initiative led by cultural activist Pupul Jayakar. This community- and collaboration-based experience would go on to shape his practice.

Working as a designer, he travelled to rural Orissa, Rajasthan, and Haryana to document traditional crafts such as Ikat and Madhubani. What he saw there impacted his early works. "Most of the weavers I met were farmers," Parekh states. "The themes of fertility and nature in my works derive from my experiences in these villages."[15]

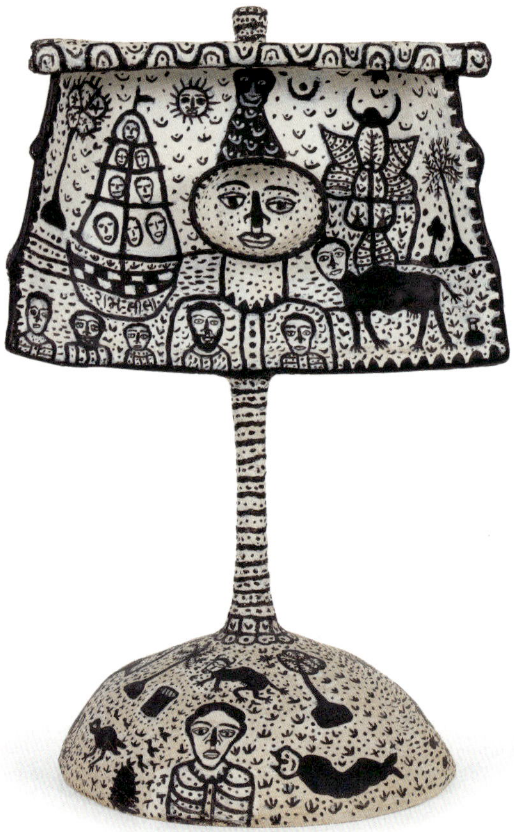

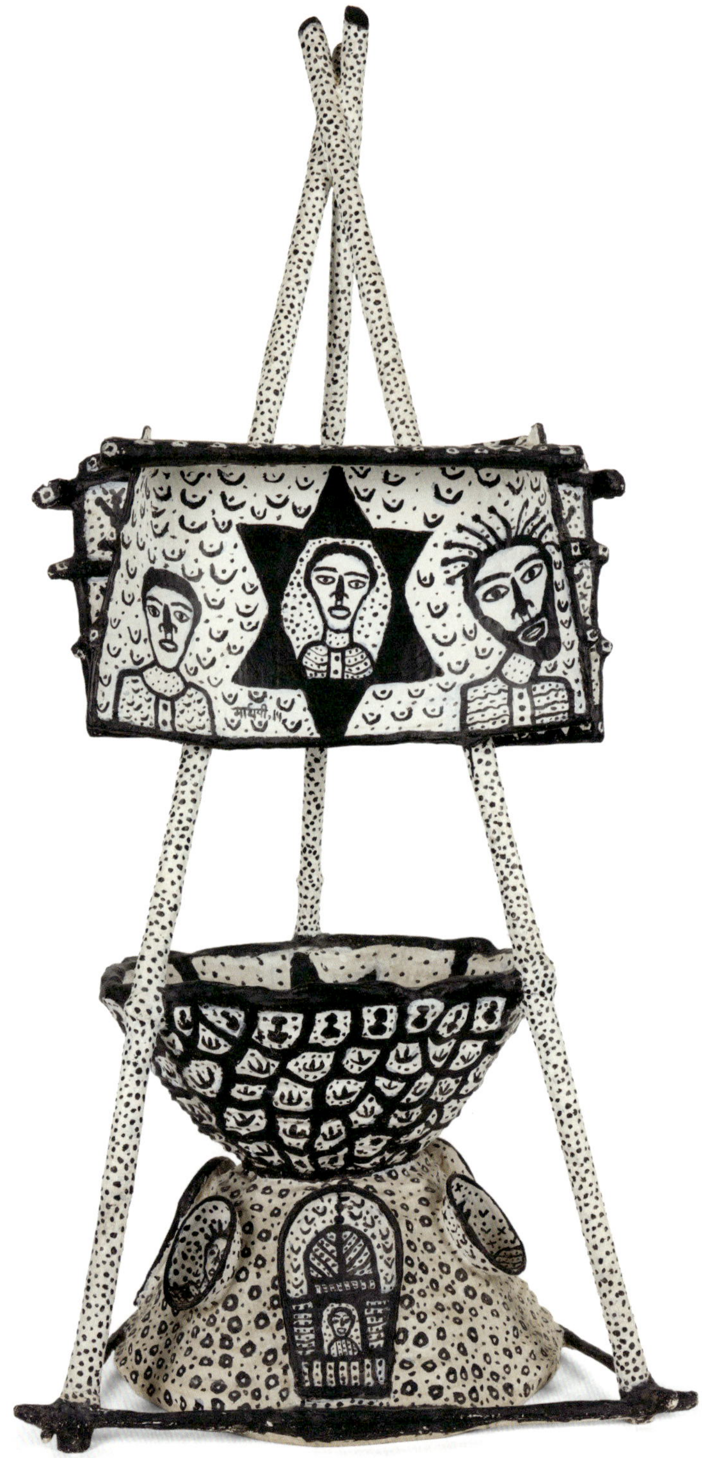

Madhvi Parekh
Kalpavriksha, 1997
Bamboo, basket, winnower, plaster of paris, painted with acrylic, 59 × 50 × 93 cm
Photo by Abner Fernandes. Courtesy of the Chanakya Foundation

Madhvi Parekh
Kalpavriksha III, 2002
Bamboo, basket, winnower, plaster of paris, painted with acrylic, 87 × 75 × 163 cm
Photo by Abner Fernandes. Courtesy of the Chanakya Foundation

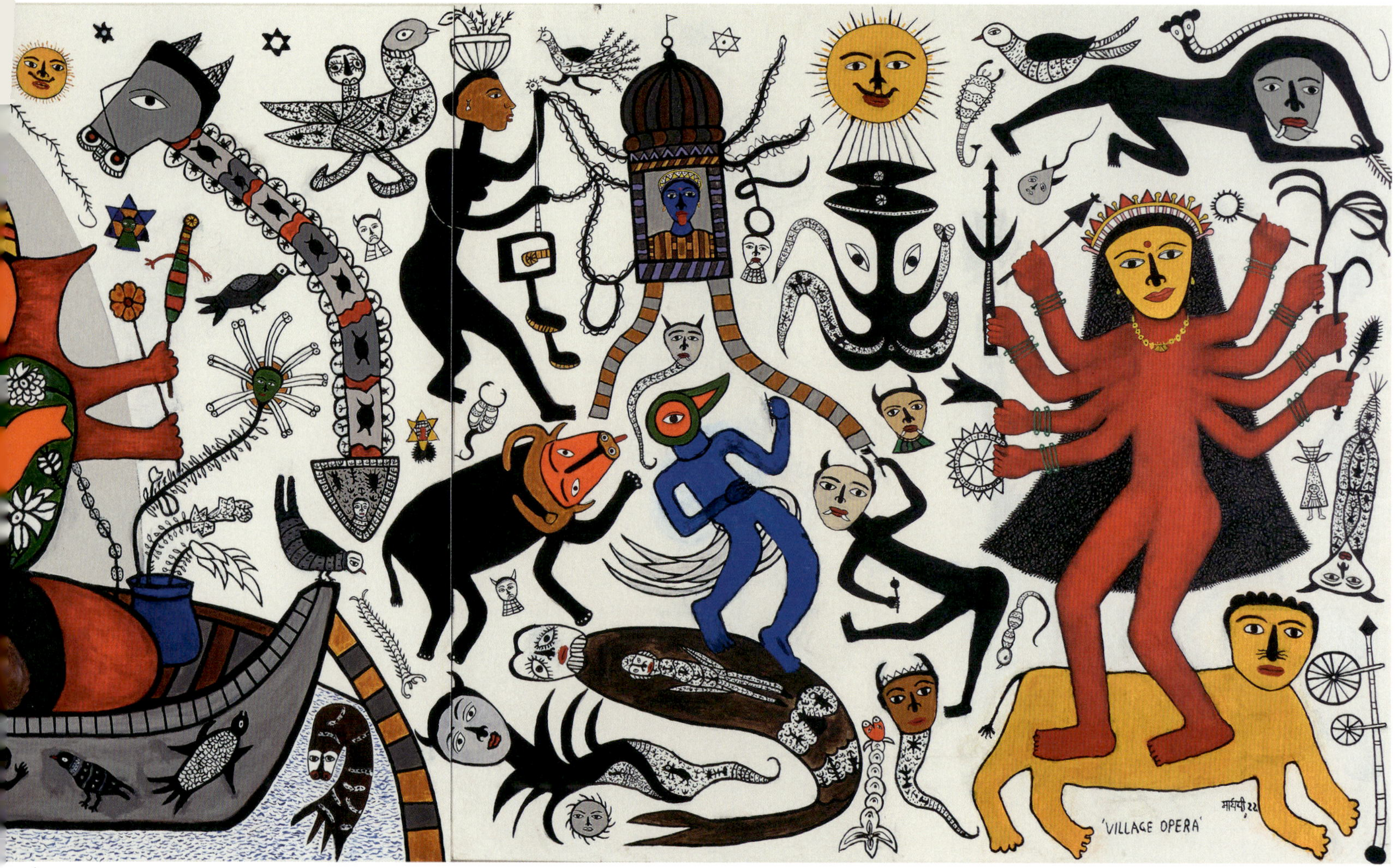

'VILLAGE OPERA'
माधवी,२२

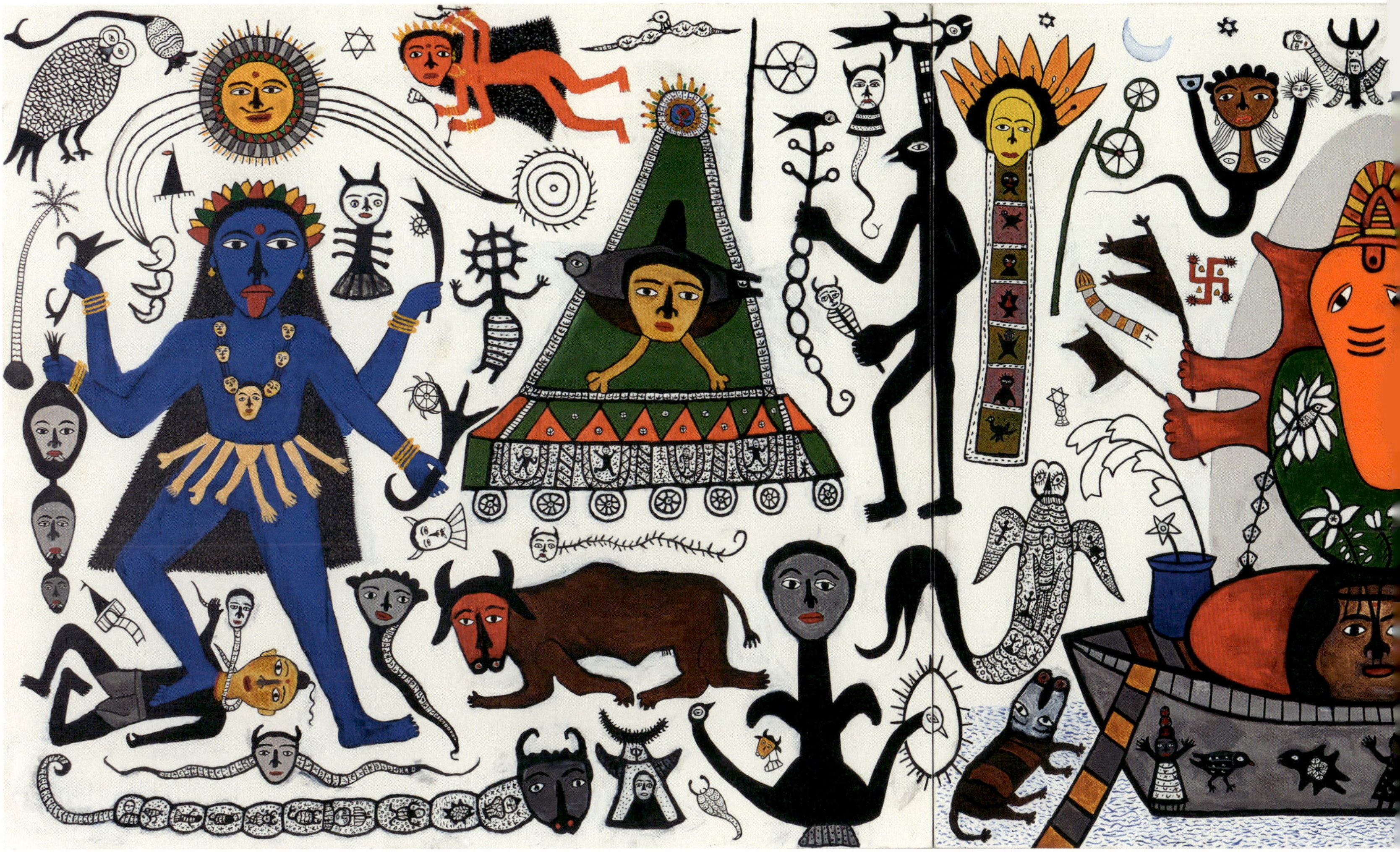

Madhvi Parekh
Village Opera, 2022
Acrylic on canvas, 612 × 186 cm
Photo Abner Fernandes. Courtesy of the Chanakya Foundation

> Manu Parekh
Chanting at Sunset, 2022 (detail)
Acrylic on canvas, 206 × 204 cm
Photo by Abner Fernandes. Courtesy of the Chanakya Foundation

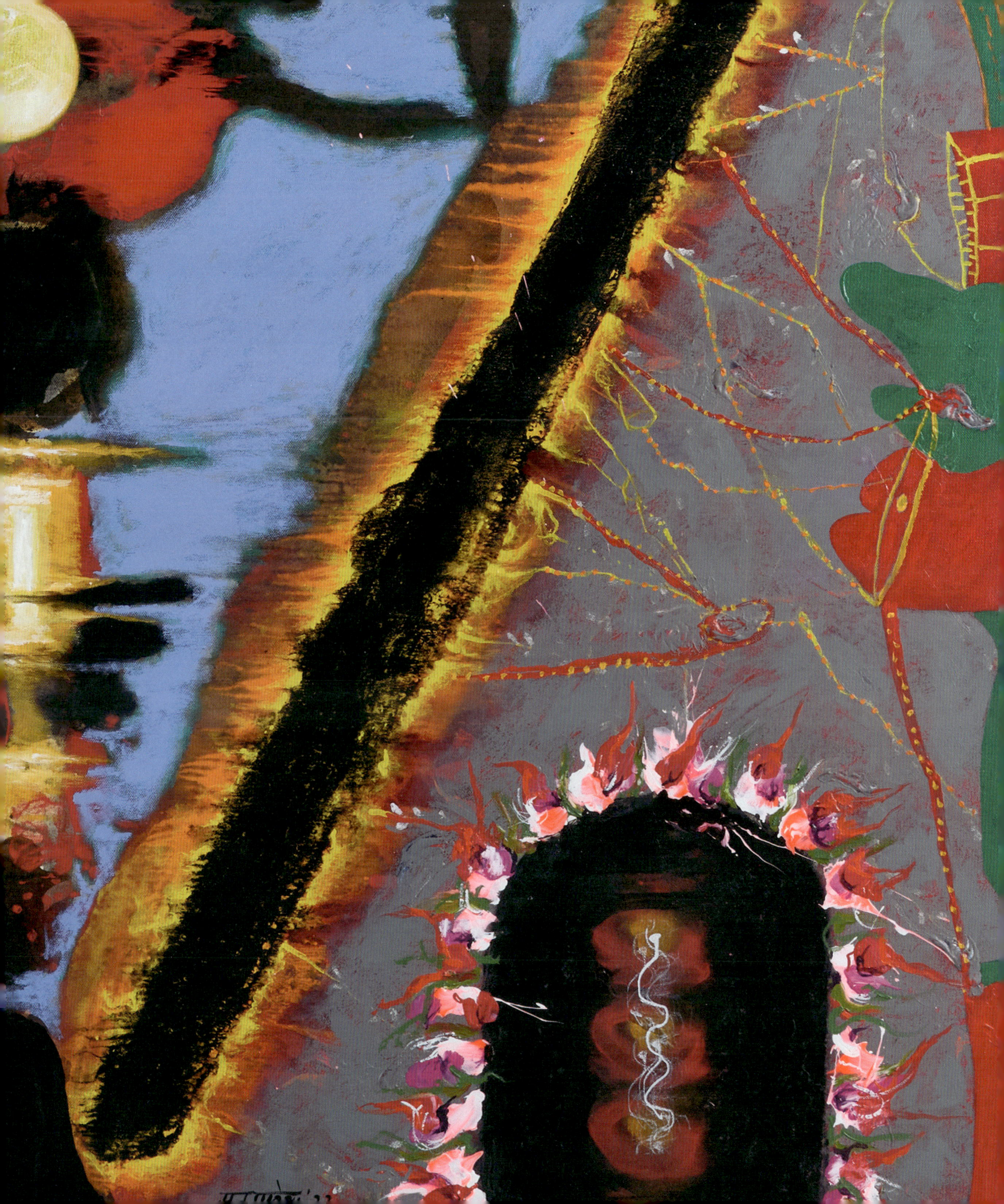

In 1963, the Weaving Centre established the National School of Design, and advised the corporation to bring in artists to act as design consultants with a view to helping weavers in India revive the country's longstanding traditions of weaving and embroidery. Manu worked alongside V.S. Gaitonde and others in its various offices,[16] which were known as Weavers Centres. This was not only an activist initiative to revive folk textiles but also an act of empowerment, intended to help generate employment.

On the surface of the canvas, his "mental landscapes" are fascinating, psychedelic, abstract representations that relate back to the Indian esoteric tradition. Shakti, feminine energy, is to be found in many of his — almost always large-scale — compositions, animated by hypnotic spiral patterns, broken lines, straight lines, and crosses that are laid over fleshy, floral patterns in vivid colours, bringing to life sensual cosmic germinations in which a plethora of coloured spurts seem to fertilise luminous uterine shapes. Bright colours dominate Manu's archetypal images, in which the male principle and the female principle fuse to create the whole. His cosmic visions appear to vibrate in unison with his brushstrokes, and these compositions — which celebrate life and its mystery — are awash with joy.

Enlightened Stones II (2010) is a powerful vision, based on just a few basic colours (red, yellow, black, and white), of the union of male and female. Shakti is a vibrant uterus surrounded by a golden halo that contains a garland of flowers. Inside it, an egg, represented by a black disc, is about to be fertilised by a sperm that seems to emanate from a series of red globular shapes occupying the whole right side of the canvas, which is split into two narrative moments.

Shiva's Tandav (The Fury of Shiva), from 2023, is an homage to Shiva,[17] one of the main Hindu deities. The canvas is divided into three sections that are separate but, at the same time, united by the rays of energy that issue forth from the rounded geometric forms represented at the centre of each section. The Shiva Tandava Stotra(m) (Sanskrit: शविताण्डवस्तोत्र, Romanised as: śiva-tāṇḍava-stotra) is a Sanskrit hymn, dedicated to the Hindu divinity Shiva. The highly rhythmic, engaging music accompanies the sacred divine dance known as the Tandava, which has vigorous, vivacious movements. When performed joyously, the dance is called Ananda Tandava, whereas when performed in a violent state of mind it is known as Raudra or Rudra Tandava.

The three paintings titled *Chanting at Sunrise*, *Chanting at Sunset* and *Chanting in Moonlight* (2022) represent three moments in the life cycle that, metaphorically, can be associated with the three phases of human life. There is a light-filled dawn, with the sun standing out like a ball of fire against an orange sun; this image of force and vitality is surrounded by a crown of flowers in bright colours (pink, yellow, and red), making it a genuine hymn in praise of life beginning. Then there is dusk — with the sun still reflecting its rays on the surface of the sea — depicted within a fiery triangle; a geometric shape that has numerous significant symbols, including the female sexual organ. The night is mysterious and sensual, with an oval surrounded by a garland of fleshy flowers that encloses a silvery moon, reflected in calm water.

Meditation on Moon (2023) is a philosophical work in which Manu transfers his vision of existence: an endless circle with no beginning or end, like the cycles of reincarnation. The circular geometric figure at the centre of the canvas is a

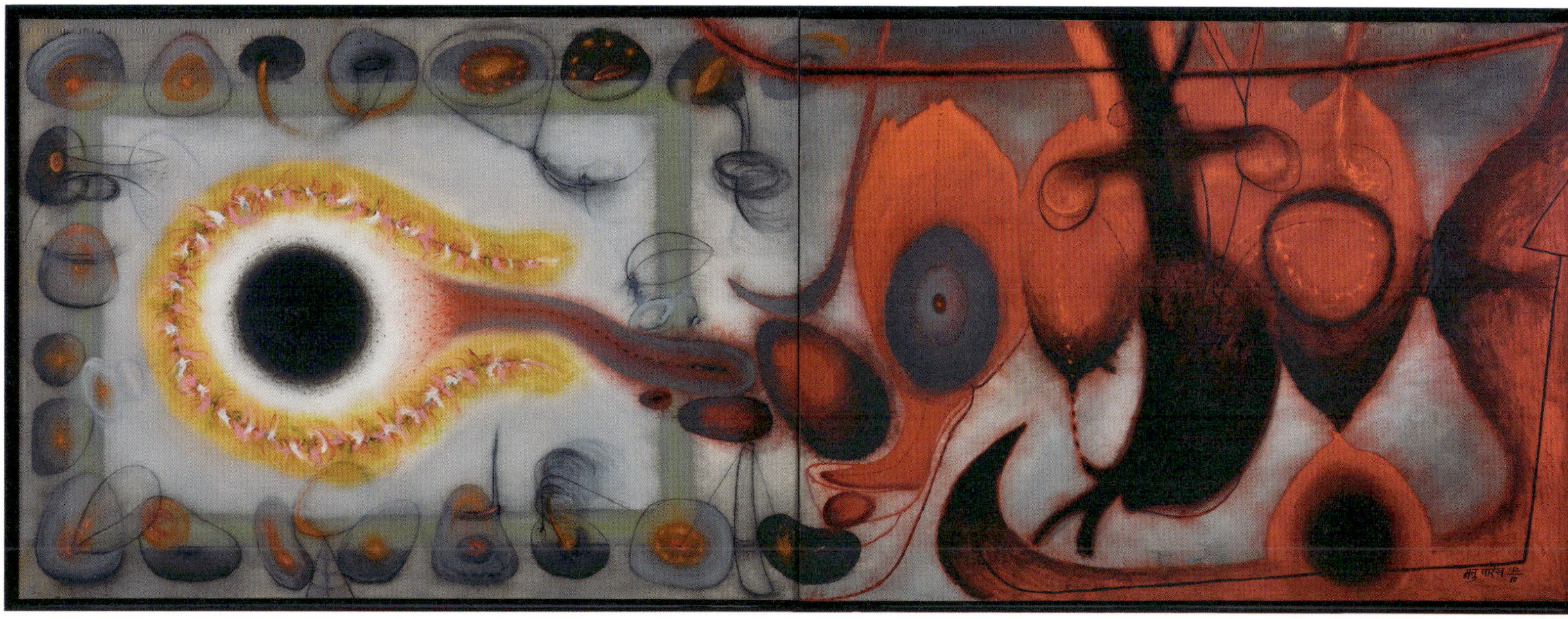

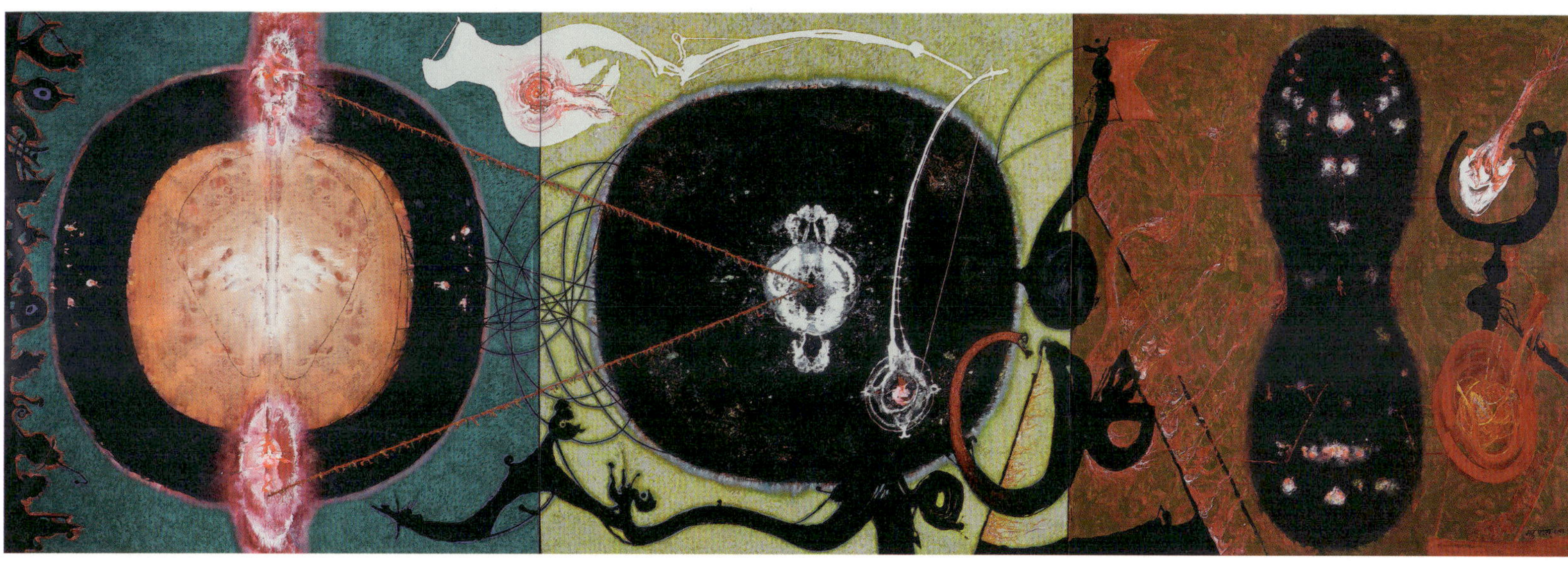

Manu Parekh
Enlightened Stoned II, 2010
Acrylic on canvas, 496 × 193 cm
Photo by Abner Fernandes. Courtesy of the Chanakya Foundation

Manu Parekh
Shiva's Tandav (Fury of Shiva), 2023
Acrylic on canvas, 615 × 204 cm
Photo by Abner Fernandes. Courtesy of the Chanakya Foundation

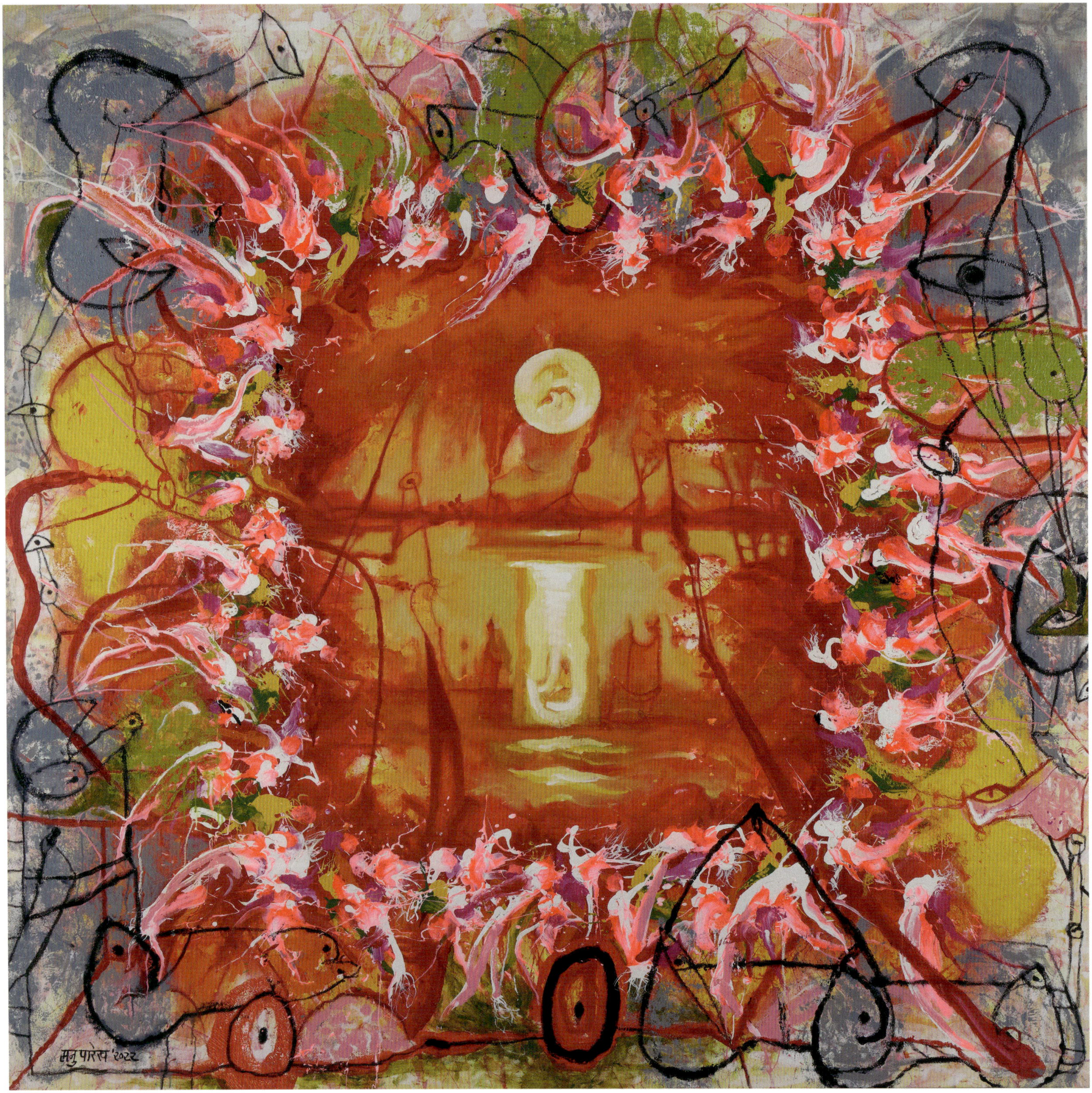

Manu Parekh
Chanting at Sunrise, 2022
Acrylic on canvas, 202 × 203 cm
Photo by Abner Fernandes. Courtesy of the Chanakya Foundation

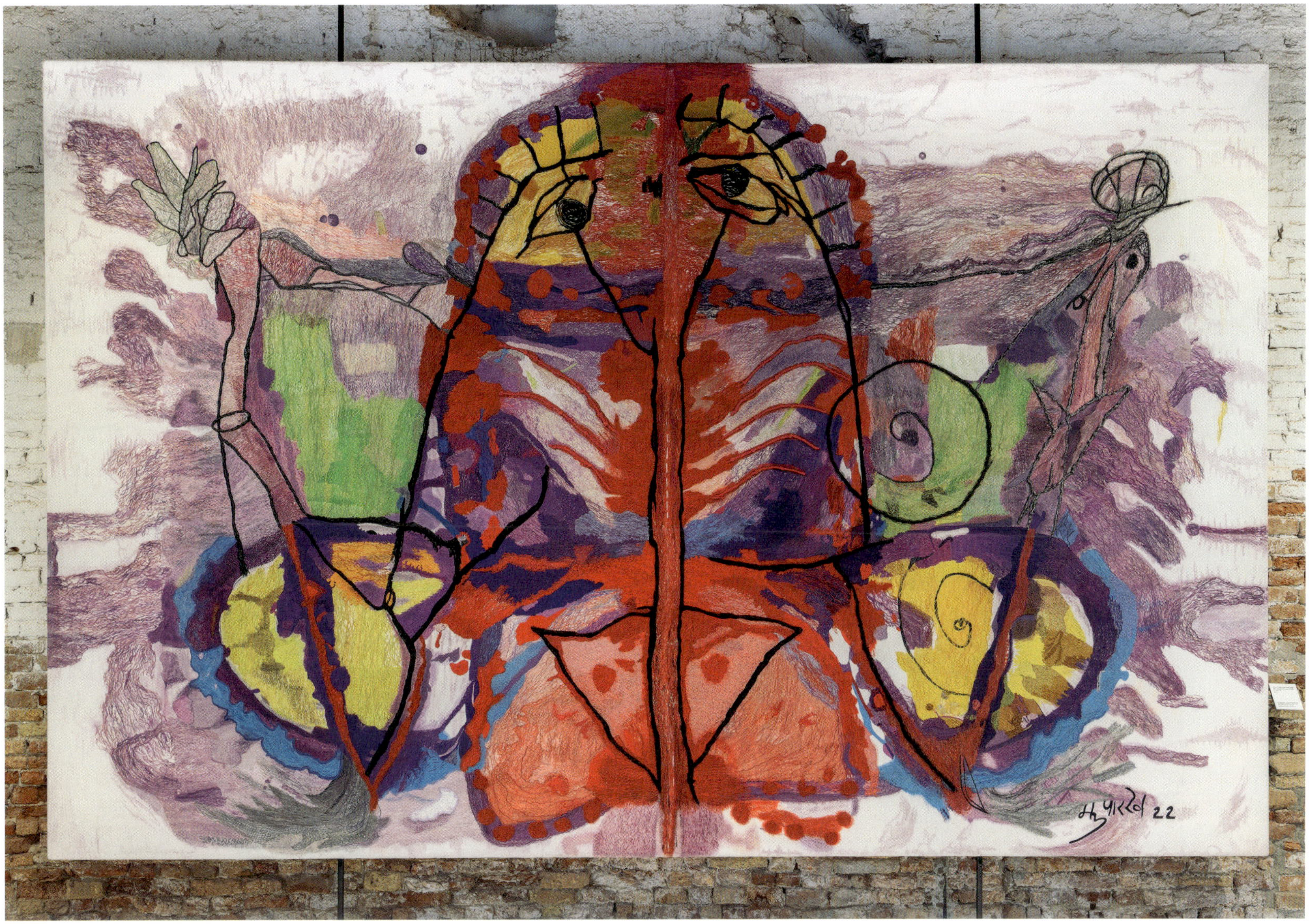

Manu Parekh, Karishma Swali, and the Chanakya School of Craft,
Untitled VIII, 2023
Organic jute, cotton, linen, and raw silk thread
on cotton textile, 282 × 432 cm
Photo by Danto Production. Courtesy of the Chanakya Foundation

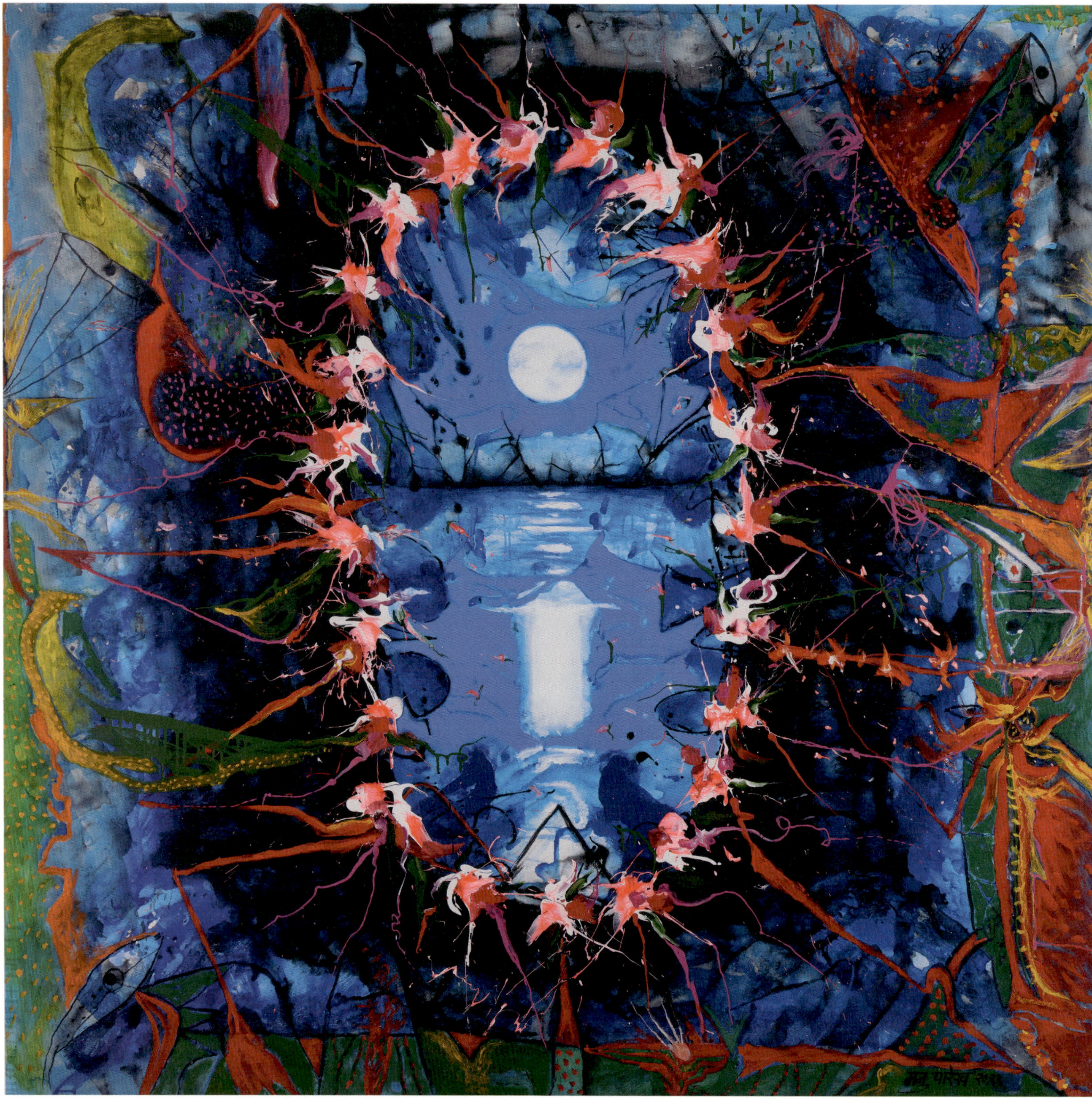

Manu Parekh
Chanting in Moonlight, 2022
Acrylic on canvas, 202 × 203 cm
Photo by Abner Fernandes. Courtesy of the Chanakya Foundation

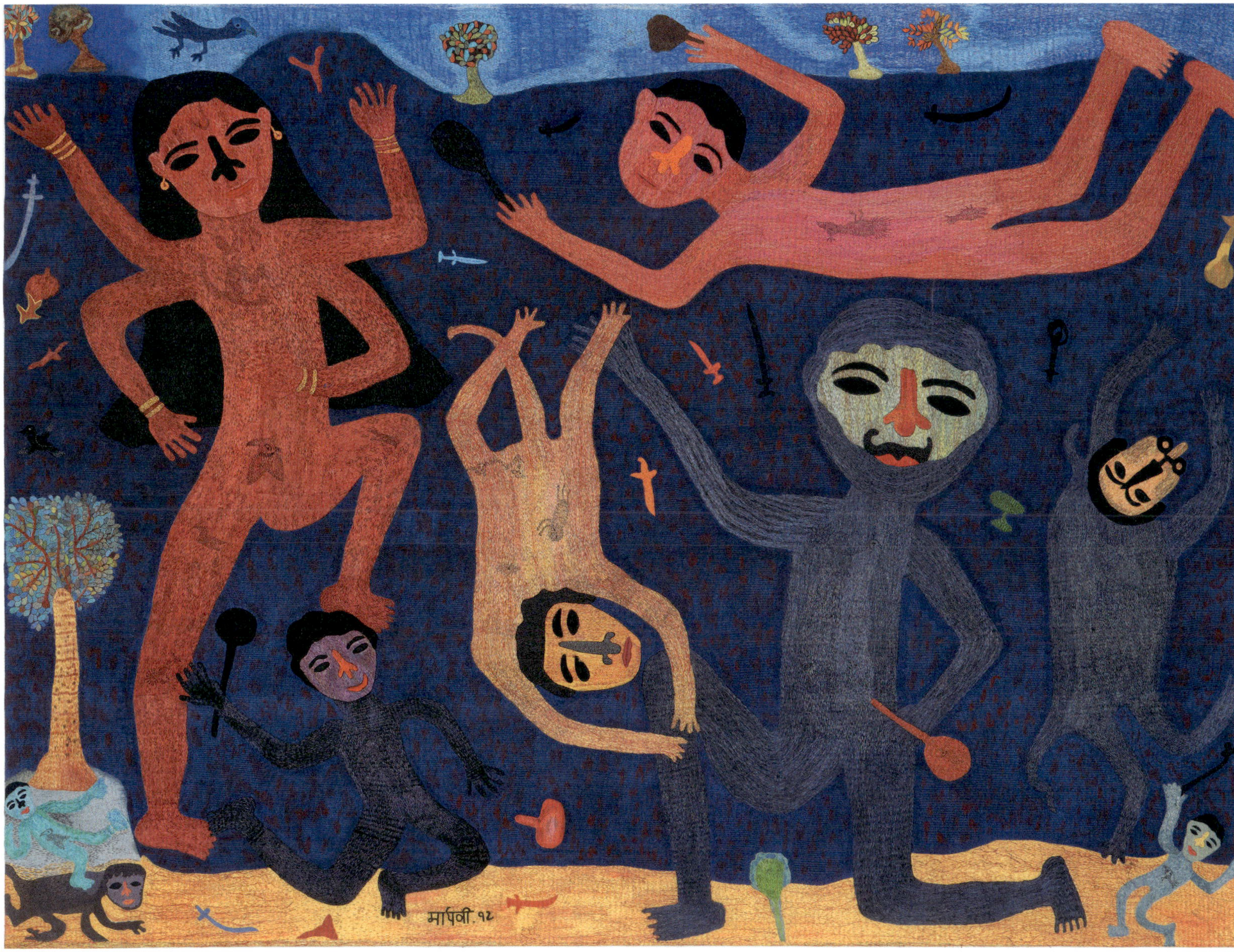

Madhvi Parekh, Karishma Swali, and the Chanakya School of Craft
Devi and Asura, 2023
Organic jute, cotton, linen, and raw silk thread
on cotton textile, 292 × 378 cm
Photo by Ryan Martis. Courtesy of the Chanakya Foundation

moon, but also the conceptual representation of our eternal return – a condition that can be stopped by an awareness of the self, which is achieved through the constant practice of meditation. The work, characterised by apparently irregular, disconnected brushstrokes, vibrates with a cosmic pulse that invites us to reflect upon our life and our intimate connection with the universe.

The purpose of *Cosmic Garden* is also to show the ongoing, fertile dialogue between three artists: Madhvi Parekh, Manu Parekh, and Karisma Swali, as well as between the pictorial works and their embroidered versions. Multimedia artworks such as *Festival in My Garden* (2021), *Resting Near the Pond* (2023), and *Devi and Asura* (2023) are quite extraordinary, highly original textile interpretations of three of Madhvi's acrylic paintings. Using more than 32 handcraft techniques and devoting innumerable hours of work to the task, the embroiderers worked together to create these masterpieces, which demonstrate to us how much this ancient manual art is far more than a "simple" craft. *Festival in My Garden* depicts a party taking place in a village in Gujarat. Represented on the square green lawn inside an indigo frame are adults, children, and pets who happily make the most of the feast day to play and to savour the natural world that surrounds them.

In *Resting Near the Pond*, the human figures — stylised in appearance and unrealistically coloured yellow, green, red, orange, and blue — rest close to a little azure lake that stands out against the pink background of the composition. The memories of his childhood in that region of India and of his home village are blended with stories bound up with Indian mythology, as in *Devi and Asura*,[18] two classes of divinities in constant battle with each other. Silk, jute, and cotton — all organic materials coloured with vegetable dyes — are interwoven and overlaid, creating surfaces that are almost three-dimensional. Many different stitches are used in combination to create surprising bas-relief effects, as in the work titled *The Third Eye of Shiva*, based on a painting by Manu Parekh in which the concentric blue, pink, and black circles — symbolising the circularity of life, with its endless deaths and rebirths — form a particular texture that embodies a perfect equilibrium between manual techniques, colour choices, and vision.

Today we can celebrate this body of work under the title *Cosmic Garden* in all its complexity, without being forced to choose between a binary either/or (either art or craft). Instead, this multivalent, interdisciplinary practice insists on both/and — both art and craft, major and minor, visual and functional, serious and beautiful. Such openness is part of what renders completely alive this form of art, with its ability to sustain multiple — at times, contradictory – reinterpretations, repositioning, and readings. This is also the hallmark of all great works of art, both fine and applied.

An ode to Shakti and its visual expressions, *Cosmic Garden* takes us on a journey of discovery that encompasses not only art but also the philosophical, esoteric, and artistic traditions of India and its exceptionally rich history.

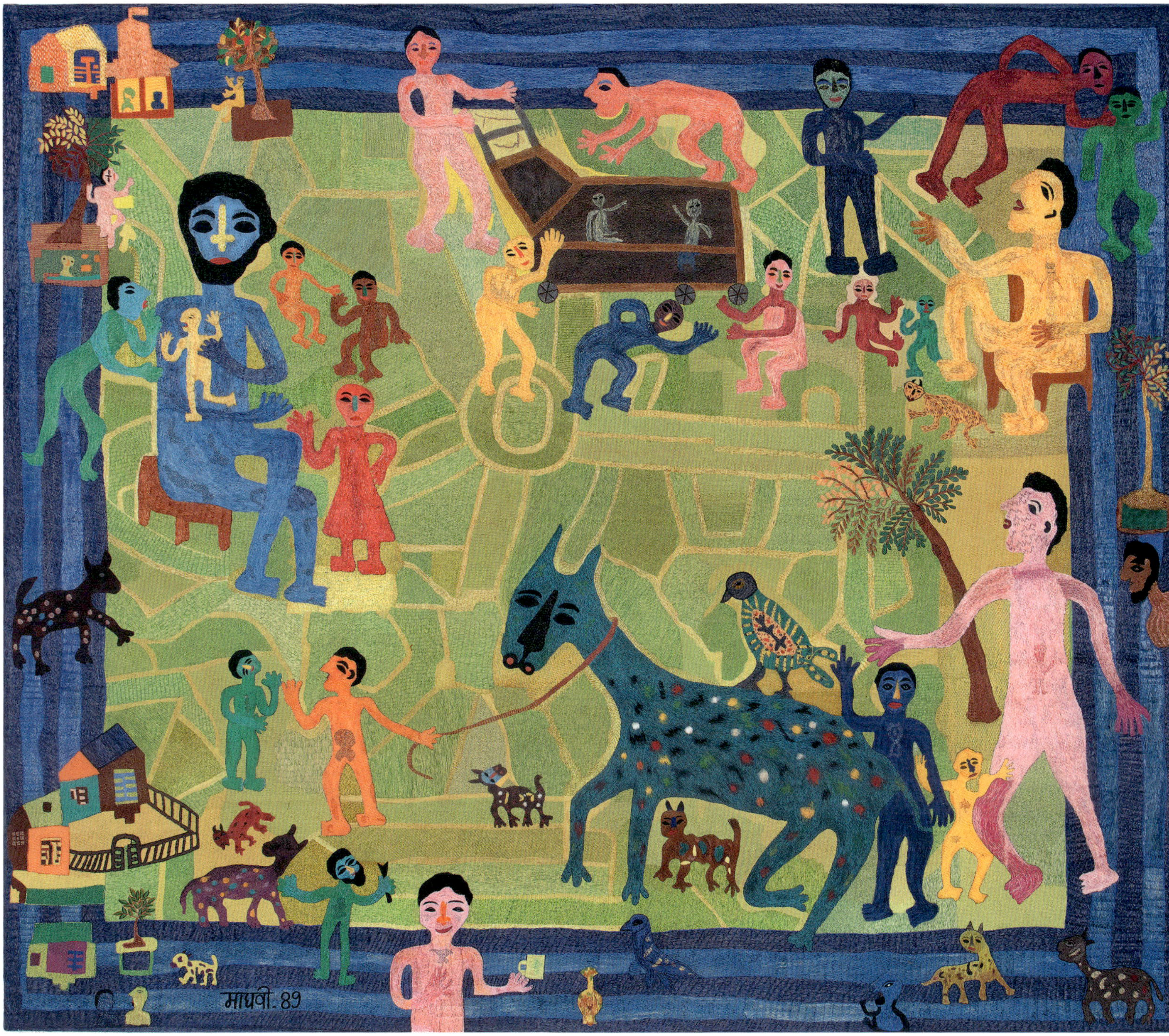

Madhvi Parekh, Karishma Swali, and the Chanakya School of Craft
Festival in my Garden, 2023
Organic jute, cotton, linen, and raw silk thread
on cotton textile, 388 × 328 cm
Photo by Ryan Martis. Courtesy of the Chanakya Foundation

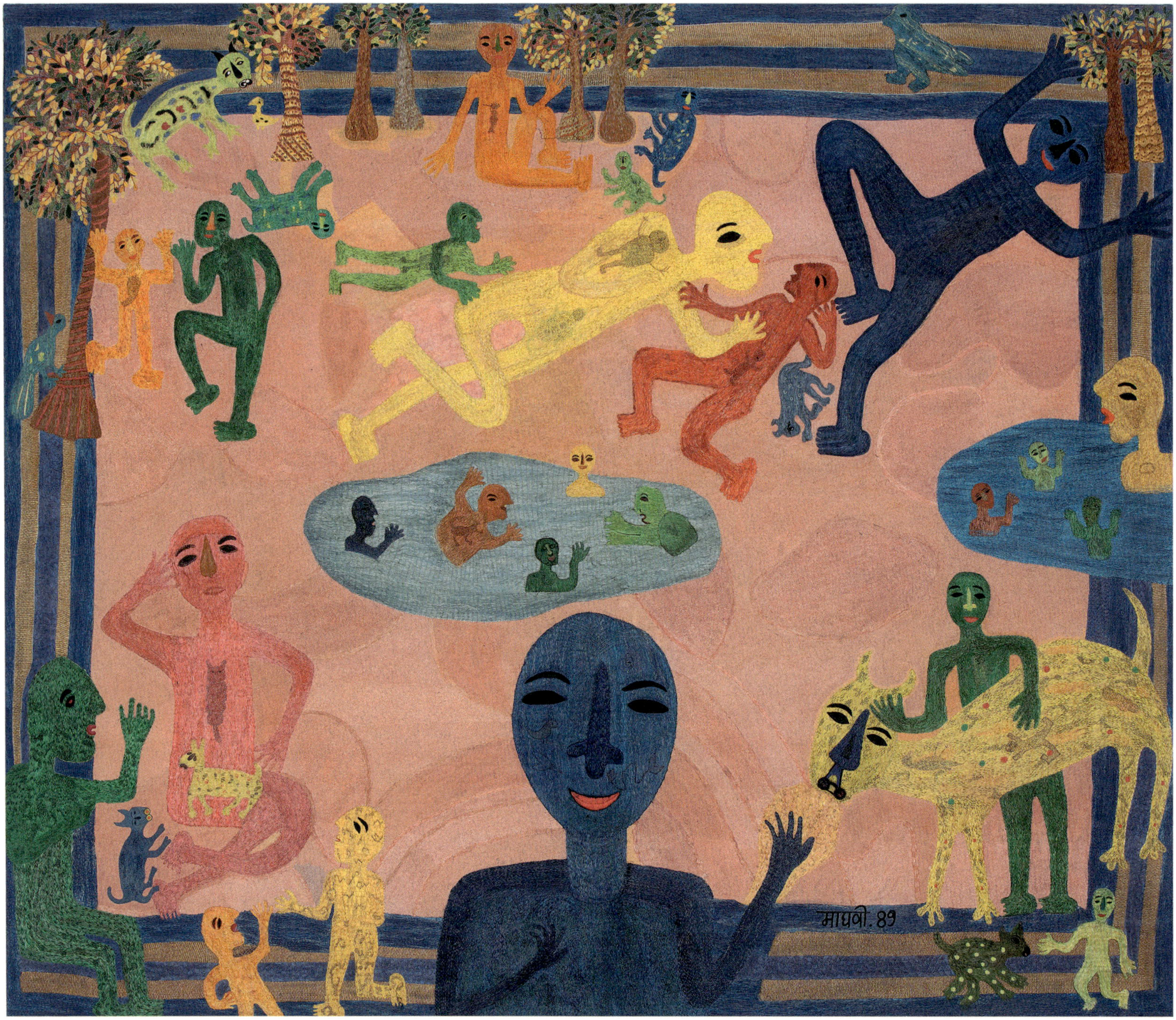

Madhvi Parekh, Karishma Swali, and the Chanakya School of Craft
Resting Near the Pond, 2023
Organic jute, cotton, linen, and raw silk thread
on cotton textile, 286 × 340 cm
Photo by Ryan Martis. Courtesy of the Chanakya Foundation

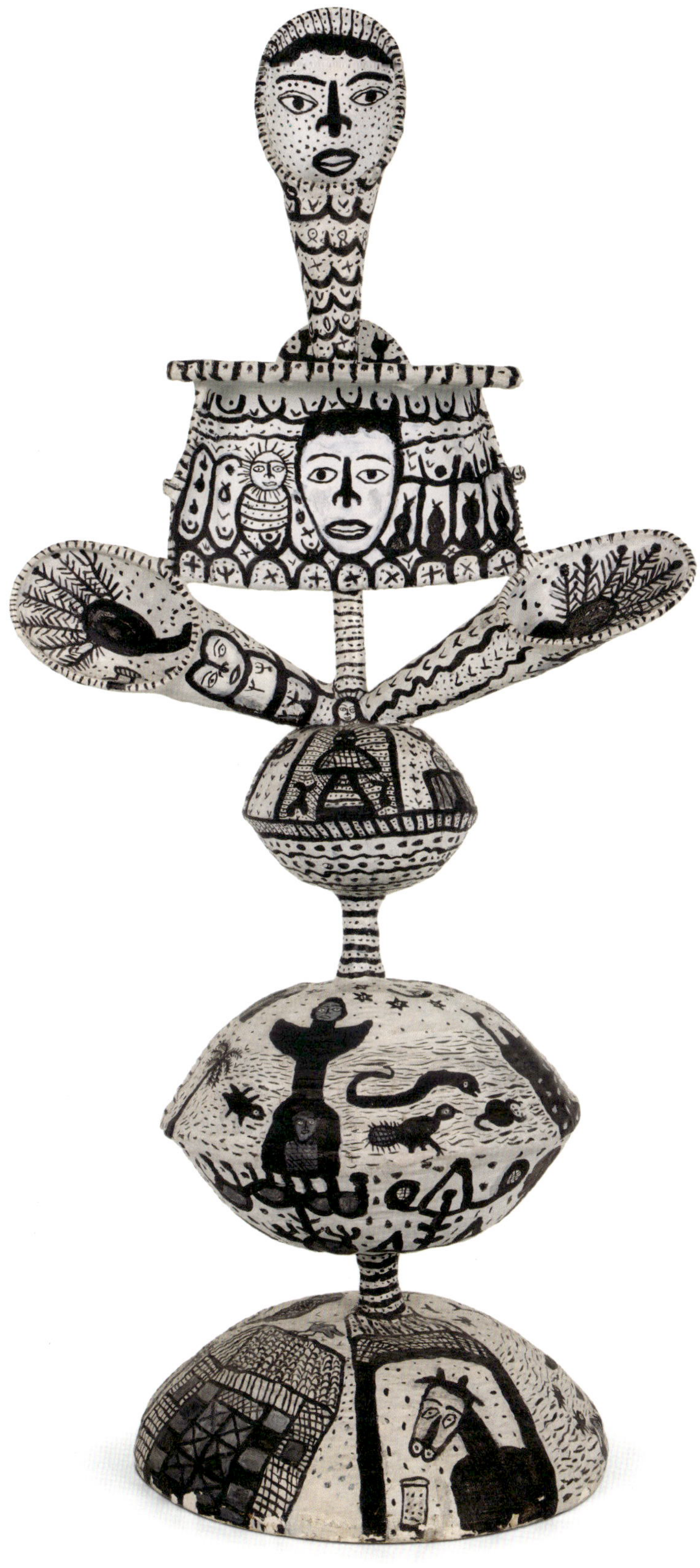

Madhvi Parekh
Kalpavriksha IV, 2006
Bamboo, basket, winnower, plaster of paris,
painted with acrylic, 71 × 52 × 155 cm
Photo by Abner Fernandes. Courtesy of the Chanakya Foundation

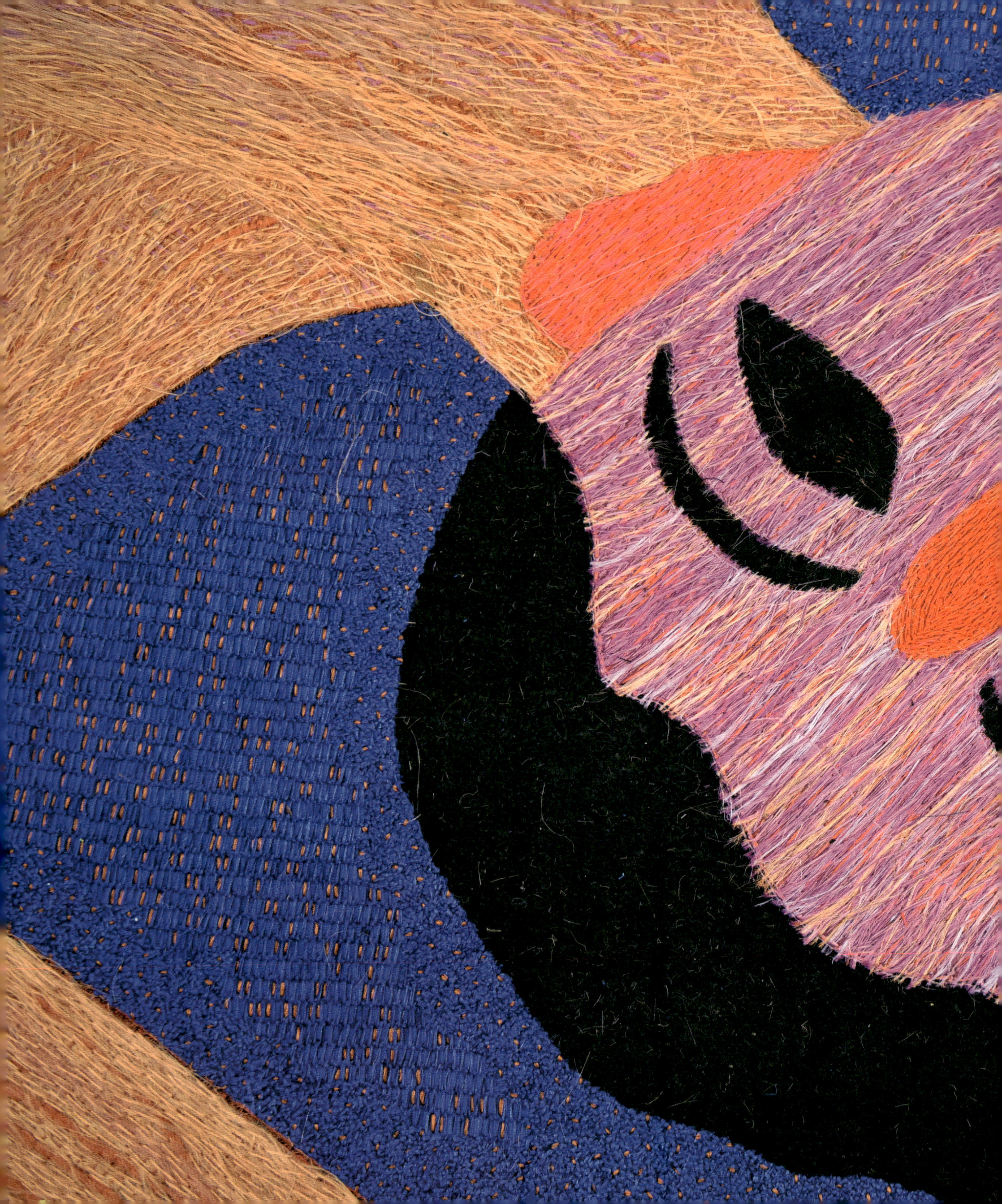

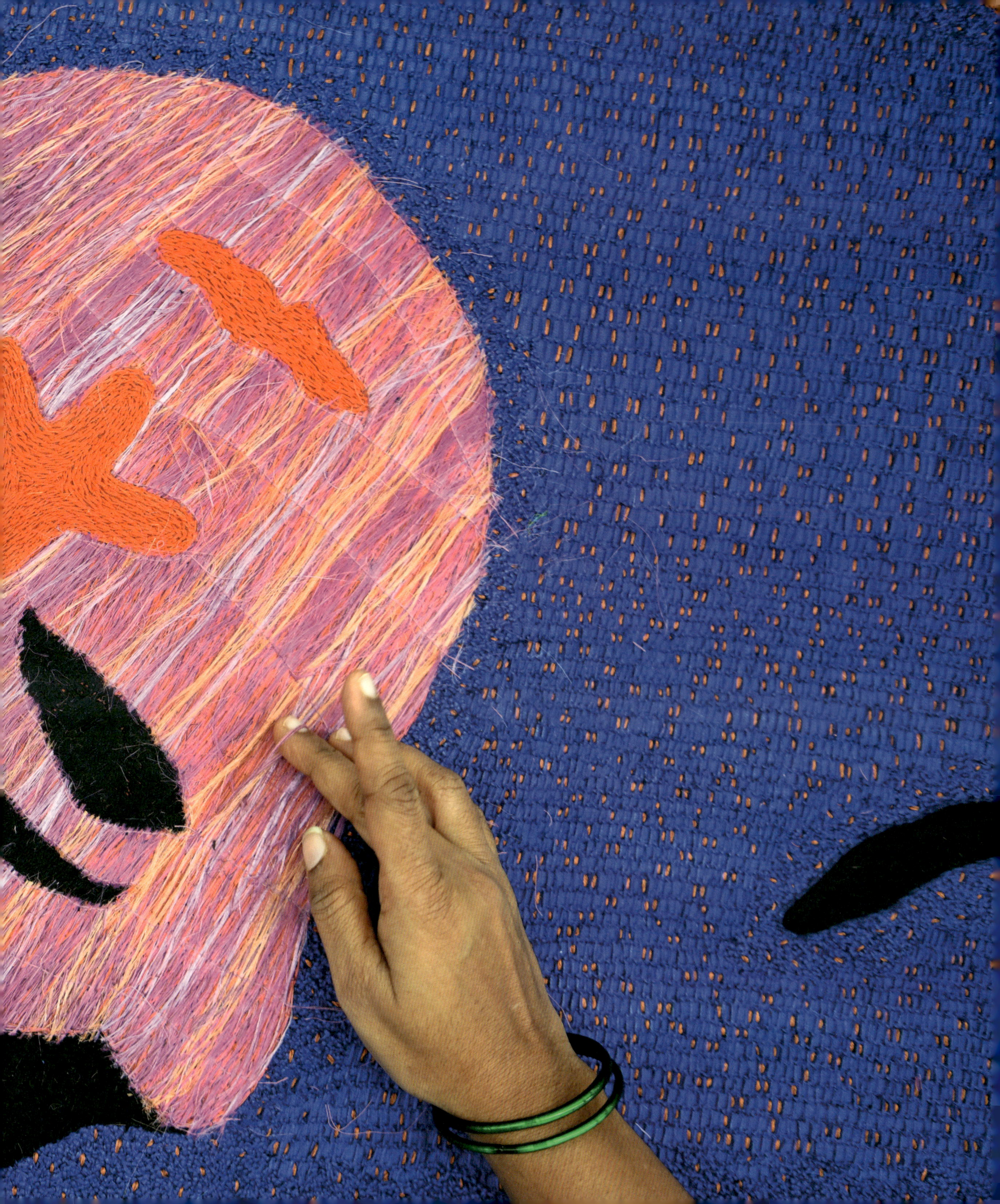

A Future Foretold

The Past, Present, and Unfolding Future of Embroidery

Dr. Ritu Sethi

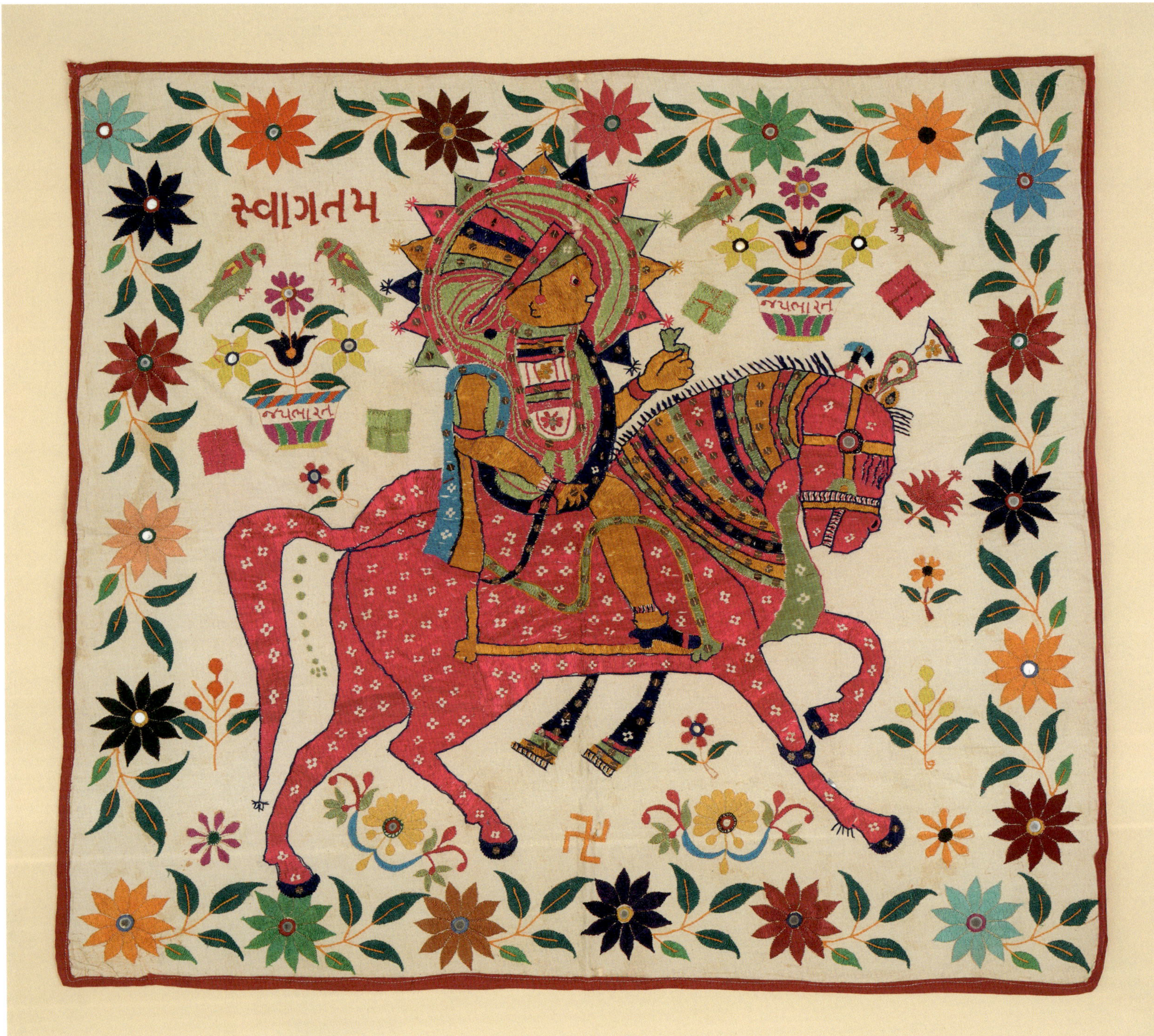

Embroidered Coverlet, Gujarat, ca. 1900
Collection of the Chanakya Archive

Few cultures can claim an embroidery inheritance as rich and enduring as that of the Indian subcontinent. Its composite sensorium emerges from the interplay of colour and vision, sound and silence, taste, touch, and texture — each heightened by the hands at work, where material and intention converge. Layered with meaning, and intertwined with history, myth, and legend, its conceptual framework can be best discerned through the *Brhadaranyaka*, Upanishad's delineation of the eightfold faculties of perception.[1] For it is through *mana*/thought, *prana*/breath, and *bhasha*/verbalisation that creation, expression, and discernment take form.

This essay examines the layered historical palimpsest of embroidery, illuminating its rich cultural significance. It begins by tracing embroidery's civilisational roots, shaped by royal ateliers, courtly traditions, and transnational exchanges. In addition, it shines a lens on domestic and personal embroideries of the everyday, recognising the contributions of who sustained and adapted these practices over centuries. This historical trajectory reveals the dynamic nature of embroidery forms and their evolution as shaped by intersecting social, economic, and cultural forces. Building on this foundation, the discussion turns to the artistic practice of Karishma Swali and the institutions she leads — Chanakya International, the Chanakya Foundation, and the Chanakya School of Craft — examining how their work challenges established hierarchies that have long separated the roles of artist and artisan. Through a focus on embroidery, these initiatives position the medium as an intellectual and material practice that engages with contemporary cultural production. By situating embroidery within a broader discourse of conceptual art, their work challenges conventional binaries, foregrounding the possibilities of craft as an active participant in the redefinition of artistic authorship and agency.

For embroidery in India is not just about fabric and thread; it is about memory and meaning, about the way the past converses with the present, about the silent eloquence of things wrought by hand and a testament to the remarkable continuity of traditions across time.

Civilisational Rooting: Indus Valley to Ajanta and beyond

Archaeological findings trace the lineage of the subcontinent's textile culture to the Indus Civilisation (2500–1700 BCE), as evidence of cloth technologies in practice extend from finds of spindles, fine copper and bone needles (with eyes), and traces of organic fibres showing credible proof of dye-knowledge.[2] Further in time, mythic literature, Vedic hymns (1500–1200 BCE), the Puranas, the great epics, and Buddhist and Jain writings, alongside other literary texts, extolled textiles through rich allegorical language. They described the opulent furnishings of courts and the attire of kings, queens, and courtiers — clothed in gold and silver, threaded with pearls and precious stones — though the specific techniques employed often remained elusive.

The *Jatakas*, stories of the Buddha's previous incarnations composed between the 3rd century BCE and the 2nd century CE, not only depicted customs, worldly existence, and the rhythms of ordinary life but also offered glimpses of dress and cloth. The *Sūci-Jātaka*, or "Quickly Threaded," recounts the tale of a young needle-maker who dared to court the daughter of the king's favoured needle-maker, renowned in a village specialising in metalsmithing in Kasi (Varanasi). To win her favour, he crafted an exceptional needle and boldly proclaimed its superiority outside her window — a daring attempt to capture her attention and admiration — reciting:

Quickly threaded, smooth and straight,
Polished with emery,
Sharp of point and delicate,
Needles! Who will buy?
Quickly threaded, straight and strong,
Rounded properly,
Iron they will penetrate,
Needles! Who will buy?[3]

A village of metalsmiths, a master needle-maker acknowledged by the king, a young skilled craftsman: all suggest the presence of embroidery, echoing the artistic sensibilities of an advanced society.

Our first real reference to embroidery appears in the 8th century, in *Kuttanimatam*, a work by Damodaragupta, who served as a minister in the court of Jayāpida, ruler of Kashmir. In his vivid portrayal of a wealthy grandee, he describes his footwear "embroidered with gold thread and decorated with a floral meander."[4] From the 12th century onwards, literary references to embroidered clothing and fashions became increasingly abundant. From the Sanskrit treatise *Manasollasa*, authored by the Western Chalukya king Somesvara, to biographies and narratives like *Puratana-prabhanda-sangraha* authored by Jain scholars in the 13th and 14th centuries, all mention embroidery among detailed lists of textile varieties.

While these and other references continue to pepper accounts, what remains shrouded in mystery is the actual appearance of these embroideries, the identities of their creators, and the processes used to craft them.

Monks, Travellers, Traders and Explorers

While no extant material evidence survives, the accounts of monks, travellers, traders, and explorers provide valuable glimpses into India's textiles and trade, shedding light on the costumes and manufactures of the period. Renowned as a pivotal entrepot connecting East and West, the Indian subcontinent lay at the axial point for exploration, learning, trade, and commerce. And while centuries of travellers to India marvelled at the richness and beauty of Indian dress, the first written description from the West dates to the 4th century BCE. Recorded in *Indica*, Megasthenes, the Greek envoy to Emperor Chandragupta Maurya's court, described the opulence of imperial life. He marvelled at the luxurious robes adorned with gold and floral motifs. Perhaps embroidered, though not explicitly stated as such.

While embroidery from India captured the imagination of overseas travellers and markets, the first recorded mention of techniques was in the

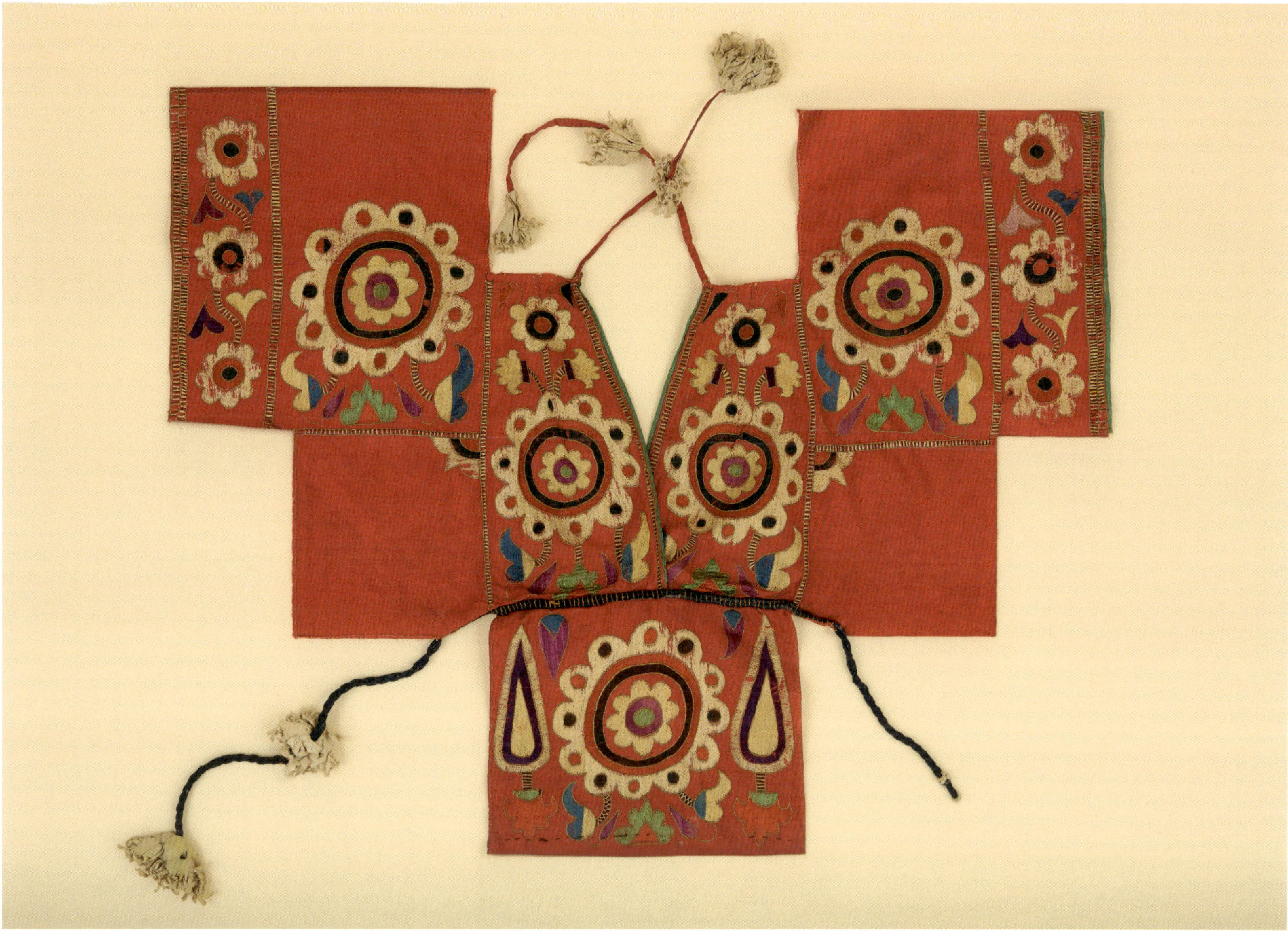

Choli, early 20th century
Collection of the Chanakya Archive

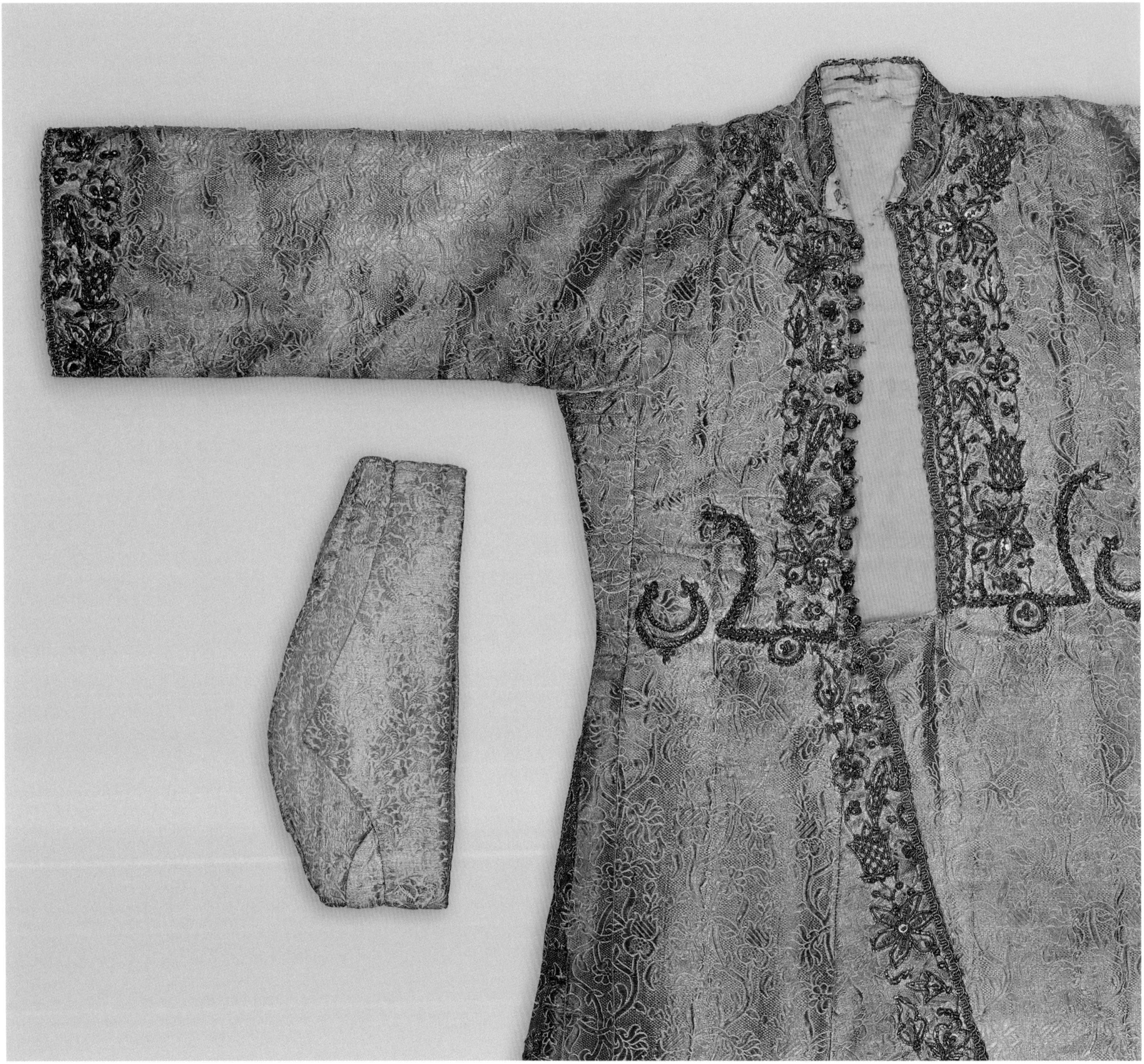

Child's robe and cap with gold thread embroidery
Collection of the Chanakya Archive

10th century. by the Arab historian and geographer Abu'l Hasan al-Mas'udi.[5] He noted that Cambay (present-day Gujarat) was renowned in the Abbasid capital of Baghdad for producing and exporting finely embroidered luxury sandals.[6] This embroidery tradition seemed to have had a continuing popularity and longevity, as almost three centuries later the Venetian explorer Marco Polo complimented these "marvellously beautiful" embroideries of Gujarat in his travelogue. These intricate chain-stitch silk embroideries from Gujarat, produced by the Mochi leatherworker and embroiderer community, using hooked needles, were by the 16th century sought after by the Portuguese and British. This tradition continues until today in modern-day Gujarat. As the survival of embroidery is rare due to the fragility of textiles, these examples of direct references to embroidery are of great importance as they provide a window into its long history.

Mughal Splendour

By the 16th century, the subcontinent's most powerful rulers, the Mughals, set aesthetic standards that produced the most spectacular and technically refined textiles. The breadth and sophistication of Mughal embroideries extended beyond magnificent clothing donned by royalty and courtiers to include all manner of furnishings from palaces to royal tents. Every aspect associated with the emperor and his court exuded opulence, including the visually stunning animal trappings of their elephants, horses, and camels. During the reign of Emperor Akbar, the tradition of imperial *karkhanas* employing skilled professional artisans came into prominence.[7] Court historian Abu'l Fazl records that Akbar paid "much attention" to the textiles commissioned for his court, changing its fashions and styles. Among the many luxurious fabrics that drew the emperor's attention was *zardozi* embroidery crafted from precious metallic yarn.

His heir, Emperor Jahangir, played a pivotal role in embedding textiles into the language of power and Mughal courtly culture.[8] During his reign, embroidered and other luxurious textiles transcended their function as clothing, emerging as potent symbols of imperial authority and favour. The gifting of the *khil' at* became a highly codified practice, signifying imperial grace while consolidating social hierarchies, extending patronage, and forging political alliances.[9] Empress Nur Jahan, Jahangir's formidable and politically astute wife, commemorated Khurram's elevation by gifting him a robe of honour, intricately embroidered with jewelled flowers and pearls — its presentation underscoring the complex interplay of power and familial ties.

The testament to the value of textiles in Mughal culture is further emphasised by their inclusion in imperial weighing ceremonies, a ritual of profound symbolic and charitable significance. During these grand events, members of the royal family were seated on massive scales and weighed against an array of precious materials, including textiles. Once weighed, these luxurious offerings were distributed among the needy and bestowed upon holy men. These ceremonies reinforced the emperor's image as a benefactor but also the deep cultural resonance and preciousness attached to textiles within the Mughal court.

The reign of Aurangzeb (1618 –1707) is widely acknowledged as a pivotal moment in the decline of the Mughal imperial power. Continuous warfare drained resources with a corresponding diminished scale of courtly patronage. Consequently, many artisans abandoned the court, migrating to provincial courts.[10] Despite the waning influence of the later Mughal courts, its aesthetic traditions endured. The legacy of the Great Mughal stands as one of the most significant creative forces, shaping and enriching the aesthetics of the textile crafts of the subcontinent for generations to come.

Indian Embroideries for British Tastes

In the early 17th century, Indian embroideries first arrived in Europe as objects of curiosity rather than commerce.[11] As their potential for wider appeal became apparent, Portuguese, French, Dutch, and British trading companies swiftly recognised an opportunity. They began commissioning Indian artisans to produce designs tailored to international tastes, marking the beginning of transcontinental commerce on the Indian subcontinent. The English East India Company (EEIC) swiftly rose to prominence within this burgeoning global trade network, setting the stage for a profound shift in the course of Indian history. Reinterpreted to suit evolving tastes and social conventions, the demand for Indian embroideries in Britain and Europe was fuelled by a fascination with the exotic. These textiles found widespread adaptation across clothing, wall hangings, bedcovers, and other decorative furnishings. These include the export of the *Satgaon* quilts from Bengal, made under Portuguese influence and worked in golden-yellow Tussur silk with dense pictorial patterning.[12] Shawls from Kashmir, *chikankari* of Dacca and Lucknow, were embroidered on fine muslin in both coloured or white thread and modelled into gowns, aprons, under-skirt petticoats, frills, and other manner of clothing.

For the wider British populace, embroidery treasures from India, valued for their rarity and cost, were publicly displayed for the first time in 1851, at the Great Exhibition of the Industry of all Nations, to "dazzle the eyes of so many thousands of European visitors."[13] Amongst the items on view were embroidered 'oriental luxuries' gifted to Queen Victoria. The Nawab Nizam of Bengal's extravagant gifts included a magnificent silver throne complete with its gold-and-silver-embroidered state parasol and canopy. The next grand spectacle showcasing embroideries took place in 1886 at the Colonial and Indian Exhibition, inaugurated in London by Queen Victoria, the newly anointed Empress of India. Her Chair of State was positioned beneath an imposing canopy of Indian cloth of gold, crowned by a baldacchino of gold-embroidered red velvet Delhi work. On the backdrop of the canopy, embroidered in gold letters and surmounted by the Imperial Crown, was the monogram of Victoria, Queen and Empress.[14]

Decline and Fall

Britain's rapidly growing mechanised textile industry had an intensified need for new designs and captive markets to absorb its expanding production output. An 1886 noting stating "India is in a position to become a magnificent customer; for to clothe but a mere percentage of such a vast population would double the looms of Lancashire."[15] This was to become a leitmotif of the decades to follow, as competition from imports of cheap mass-produced cloth from Britain, which offered embroidery lookalikes, led to a downturn in embroidery trade and production.

The evolving dress codes of royalty, aristocrats, and the elite — men, women, and children now dressed in either European fashions or modern, minimalistic interpretations of tradition — had a corresponding impact on embroidery ateliers. This shift extended to more quotidian attire, from school and army uniforms to the acceptable clothing of Indian employees across all levels of service, all reflecting British sartorial codes. Consequently, the demand for embroidered clothing experienced a marked decline.

The arrival of the sewing machine in the 1900s further contributed to the gradual dissolution of the intricate interdependencies between embroiderers and garment-makers. Traditionally, the geometry of embroidery was integral to the construction of a garment, shaping it to the human form. Imaginative stitchery not only assembled the various components of a dress but also harmonised aesthetics with structure and function. Borders, joints, and seams were transformed into elements of the embroidered design, while buttons, fastenings, braiding, and hems ensured the garment's fit and fall. Embroidered patchwork panels added flair, each stitch contributing to a cohesive visual language — a skill that slowly faded into obscurity.

The decline of these celebrated professional embroideries, once prized both within India and overseas, marked the end of an era. The exquisite fineness of historical manufactures became little more than a memory of the past.

Changing Times and Change-Makers

The ground reality at the dawn of Indian independence in 1947 was an economy that was primarily agrarian. 83% of India's rural-based artisanal population suffered from chronic underemployment and meagre incomes.[16] The intense disruption caused by the partition of the country, coupled with a stark acknowledgment of artisanal distress, underscored the challenges that lay ahead. In response to this pervasive decline, two pioneering figures — Kamaladevi Chattopadhyay and Pupul Jayakar — spearheaded efforts to regenerate India's handicrafts. Their visionary initiatives created enduring patterns of pan-Indian impact and influence in the field of crafts and textiles.

Alongside broader textile initiatives, they focused on revitalising domestic embroidery practices that lay at the heart of India's heritage. These personal expressions of rural and tribal traditions ranged from the vibrant embroideries of Kutch and Saurashtra in Gujarat to the intricate work of the Toda tribe of the Nilgiri Hills and the Banjara traveller community. They included the embroideries of pastoralists, diverse quilting traditions, and countless other forms of personal expression practiced across India's vast geography. Embroideries were created for rites of passage, festivities, and worship, as well as for the home, oneself, and family, with an extraordinary array of remarkable work intended for everyday use. Crafted within the confines of homes and communities, these practices endured through generations, with knowledge passed from mother to daughter, ensuring continuity and cultural resilience.

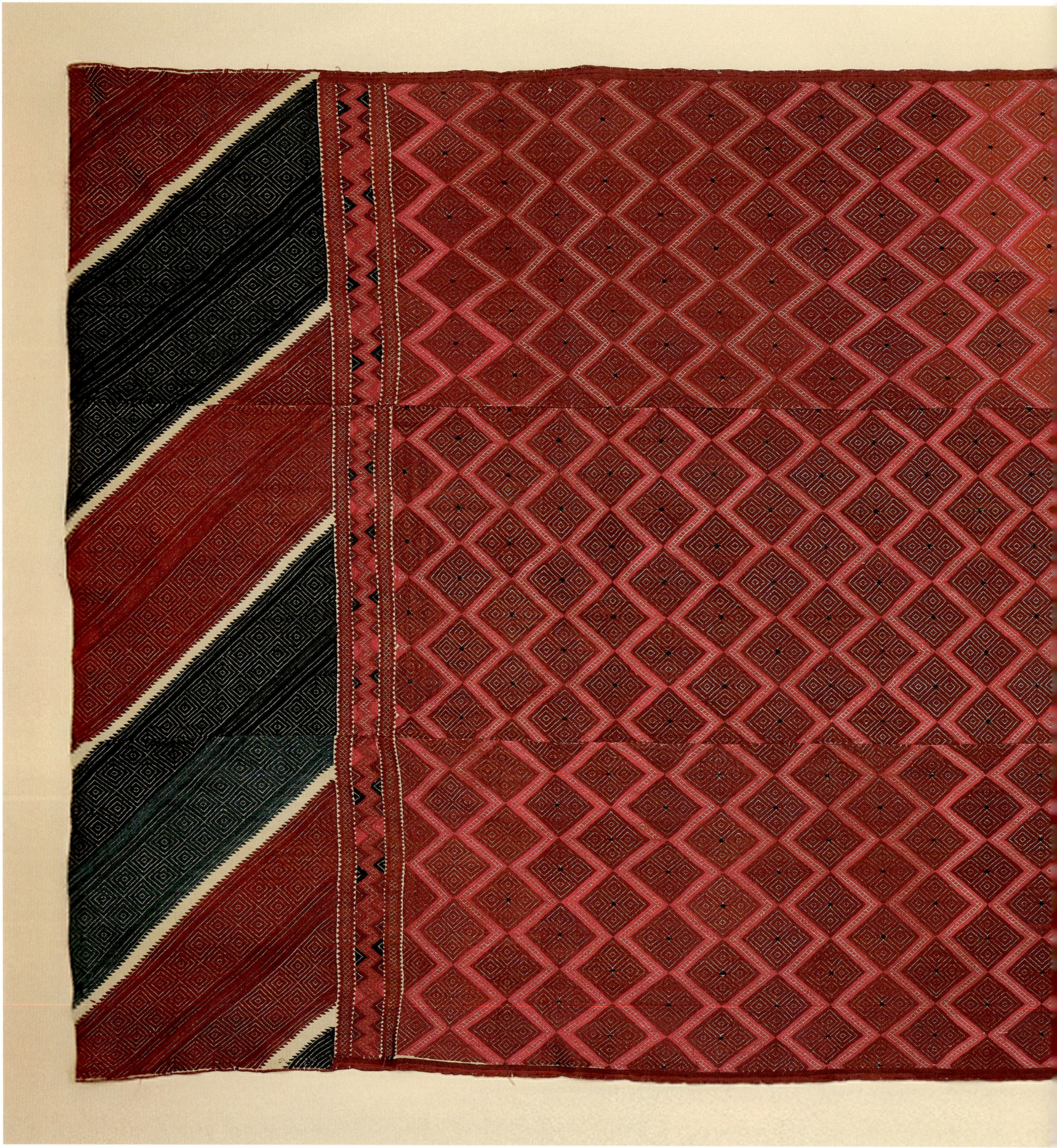

Phulkari bridal veil, Punjab, India, cotton base, silk, floss silk
Collection of the Chanakya Archive

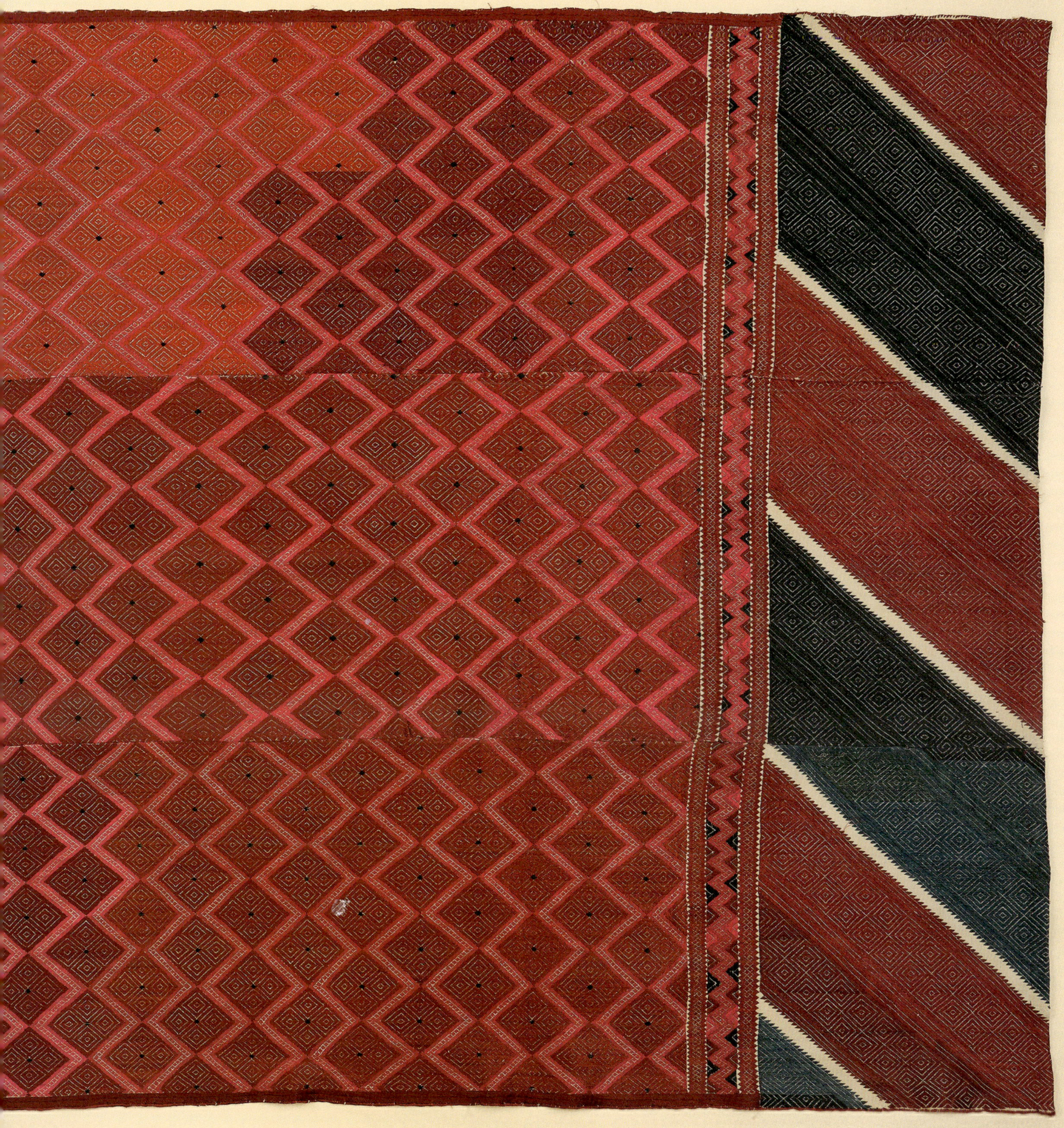

In Kutch, the 1960s was a period of unremitting drought. Relief programs offered backbreaking physical labour for meagre remuneration. In 1969, Chanda Shroff, part of a relief team, saw the commercial possibility of the embroideries of herding and pastoralist communities.[17] Leveraging the women's inherent skills, providing home-based work, she initiated the process of embroidering for sale in urban markets. Beginning the project with the women of the *Ahir* community and one village, Shrujan, the NGO she set up now, works with more than 3500 women in over 120 villages.[18] Similar work was also initiated by SEWA, Gujarat, under the leadership of Ella Bhatt. The work of Judy Frater at *Kala Raksha* connected embroidery makers to markets, remaining within community traditions to create contemporary textiles for the cognoscenti.[19] Meanwhile, she established India's first design and entrepreneurship school for traditional artisans, where many graduates went on to specialise in embroidery.

Renewing Professional Embroideries

Artisanal distress among commercial embroiderers became widespread following shifts in dress norms. Resilient artisans, now working at the margins, struggled to maintain their foothold in the trade amid challenging circumstances. However, innovative experimentation in the 1980s led to a steady rejuvenation of storied embroidery traditions, reviving some practices while inspiring new expressions. Notable examples include *zardozi* and *chikankari*.

Zardozi, the opulent gold and silver metallic embroidery traditionally crafted by professionals in *karkhanas* (workshops), was once a ubiquitous art form across India, distinguished by regional specificities. These commercially produced frame-embroideries catered to an exacting elite accustomed to the finest luxury and refinement. Historically used to adorn lavish interiors and garments during the Mughal era, *zardozi* faced a sharp decline as changing fashions and dwindling orders took their toll. This decline was further compounded by the Gold Control Act of 1962, which decimated the production of real gold *zari* yarn, and by the withdrawal of aristocratic patronage following the Privy Purses Amendment of 1971, which stripped India's erstwhile royalty of their privileges and allowances.

Though these embroideries continued to be produced, they gradually lost their sophisticated, fashionable appeal. The work became crude and rough, lacking the aesthetic finesse of its former glory, while its makers were pushed to the margins. Words like tawdry, cheap-looking, gaudy, and tasteless became common descriptors for *zardozi*. Its revival in the 1980s, however, was spearheaded by designer Ritu Kumar, whose eponymous boutiques showcased handcrafted clothing, including gilded wedding and eveningwear embroidered in refined *zardozi*. This renewed focus gave a significant fillip to the craft.

Similarly, white-on-white *chikankari* received its much-needed boost in the mid-1980's. Lacking the aesthetics of their glory days, the embroideries being churned out were a crude, rough, low-cost, low-value product that bore no resemblance to the sophistication of the past. The predominantly women embroiderers faced deep poverty and debt, were largely unlettered, lived in purdah, and remained vulnerable to exploitation by wholesale traders. In 1984,

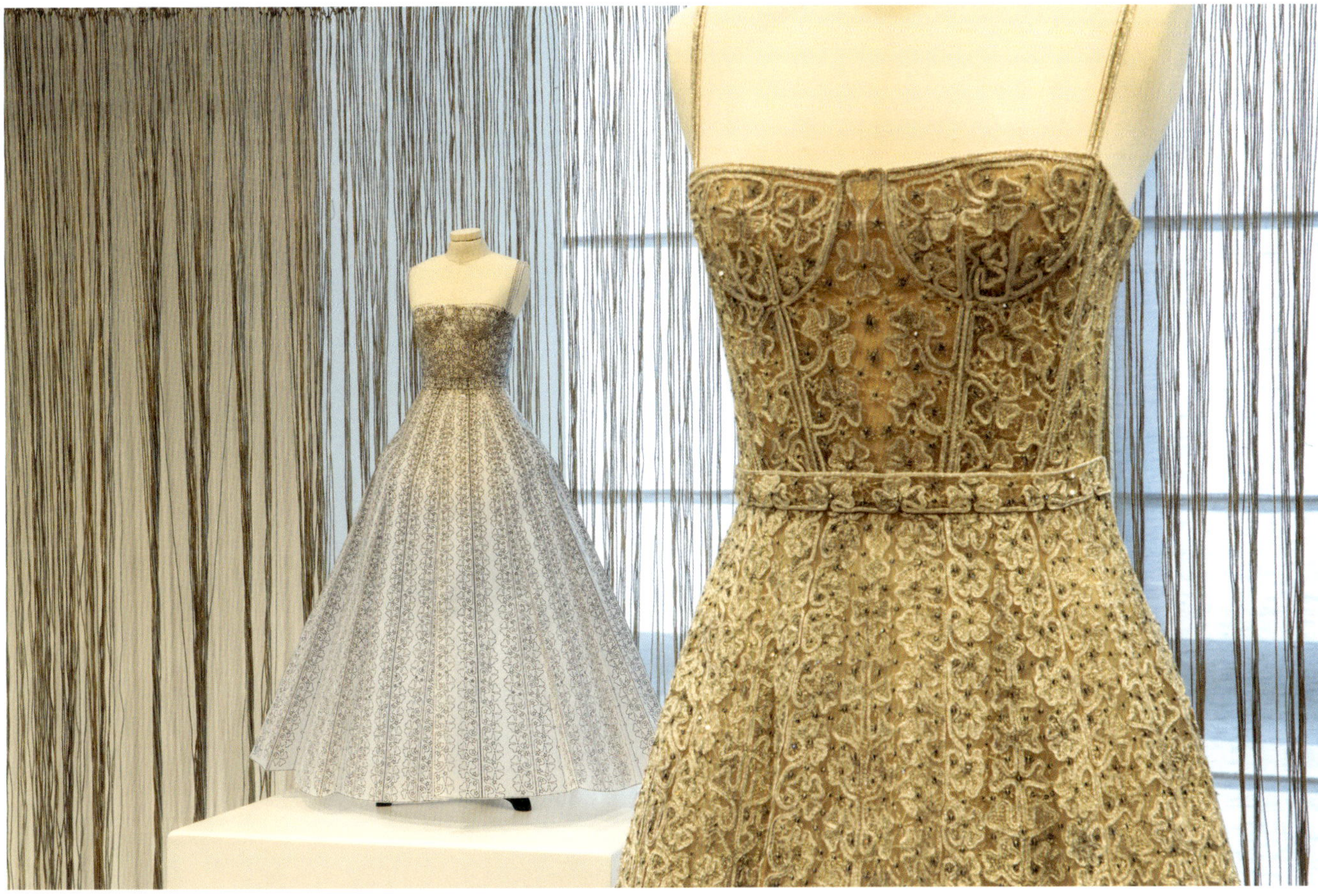

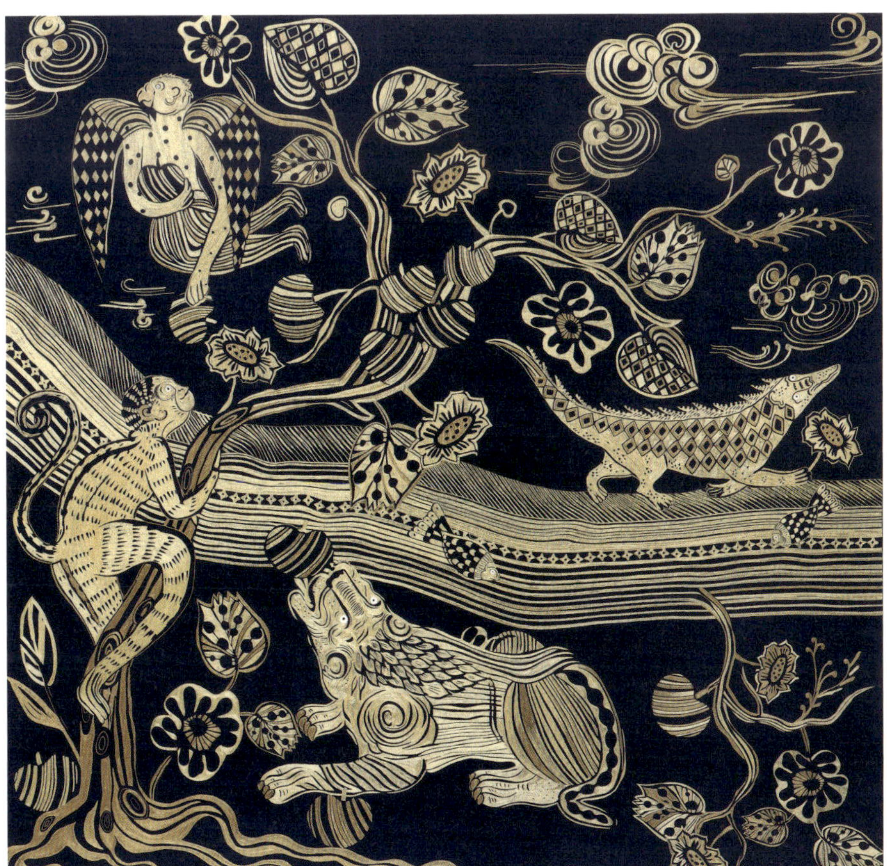

Chanakya revitalises traditional craft techniques through innovation. One such revival is the Chand *jaal*, an intricate lace of coiled pure silver threads, once favored by the Mughals. Courtesy of Dior

Karishma Swali and the
Chanakya School of Craft
Untitled, 2024
Natural tussar and muga silk on khadi
Courtesy of the Chanakya Foundation

the civil society organisation SEWA Lucknow, under the leadership of Runa Banerjee, sought to break this stranglehold by establishing an autonomous association aimed at empowering *chikan* workers.[20]

At its very start, designer Laila Tyabji[21] worked with the embroiderers to revitalise their skills and restore the stitch repertoire that was by then largely unused and almost forgotten to reclaim the aesthetics.[22] The embroidery now took its place at fashion shoots and red carpets, reviving the elegance of Mughal courts and Oudh aristocracy as its floral *butis*, paisleys, and geometric *jaal* motifs regained their excellence. With altering perceptions *chikankari* recovered its position as a textile of choice for the long sweltering months of summer, with the number of embroiderers, at the last count, reckoned to be more than a lakh.[23]

These commercial interdependencies between entrepreneurs, designers, and embroiderers worked to the benefit of all: reviving techniques, empowering practitioners, and introducing innovative styles and fashions for an expanding customer base. However, these were not the only genres to experience a resurgence. Other admired embroideries also received a much-needed fillip, rejuvenating once-lost visual languages. Parallel developments further spotlighted master artisans, drawing them out of anonymity through systems of recognition and awards that honoured their practice.[24]

This was when the government inaugurated the seminal, decade-long Festival of India in the 1980s, which opened up the textile landscape and introduced Indian crafts to the global market. These festivals, held in Britain, USA, Russia, Japan, and France, were a major series of high-profile events, and included exhibitions of contemporary textiles focused on the continuity of skills and tradition.[25] Spanning over a decade, these festivals repositioned hand-crafted products and ignited global interest in Indian textiles. While the focus largely centred on woven, printed, and painted textiles, the exhibition *The Costumes of Royal India*, displayed at the Metropolitan Museum of Art, New York, in 1985–86, showcased some of the most magnificent embroideries. Curated by Martand Singh, the curator and exhibition designer of the festival, it highlighted the richness of India's textile heritage. The overall impact of the festival was profound, opening new commercial prospects for handmade goods and revealing the inventive possibilities offered by their makers.

As this creative ferment took hold, both professional and domestic embroideries began to seep out of *karkhanas* and homes. The seamless integration of an entire ecosystem — designers, retailers, exporters, and buyers — with embroiderers fostered innovation, unlocked commercial potential, and propelled the craft into the contemporary landscape.

Parallel to this was the rise of commercial and entrepreneurial activity embracing a global design sensibility, producing fashion and bespoke embroideries for international couture houses. Yet, in the early 2000s, 'Made in India' embroideries rarely found mention on Western designer labels. Indian craftsmanship remained the invisible hand behind global fashion, despite the well-known industry axiom that 90% of all hand-embroideries worldwide — from haute couture garments to luxury interiors — originated in India. This imbalance took time to correct, but its reversal is now evident, echoing patterns that have shaped global fashion for centuries.

Material as Metaphor

Indian embroidery is enjoying a day in the sun, moving beyond set boundaries that in the past confined creativity within rigid dualities dividing the arts from the crafts. Embroiderers, embroidery ateliers, and artists are pushing the limits of possibility, challenging conventional notions of what can be achieved. Among the contemporary initiatives that merit special attention is the work of Chanakya International, led by Karishma Swali, whose vision has propelled the organisation to the forefront of textile innovation and cultural preservation.

Established over four decades ago, Chanakya International has remained steadfast in its mission to elevate and sustain India's rich craft heritage. At its core is a distinguished lineage of 13th- and 14th-generation master artisans — many of whom have been integral to its journey since its inception — whose expertise reflects centuries of accumulated knowledge and skill. Under Swali's leadership, Chanakya has built enduring creative partnerships with over 40 global fashion houses and celebrated artists, positioning Indian embroidery within the highest echelons of contemporary visual culture. With a career spanning 25 years, Swali has championed a model that reshapes the discourse surrounding embroidery, advancing its status from a historically marginalised craft to a celebrated medium within the rarified global art ecosystem.

By positioning embroidery within major international exhibitions and institutions, Swali has facilitated a critical re-evaluation of its artistic and cultural significance. This shift underscores a broader transformation in contemporary art, wherein textile-based practices are no longer relegated to the periphery but are acknowledged as vital contributions to the field. At the heart of this movement is a dual engagement: on one end, a profound and intimate collaboration with artisans whose knowledge spans generations; on the other, an unprecedented integration of these works into the global discourse of contemporary art. This confluence — where the deeply local meets the universally resonant — signals a radical departure from past perceptions, positioning embroidery as an autonomous artistic practice that demands recognition on its own terms.

Textile as Thought

Swali's leadership reflects an emphasis on reverence for traditional crafts and a forward-thinking approach to design and innovation. Alongside Sally Holkar,[26] Reema Nanavaty, and others[27] who advocate for India's handloom sector, Swali's contributions focus on the intersection of craft preservation, skill development, and socio-economic empowerment. Like Holkar and Nanavaty, Swali has championed platforms that not only sustain but also transform traditional practices, ensuring their resilience and relevance within a globalised economy. Her professional trajectory demonstrates a deliberate effort to challenge the reductive framing of Indian craft as a cost-efficient export, instead viewing it as a form of soft power that holds significance beyond economic value. By advocating for craft's intellectual and artistic merit, she advocates for its role in shaping cultural narratives, thereby redefining its place within the international creative economy. This philosophy is deeply rooted in her early exposure to the craft sector, shaped by her family's longstanding engagement with the

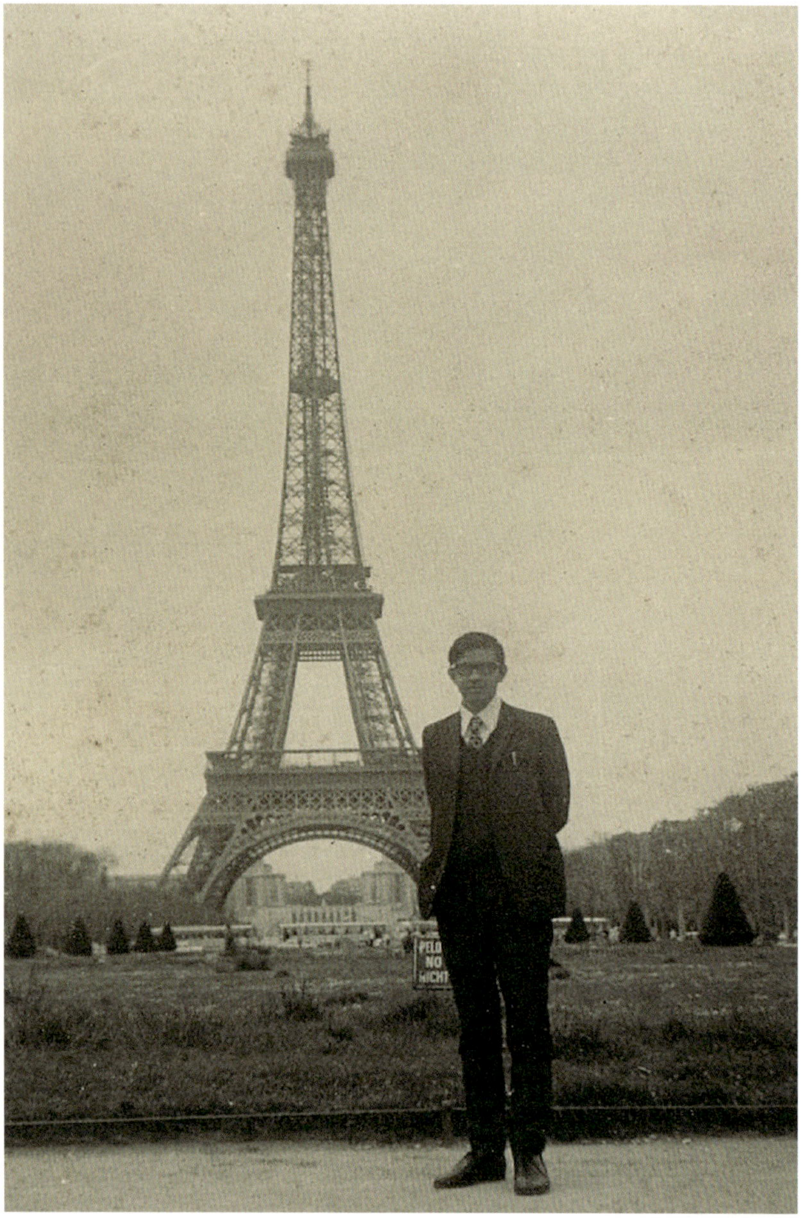

Mr. Vinod Shah, Founder of Chanakya, in Paris, 1970s
Courtesy of the Chanakya Foundation

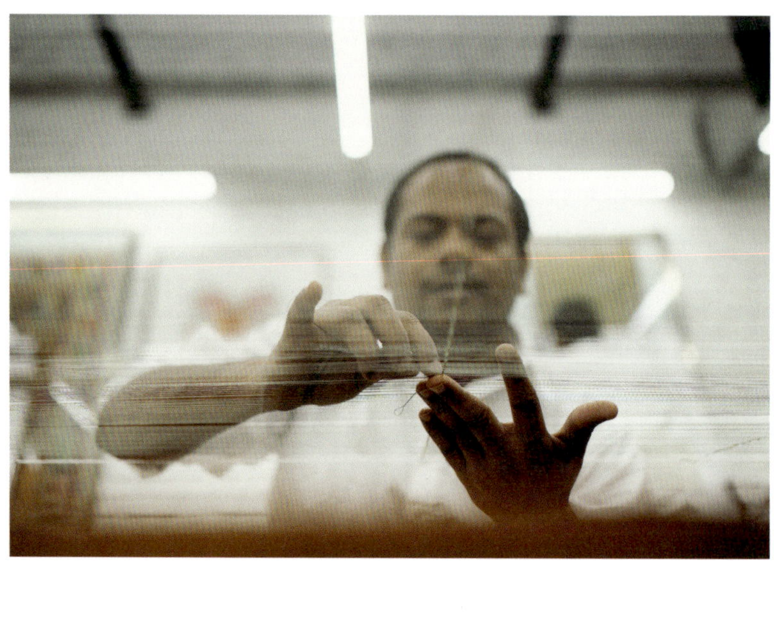

Living museum at the Chanakya Cultural Centre. Photo by Hashim Badani
Courtesy of the Chanakya Foundation

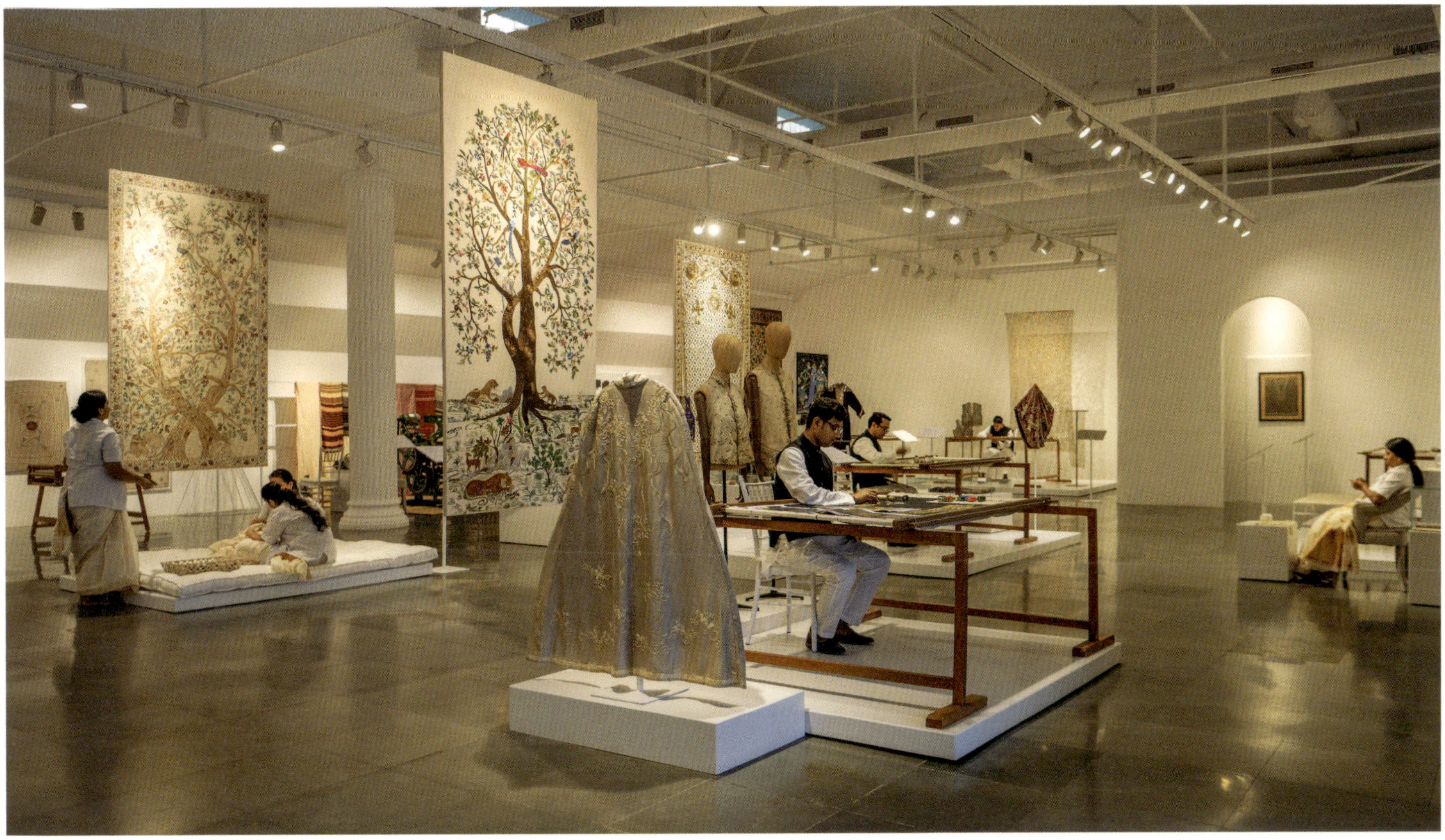

Living museum at the Chanakya Cultural Centre. Courtesy of the Chanakya Foundation

field, particularly under the guidance of her father, Vinod Shah, who founded Chanakya International in 1984.

Swali's engagement with craft began in her formative years, shaped by regular visits to the Chanakya ateliers. Conversations surrounding art, culture, and craftsmanship were central to her upbringing. At the age of eleven, Swali began observing artisans engaged in their craft, recognising the role of systematic practice, or *riyaaz*, in the mastery of embroidery techniques. This early exposure led her to view artisans as practitioners of a highly specialised skill set, contributing to cultural production rather than solely engaging in utilitarian labour. Her professional development included an apprenticeship under her father's guidance, providing her with a comprehensive understanding of embroidery traditions across India — ranging from the *zardozi* of Awadh to *kantha* embroidery in Bengal, each characterised by distinctive regional styles and historical contexts. This experience informed her later work at Chanakya International, where she advocated for artisans to be recognised as equal stakeholders in the creative process. Her work also emphasises cultural sustainability through documentation, research, and practice. Chanakya International has developed an archive of over 10,000 historical references and 100,000 artistic explorations, cataloguing the historical, symbolic, and regional contexts of various embroidery techniques. This archive serves as both a reference for contemporary design projects and an educational resource for future generations. By positioning artisans as active participants in creative dialogue, Swali's initiatives aim to counter the marginalisation often faced by craft communities in the modern economy.

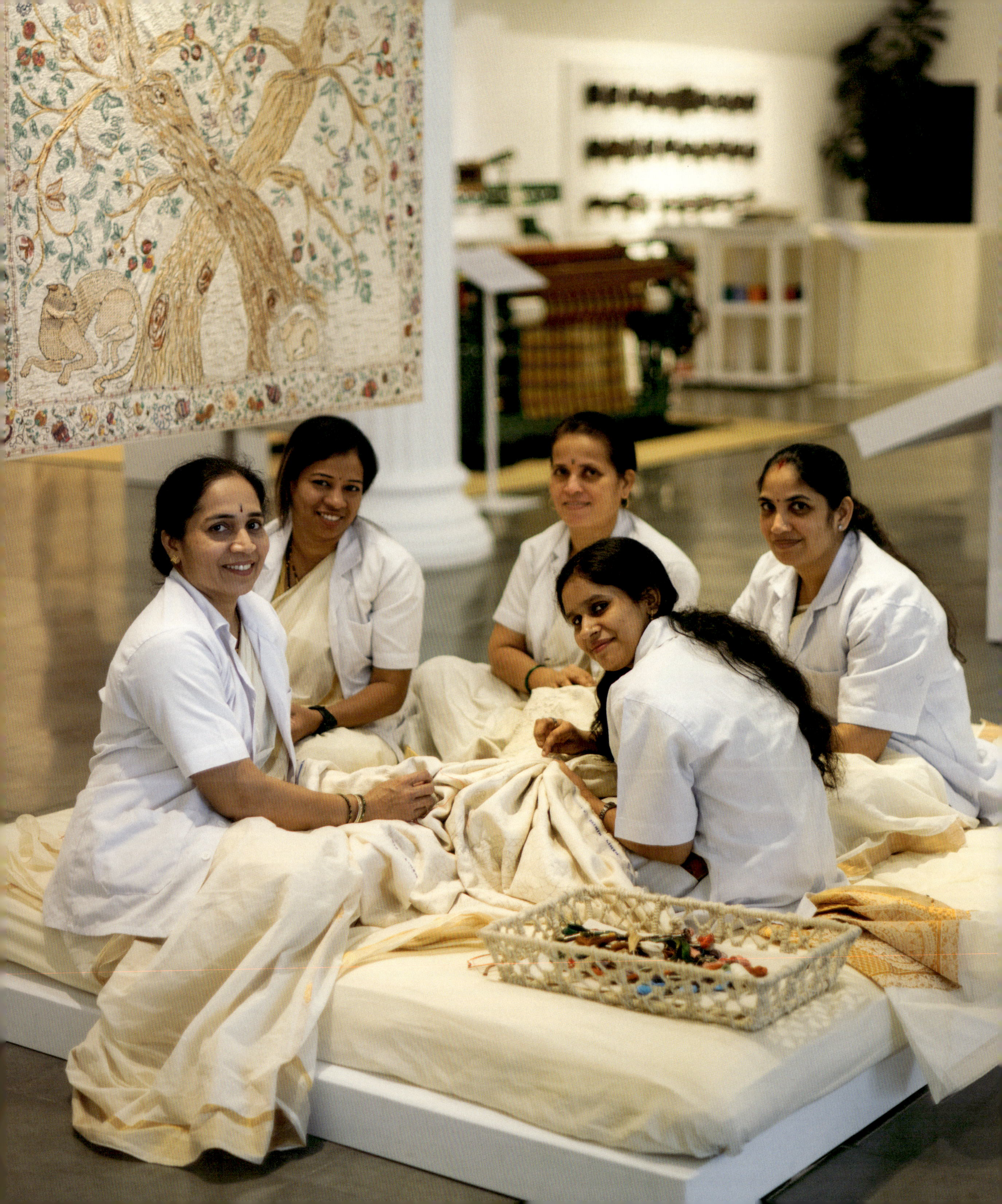

Between Tradition and Transformation

India's craft traditions rely on the expertise of makers, practitioners, educators, and innovators who sustain and adapt these practices, integrating ancestral knowledge with contemporary insights. In an era characterised by rapid change, preserving these crafts not only maintains cultural narratives but also offers an alternative to homogenised production systems.

Acknowledging the imperative need to sustain and nurture the artisanal community, the Chanakya School of Craft was established in 2016 as a non-profit institution dedicated to craft, culture, and the creation of new autonomy for women. This pioneering school offers a comprehensive curriculum that encompasses both traditional techniques and contemporary design principles, so that students are well-equipped to navigate and contribute to the evolving landscape of art and fashion. This perspective has led to numerous artistic endeavours that blur the boundaries between these disciplines, resulting in works that are both inventive and deeply rooted in tradition.

Functioning as the philanthropic arm of Chanakya International, the Foundation amplifies its mission through its educational endeavour — the Chanakya School of Craft — positioning itself at the front line of a transformative engagement with embroidery and other artisanal traditions. Central to its philosophy is a profound re-evaluation of the conventional hierarchies that have historically delineated the roles of artist and artisan. By fostering a renewed discourse, it challenges these long-standing distinctions, recognising embroidery not merely as a decorative technique but as a medium of conceptual and material innovation.

A distinctive feature of the school is its emphasis on empowering women from underserved communities. In an industry where female artisans have long been underrepresented and, as a result, undervalued, the Chanakya School of Craft offers a vital space for women to develop specialised skills, gain financial autonomy, and assert their creative voices. This empowerment is not confined to the individual; it reverberates through entire communities, strengthening social structures and contributing to a larger, evolving dialogue on gender equity within the arts. The school's mission is encapsulated in its commitment to preserving global master crafts and hand embroidery, investing in their reinvention and innovation, and creating a more inclusive future that consciously preserves communities, craft, and the environment. This perspective has led to numerous artistic endeavours that blur the boundaries between these disciplines, resulting in works that are both inventive and deeply rooted in tradition.

The collaborative efforts between the Chanakya School of Craft and renowned artists have resulted in projects that have received global acclaim. One such collaboration is with artist Judy Chicago, commissioned by Maria Grazia Chiuri, for the Dior Spring / Summer 2020 haute couture collection. The installation, titled *The Female Divine*, comprised 22 monumental appliqué, handmade brocade, and velvet banners, each with a query that related to the work's driving proposition, which was written across a central banner: "What If Women Ruled the World?" The prompts ranged from the material — "Would Buildings Resemble Wombs?" — to the political and social: "Would God Be Female?" and "Would There Be Violence?". Under Karishma Swali's

< Living museum at the Chanakya Cultural Centre
Courtesy of the Chanakya Foundation

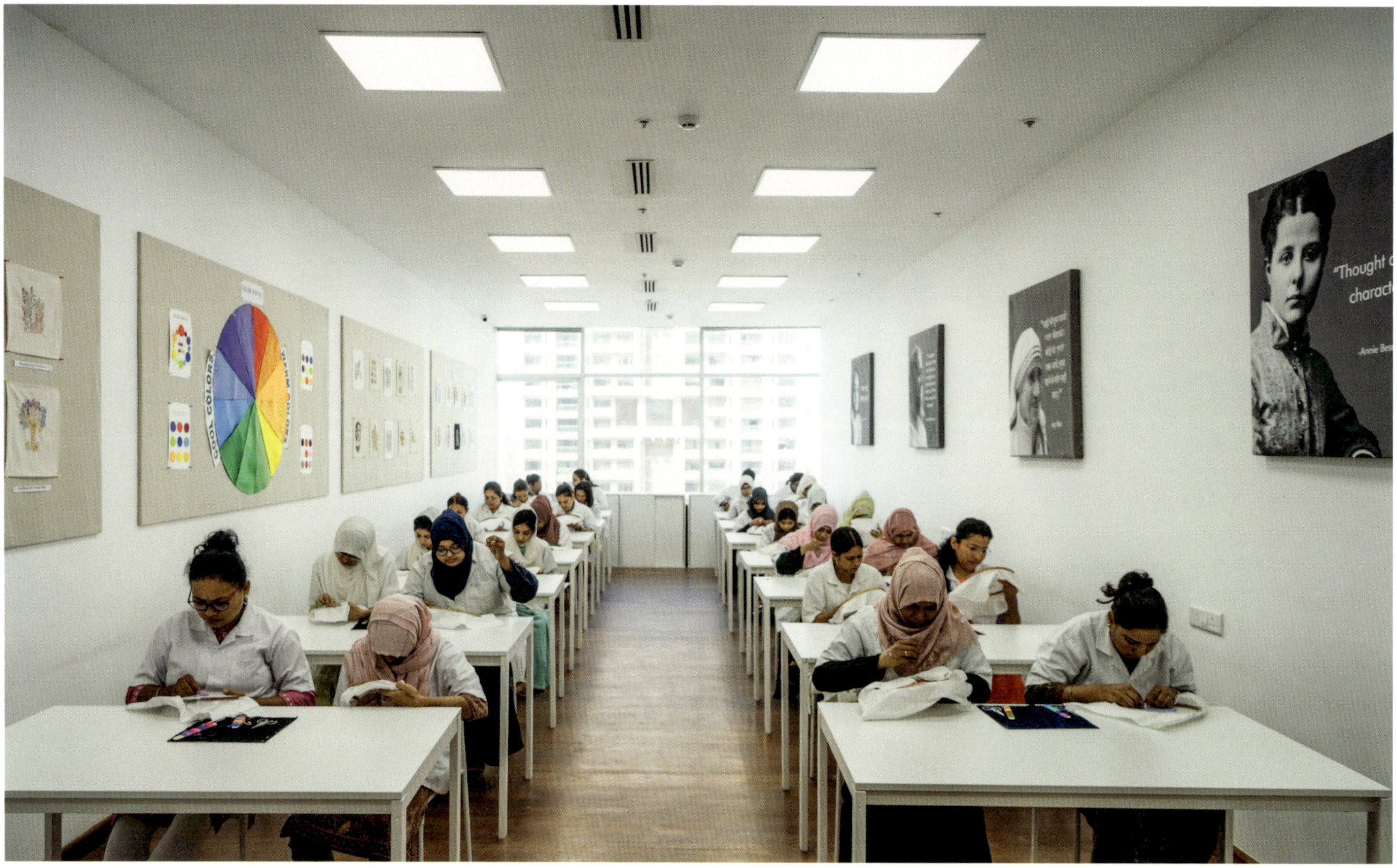

guidance, the female graduates of the Chanakya School of Craft, alongside master artisans from the Chanakya ateliers, meticulously handcrafted the textile banners. These works confront viewers with provocative questions, challenging gender stereotypes and cultural norms through powerful messaging.

Another, more recent collaboration is with Indian artist Rithika Merchant for Dior's Spring / Summer 2025 haute couture collection. Titled *The Flowers We Grew*, the installation featured 37 large-scale embroidered textile panels based on Merchant's watercolour paintings. These textiles, fabricated by the artisans of Chanakya International and students of the Chanakya School of Craft, were showcased at the Musée Rodin in Paris. Both projects, deeply rooted in a feminine narrative that aligns with the school's ethos, show just how harmoniously traditional craftsmanship can evolve within contemporary artistic frameworks.

Beyond their celebrated collaborations with leading contemporary artists, Karishma Swali and the artisans of the Chanakya School of Craft engage in a deeply introspective artistic practice that transcends conventional boundaries of craftsmanship, positioning textiles, hand embroidery, stone carving, and other tactile mediums as tools of exploration and cultural discourse. This approach materialises in bodies of work such as *Belong* and *Towards Light*, where the interplay between materiality and meaning underscores the practice's intellectual rigor. Highlighting artisanal excellence, the collective examines the socio-historical trajectories, symbolic frameworks, and regional distinctions that shape each craft tradition. By situating these practices within their broader cultural

Female students working on class assignment at the Chanakya School of Craft. Photo by Hashim Badani. Courtesy of the Chanakya Foundation

> Female students with Karishma Swali, Creative Director of the Chanakya School of Craft and Anisha Shetty, Head of Atelier. Photo by Hashim Badani. Courtesy of the Chanakya Foundation

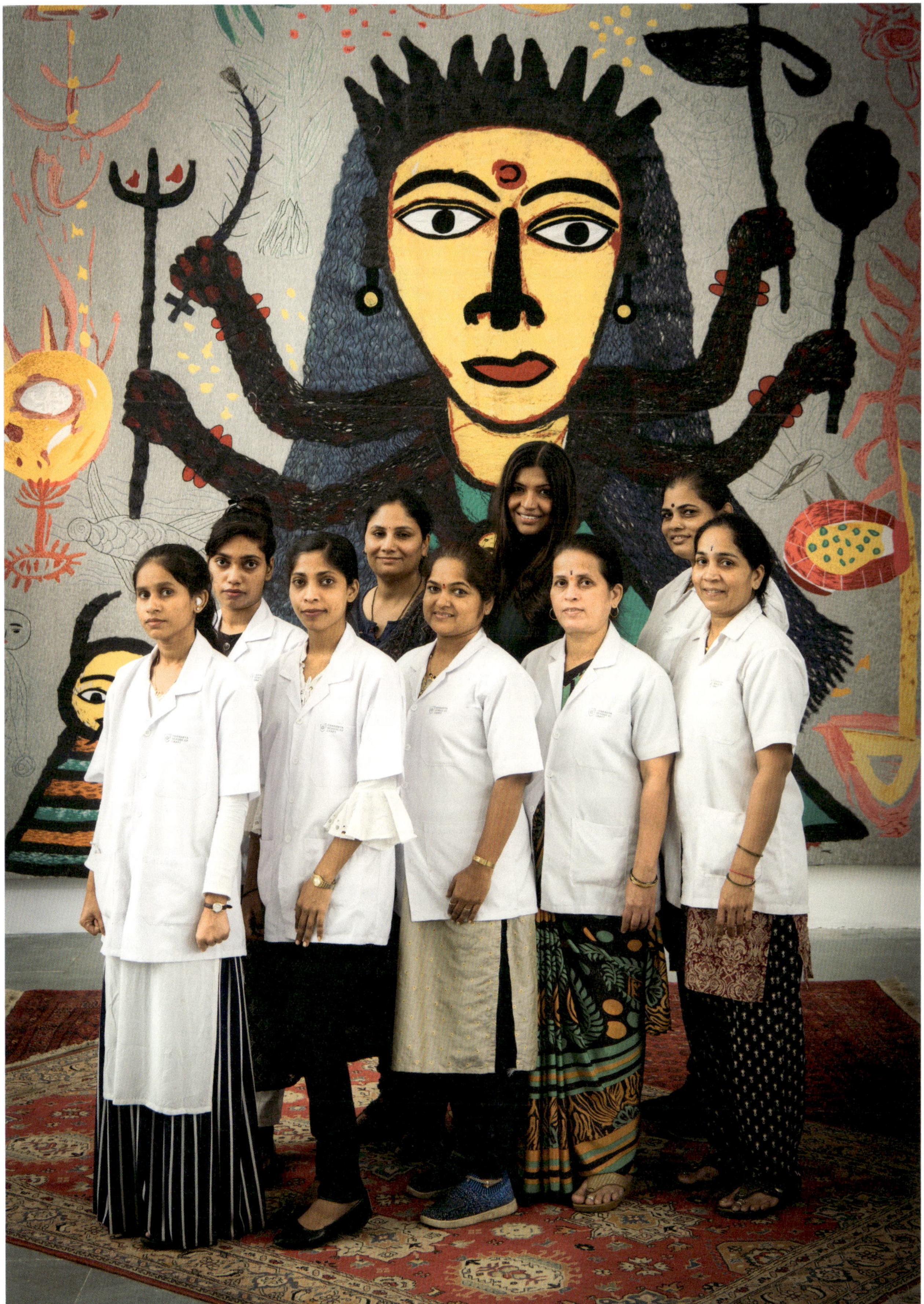

and historical contexts, it emphasises their role as evolving sites of knowledge, continuity, and reinterpretation. Through this lens, craft is not perceived as a static cultural artifact but as an evolving discursive space wherein contemporary concerns — identity, belonging, and resilience — are articulated. In foregrounding these narratives, the collective challenges hegemonic hierarchies within the art world, asserting craft's relevance in both historical and contemporary contexts while gesturing toward its transformative potential in shaping cultural memory and shared identities. Their works are now enshrined in the permanent collections of global private collectors, the Kiran Nadar Museum of Art, and the Durjoy Bangladesh Foundation, among others.

These initiatives redefine its living practice, where embroidery is not an auxiliary embellishment but a medium of articulation. Within this approach, embroidery becomes a vessel for storytelling, a means of reclaiming narratives, and a means for engagement with contemporary issues, reinforcing the interconnectedness of materiality, skill, and creative vision. This renewal also speaks to the resilience of a culture determined to reclaim and reimagine its aesthetic and artisanal legacy in a global world. What lies at its core of these engagements is the remarkable versatility of its embroiderers. By sustaining the vitality of embroidery as a living, evolving practice, it continues to captivate the imagination — not only in the present but, one hopes, well into the future. India, often described as a locus of creation and renewal, embodies this ethos. It is said that within its vast cultural landscape, one finds everything one seeks, and what remains undiscovered here is unlikely to be found elsewhere.

A Turning Point

This ethos was fully realised in the *Cosmic Garden* exhibition, unveiled as a Collateral Event at the 60th Venice Art Biennale in 2024, which epitomised the collaborative spirit and vision that define Chanakya's practice. Curated by Maria Alicata and Paola Ugolini, the exhibition was conceived as an immersive environment, bringing together paintings, large-scale embroidered artworks, and sculptures informed by Indian mythology, nature, and cosmic symbolism.

Under the direction of Karishma Swali, artisans at the Chanakya School of Craft reimagined the works of contemporary artists Madhvi and Manu Parekh, translating their paintings into expansive textile and sculptural forms. This process, rooted in both technical proficiency and material innovation, redefines the intersection of traditional craftsmanship and contemporary art. Working with organic materials such as raw linen, jute, silk, and cotton, artisans employed contemporised handcraft techniques to reinterpret the artists' compositions in a tactile, multidimensional format. In a striking extension of this approach, ten figures from Madhvi Parekh's paintings were extracted and rendered as three-dimensional sculptures, constructed from metal wire, paper-mache, and organic limestone and layered with embroidery. The shift from visual to textile art in *Cosmic Garden* considers the historical association between women and needlework, expanding its significance beyond domestic and decorative spheres.

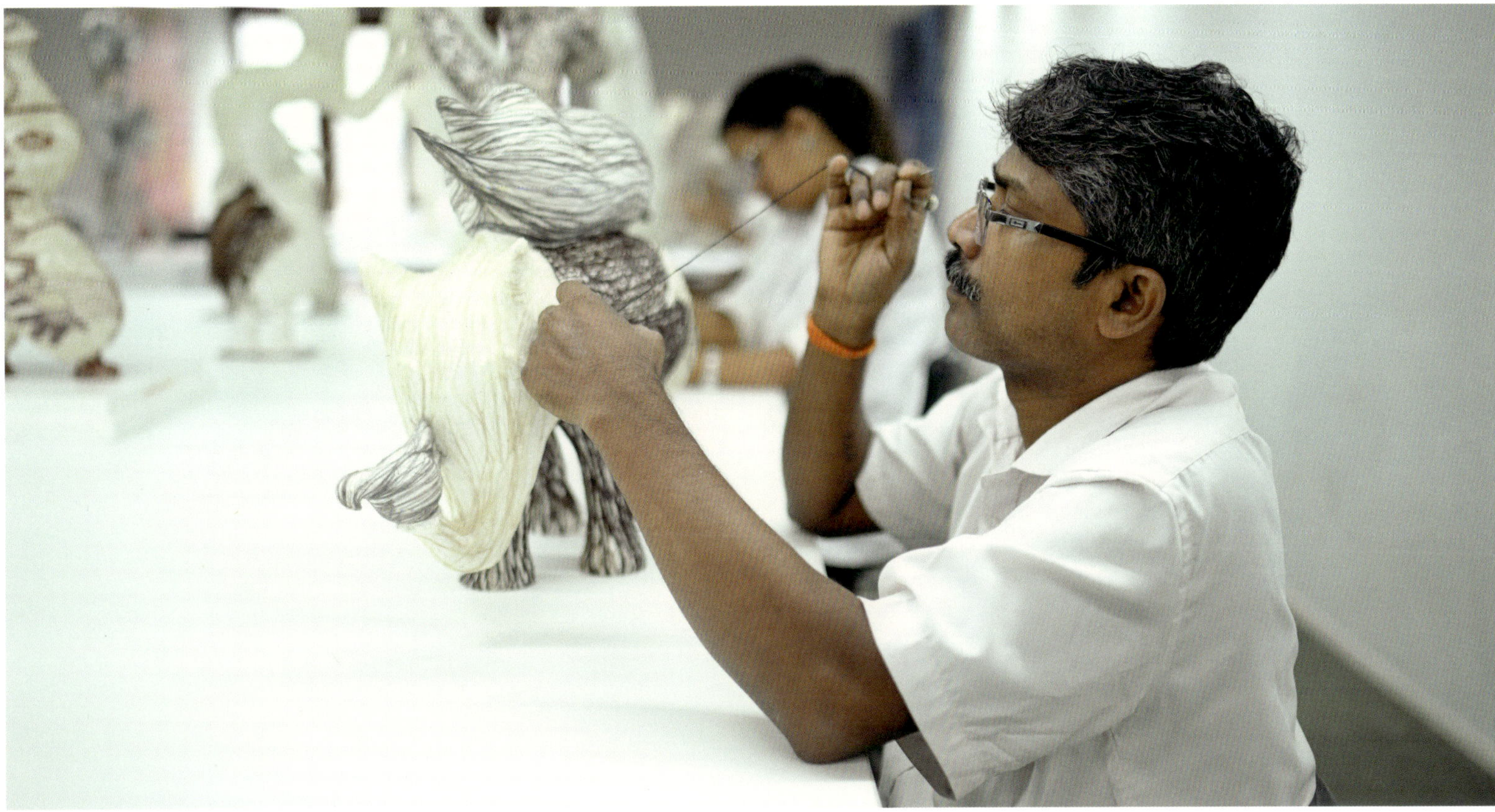

Master artisans crafting paper-mache sculptures
Photo by Hashim Badani. Courtesy of the Chanakya Foundation

Far from being a nostalgic gesture, this approach demonstrates how traditional craftsmanship, when nurtured within a progressive, cross-disciplinary framework, can evolve into a powerful medium of contemporary expression. It reflects Chanakya's broader engagement with cultural sustainability — treating heritage not as a fixed archive of the past but as an evolving practice that informs the future of art, fashion, and design. Through this, Chanakya International, the Chanakya School of Craft, and the Chanakya Foundation contribute to ongoing dialogues surrounding craft and contemporary art, both within India and across global cultural networks.

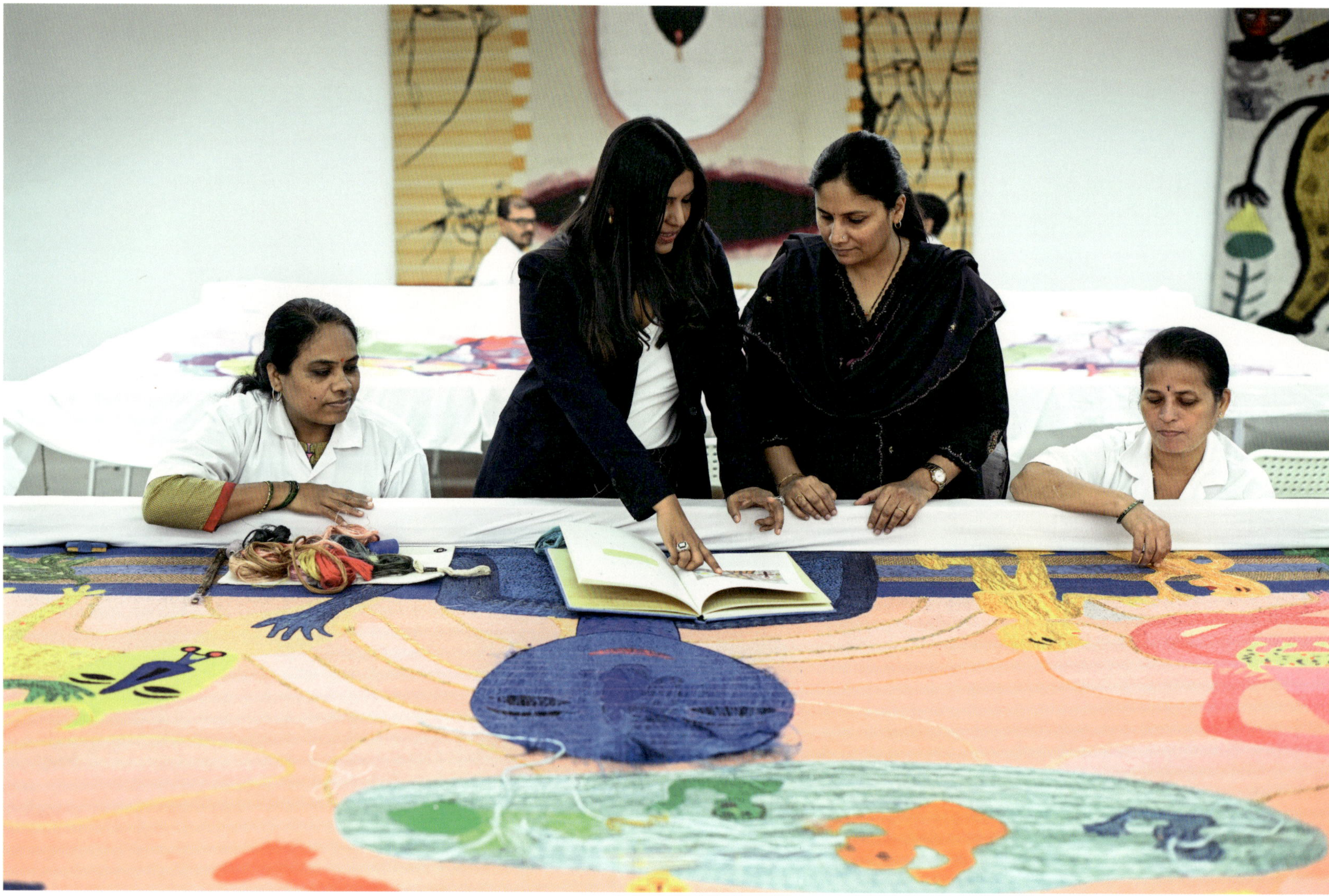

Karishma Swali, Creative Director of the Chanakya School of Craft, and Anisha Shetty, Head of Atelier, discussing *Resting Near the Pond*. Photo by Hashim Badani. Courtesy of the Chanakya Foundation

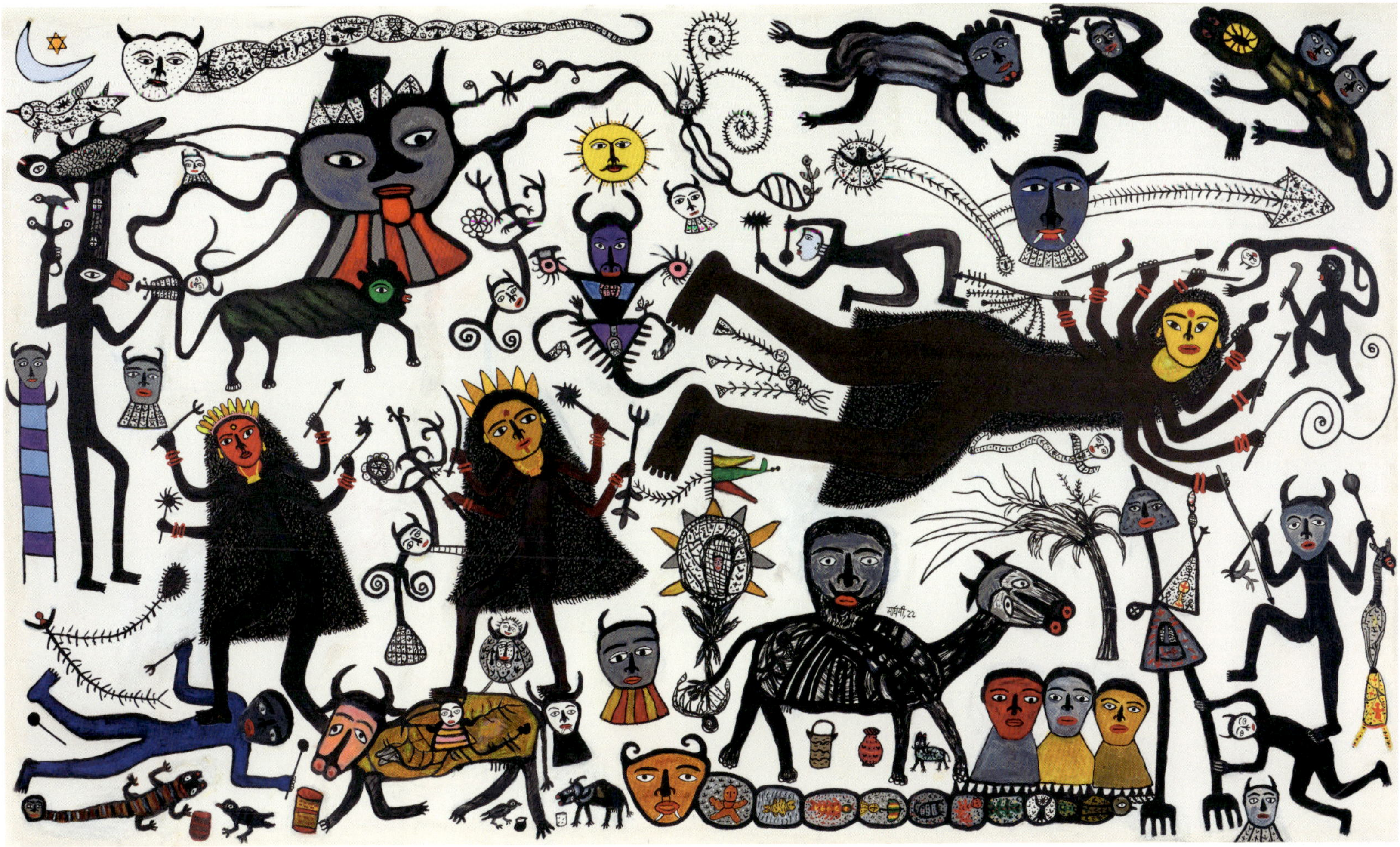

Madhvi Parekh
Flying Durga, 2022
Acrylic on canvas, 303 × 184 cm
Photo by Abner Fernandes. Courtesy of the Chanakya Foundation

Is Collaboration the Fragrance of the Cosmic Garden?

Sumesh Sharma

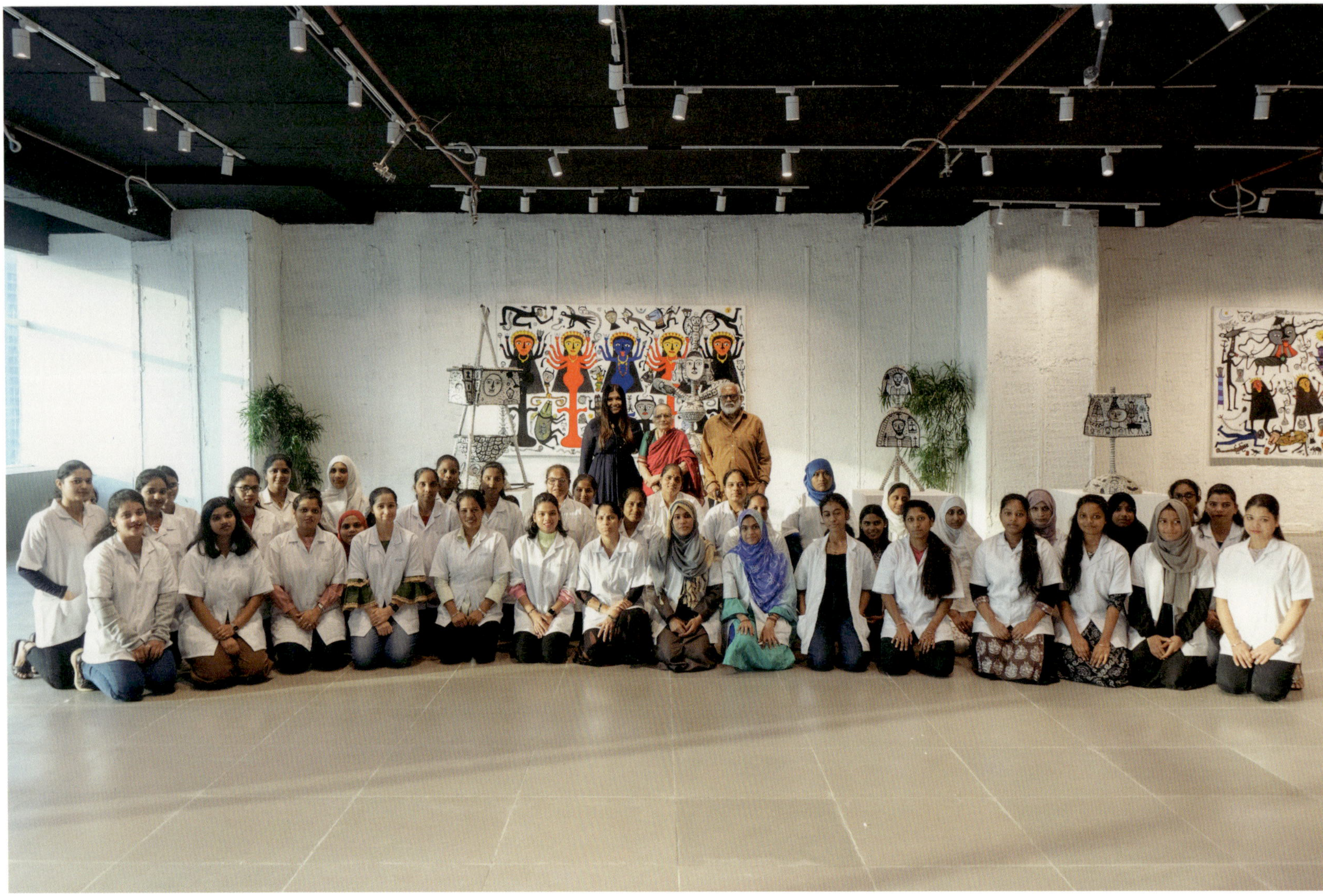

Karishma Swali, Madhvi Parekh, and Manu Parekh
with the students of Chanakya School of Craft
Photo by Vismay Mirgal. Courtesy of the Chanakya Foundation

Since Indian independence, various initiatives, both state-sponsored and privately led, have sought to reawaken the subcontinent's vast and multifaceted textile heritage. *Cosmic Garden* presents itself as an assertive gesture within this unfolding narrative, re-establishing the continued relevance of embroidery as both an inherited craft and a language of contemporary artistic expression. At its heart lies a deeply considered collaboration between the Chanakya School of Craft, its founder and patron Karishma Swali, and the celebrated veteran artists Manu and Madhvi Parekh. Together, they shape a practice that now holds a meaningful place within Indian art and craft history — one that honours lineage while opening new realms for reflection and reinvention.

This collaboration exudes a palpable intensity — both conceptual and affective — that underscores the values of craftsmanship, ephemerality, integrity, and aesthetic vision. These principles, long cultivated by the Parekhs, are brought into reanimated articulation through their engagement with Karishma Swali. What emerges is an evolving and dialogic practice rooted in rigour, investigation, and critical continuity. Manu Parekh's early experience at the Weavers' Service Centre, Benaras and Madhubani, among others, instilled in him the importance of narrativity in craft and perseverance of the practice. At the same time, Madhvi Parekh's natural and inherent process of delving into folk forms, palettes, and untouched experimentation, driven by childhood innocence and formal pursuit, allows a novel representation with determination and vehement trust. As a result, the Parekhs' visual language, once confined to painting, now expands into an interdisciplinary realm — melding painting, sculpture, and material into a bold new addition to their oeuvres. Within the framework of *Cosmic Garden*, embroidery is recontextualised as a potent site of cultural expression, subjectivity, and cross-cultural exchange.

Historically embedded as a mode of domestic and collective storytelling, embroidery here acquires restored semiotic charge through its negotiation with contemporary, socio-political realities. It ceases to function as a static emblem of tradition; instead, it becomes a fluid, evolving signifier — mediating between the archival and the experimental, the inherent and the reimagined.

This essay examines the evolution of this expanded practice. It situates the Parekhs' artistic production within a wider discourse on craft epistemologies, folk knowledge systems, and their intersections with contemporary art. Furthermore, it recognises the pivotal role of Karishma Swali and the Chanakya School of Craft in enabling new platforms of artistic engagement, foregrounding a vision that is simultaneously pedagogical and collaborative.

The Embedded Narrative of Embroidery

The large-scale interdisciplinary works have captivated both national and international audiences, evoking a profound and lingering sense of wonder. These pieces speak of the meticulous and intuitive direction guided by Karishma Swali and the artisans of the Chanakya School of Craft — an approach that transforms embroidery into expansive, immersive compositions, whether rendered in two or three dimensions. The lineage of embroidery holds a length of the Indian subcontinent and beyond in deriving its current excellence, historicity, and appraisal. Hence, embroidery is a noted, measured, and concrete language of its own. To understand a collective portrayal of embroidery in India, this section attempts to share a short, concise, and common glimpse into a few well-known forms and their socio-cultural impact.

India's rich embroidery heritage, among many, includes *phulkari*, *chikankari*, *zardozi*, *kantha*, *kashida*, *kasuti*, *gota patti*, *sujani*, *shisha* (mirror work), Banjara, Toda, appliqué (pipli), and aari, each reflecting its region's unique culture and artistry. For instance, *zardozi* was introduced in India around the 14th century via patronage of the Mughals from Iran. With the migration of Persian artists, distinct designs of embroidery inspired by nature were interlaced with animal motifs, assimilating with the indigenous Indian aesthetics. A distinct imagery inspired by this narrative, which Indian painting has traditionally held, was then interspersed with simple cloth decoration.

Subsequently, the subtle craft of embroidery holds a profound narrative that contextualises several social, economic, ecological, and cultural narratives of each state in India. Each style of embroidery stitch from a particular region represents a lineage of a community's customs, traditions, and folklore. Moreover, it also associates with gender, purpose, identity, status, hierarchy, functional attributes, and building reasons in the technical process. For example, Toda embroidery from Tamil Nadu, which is red and black geometric designs stitched on white cloth, is practised by Toda women and bears a sign of respect and status within the community. At the same time, *kantha* embroidery from Bengal strongly associates with women who lyrically recite folk routines during the act.

Embroidery, often as a narrative script, has existed through subtle layers of women's work. Across different regions, women have traditionally been the primary practitioners of embroidery, passing down skills from generation to generation. One of the most famous embroidery traditions is *phulkari* from Punjab, where women stitch compelling floral patterns on shawls and *dupattas*. In this case, *phulkari*, from its memory, narrates the social system of dowry, with mothers and grandmothers embroidering these pieces for their daughters. Similarly, *kantha* embroidery from West Bengal and Bihar involves women stitching intricate running stitch patterns on old sarees and fabrics, often depicting folklore, animals, or daily life scenes.

In the western part of India, Gujarat and Rajasthan, mirror work and Kutchi embroidery are predominantly practiced by women from rural communities like the Rabari and Ahir tribes. Comprising bright threads, tiny mirrors, and elaborate motifs, these embroideries are evoked as a solution to the immediate need for peripatetic or Banjara sustenance. Embroidery is used to enhance the coloured traditional garments such as *ghagras* (skirts), *odhnis* (veils), and *cholis* (blouses) to reflect their presence from the far stretched deserted lands.

Inspired by Jammu and Kashmir's natural beauty, *kashida* embroidery features motifs like *chinar* leaves, birds, and blossoms, and it was done by women. Despite celebrating local aesthetics and contributing to the region's textiles, it confined women's creativity to a decorative craft that was often undervalued in comparison to male-dominated art forms like carpet weaving. Historically, *kashida* shed light upon a redundant legacy where women's labour was romanticised as tradition without being acknowledged as an economically viable livelihood option.

Beyond tradition, with several public and private campaigns and initiatives, embroidery has become a source of financial independence for women, especially in rural areas, flipping the times when it was contradictory and surpassed by the patriarchal domain. Nevertheless, despite advancement, embroidery remains an enduring symbol of feminine creativity, a symbol of nuanced craftsmanship and resilience in India.

Shifting from the historic ethos of embroidery that was embroiled in a conservative, confined space, the *Cosmic Garden*, apart from being a torchbearer of tradition-revival, significantly allots an altogether resurrected status to the craft just like canvas and brushes in painting have had over centuries. *It allows the audience to relook at contemporary pieces with the hope of the material that had been hidden in the crevices of routine oblivion.*

However, what is the inherent bond of embroidery/craft with Manu and Madhvi Parekh?

Manu Parekh: Narrating the Art and Craft of Life

The answer to the question lies indirectly within the lives of the Parekhs. Born in Ahmedabad in 1939, Manu Parekh reflects an affinity to conversation, a raconteur who has a vivid memory, exemplifying an artistic practice with a visual — a raconteur with a vivid memory, exemplifying an artistic practice through a visual framework that reflects versatility in form, muse, and context. During his time at high school in Ahmedabad, his drawing teacher, Mukund Shroff, inspired and nurtured his talent, while at the Sir JJ School of Art, he had the privilege of studying under the guidance of artist and pedagogue Shankar Palsikar. At the JJ, through landscape and miniatures studies, he attempted to bring multiple elements together in a singular perspective.

Within six months of relocating to Calcutta in 1965 — aged 26 years old — he became an active member of the Society of Contemporary Artists, working closely with Shyamal Dutta Ray, Ganesh Pyne, Bikash Bhattacharjee, and Somnath Hore — figures who significantly shaped the landscape of modern Indian art. His time in Calcutta and his professional engagements there afforded him a rare versatility, enabling a dynamic evolution of style that shifted with each solo exhibition. Also, he began to draw characters, imbibing their nature and soul in the painting; it was here ritual became important to Parekh. The theatrics of ritual were well placed, especially in a city such as Calcutta. Calcutta was seen as a difficult posting because of the overpopulation, poverty, and general chaos.

Manu Parekh's visual journey has been shaped by, among other things, his regular and long stays at various towns and cities of India — informing his timely formal alterations, conceptual turns, and essentially the belief in the innate artistic practice. Having studied in Mumbai and having been inspired by the legacy of Paul Klee at the J.J., Manu Parekh was fortified by the essential ground of formal training, which also became a source from where Madhvi Parekh eventually realised her narrative. Apart from the modern education of the times, the professional association with the craft community during his several work tenures and his deep connection with Benaras, Delhi, Gujarat, etc., provided him with a solid stimulus to flower the artistic/ spiritual foreground

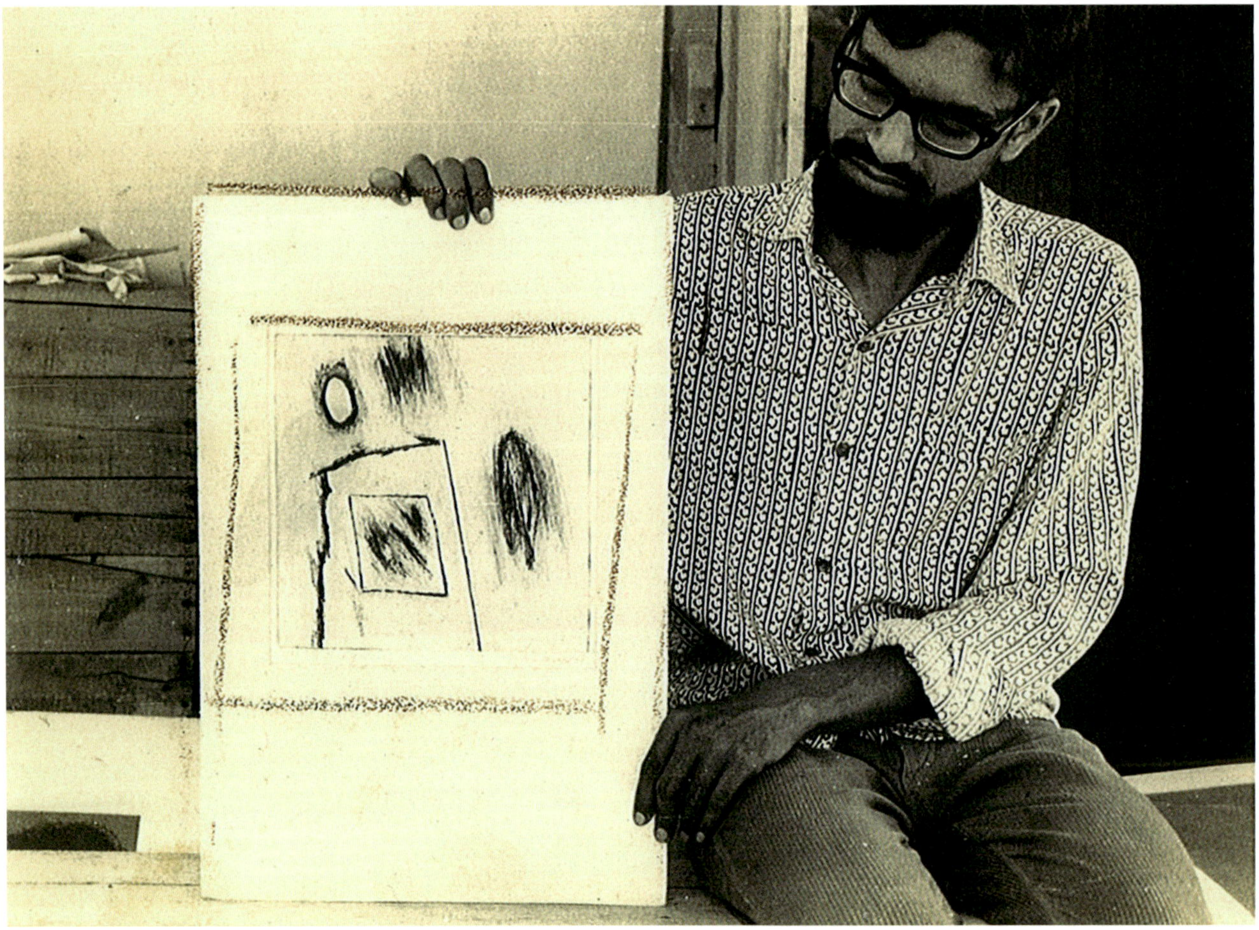

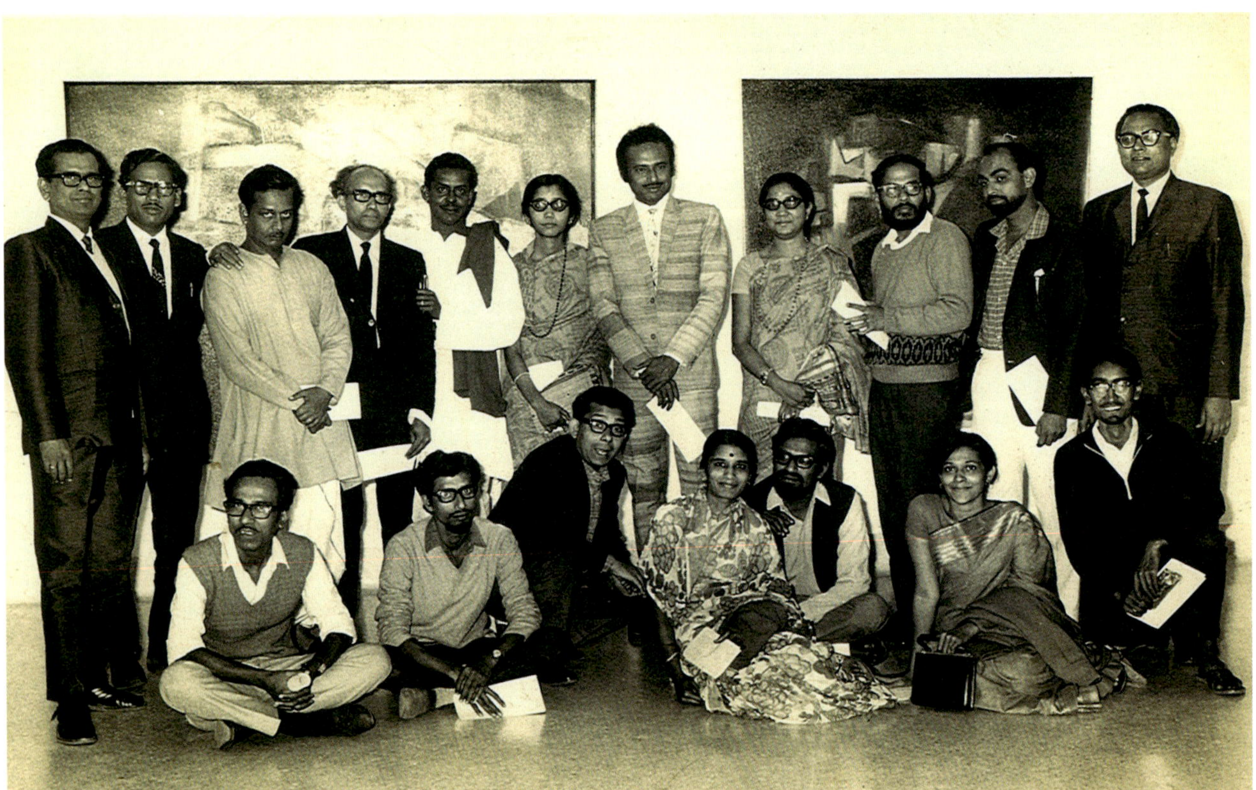

Manu Parekh in his Calcutta home
Courtesy of Manu Parekh and Madhvi Parekh

Image from an annual show at the Birla Academy, Calcutta
Courtesy of Manu Parekh and Madhvi Parekh

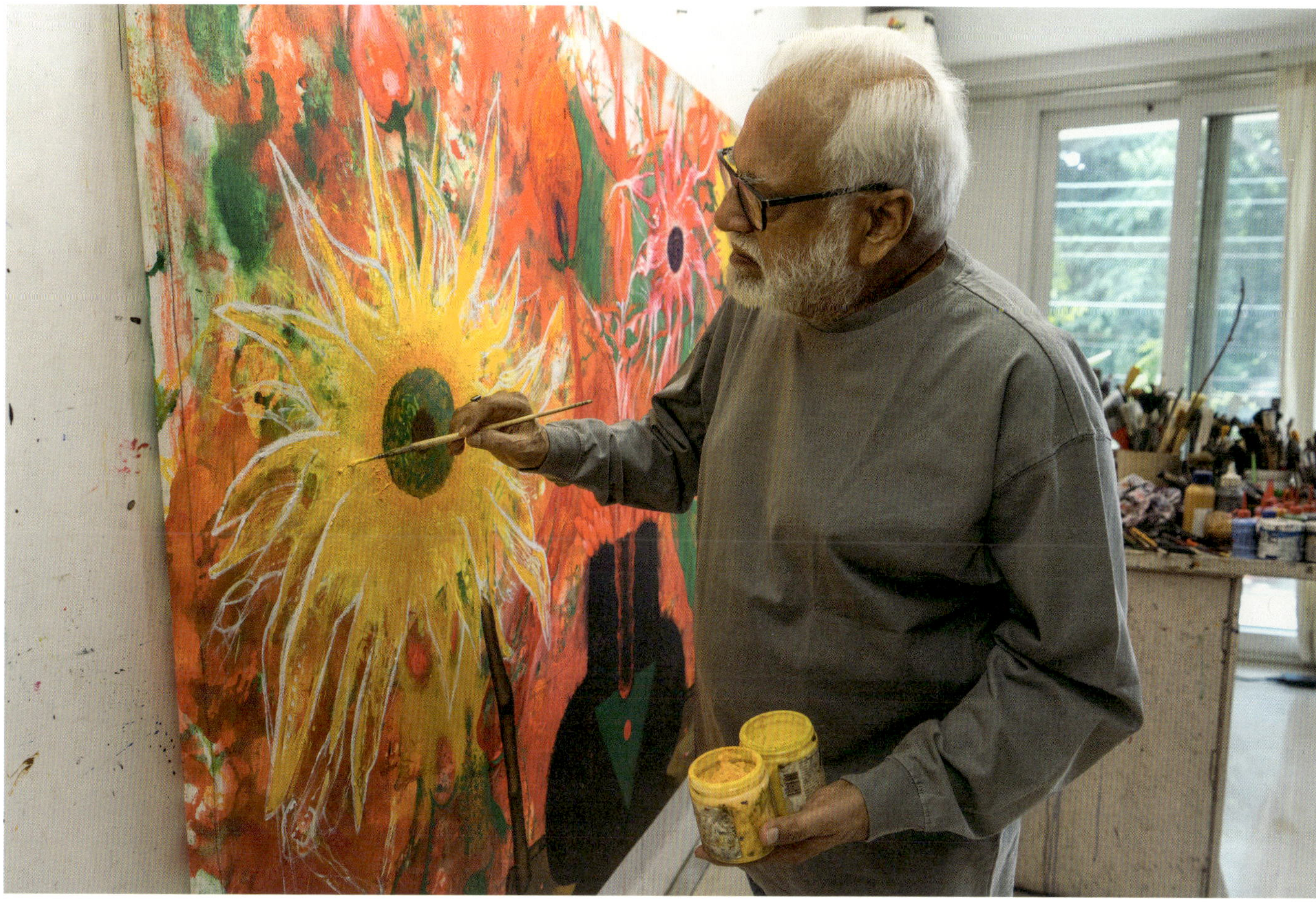

Manu Parekh at his studio in New Delhi
Photo by Sahiba Chawdhary. Courtesy of the Chanakya Foundation

into several series of paintings. Specifically, his paintings have been at the disposal of regular exploration into natural objects and scenes, armed with his passion, curiosity, and timely epiphanies.

Apart from his formal association with the Weavers' Service Centre, Mumbai, Manu Parekh had also joined the Handloom and Handicrafts Corporation of India, New Delhi, founded by Pupul Jaykar.

In 1972, Manu and Madhvi were invited to visit Madhubani by Bhaskar Kulkarni, who was an aid worker with the Government of India. Just after the Bihar Famine of 1967, Pupul Jayakar visited Madhubani to help the people of Mithila under the aegis of the Handicrafts and Handloom Corporation of India.

Madhvi noticed the freedom with which these women worked on their images of flora, fauna, and divinities from the Hindu pantheon. Also, Manu Parekh began interacting with the artists, and this interaction led to a indirect influence in the forms that Madhvi Parekh would use in her paintings to depict goddesses and animals.

Encountering Benaras: A Spiritual City as a Muse

In 1980, just after the death of his father, Manu Parekh was invited by Latika and Balbir Singh Katt[1] to Benaras. Benaras was not immediately inviting to him as an

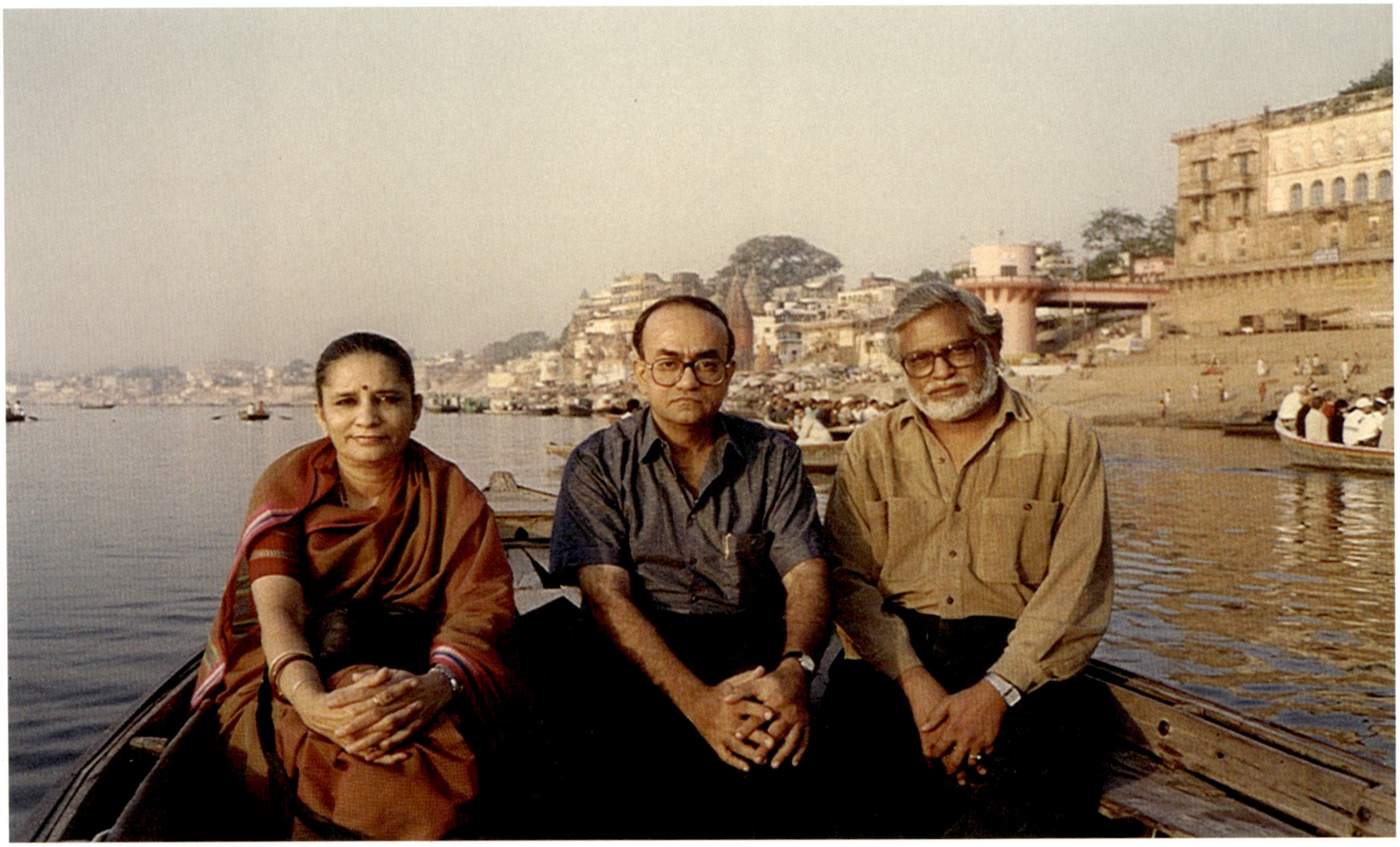

Collector Pradeep Joshi with Manu Parekh and Madhvi Parekh in Benaras. Courtesy of Manu Parekh and Madhvi Parekh

artist who was failing to see the city with the prospect of the muse. One evening, Manu took a boat from the Banaras Hindu University (BHU) to the Kashi Railway Station rather than making the trip by road. During the sunset, he witnessed an absurd architectural landscape on the banks of the river: minarets, temples, and palaces jostled with each other. On the banks, people washed, bathed, and sat under palm umbrellas, cremated corpses, and pilgrims offered lamps to the river. Crowds gathered at certain spots, leaving others desolate. The sinking sun and light that had sprung to battle the darkness created an orange hue. Indian town planning can be well described as an organic huddling together of various elements that may or may not blend into the perspective. Here was his painting!

Parekh witnessed the maze and chaos Benaras offered: the bereaved cremating their loved ones and the enthusiastic pilgrim commissioning a ritual through a priest. Parekh's attraction to Benaras arose from the profound influence that the idea of painting had on him. At times, he has described it as a process of devotion based on service, popularly associated with the Bhakti Movement.[2] For Manu Parekh, Benaras revealed itself as a profoundly layered and performative space — where devotion, mortality, and daily life converged in complex and often contradictory ways. Along the banks of the Ganges, he witnessed a continuum of human experience: the solemnity of funerary rites, the hopeful presence of pilgrims, and the everyday rhythms of trade and ritual.

This professional obligation of examining the crafts, ethereal ambience of Indian towns, and an impeccable sublimity of traditional arts in India gradually became a source of an informal trajectory that would eventually be one of his

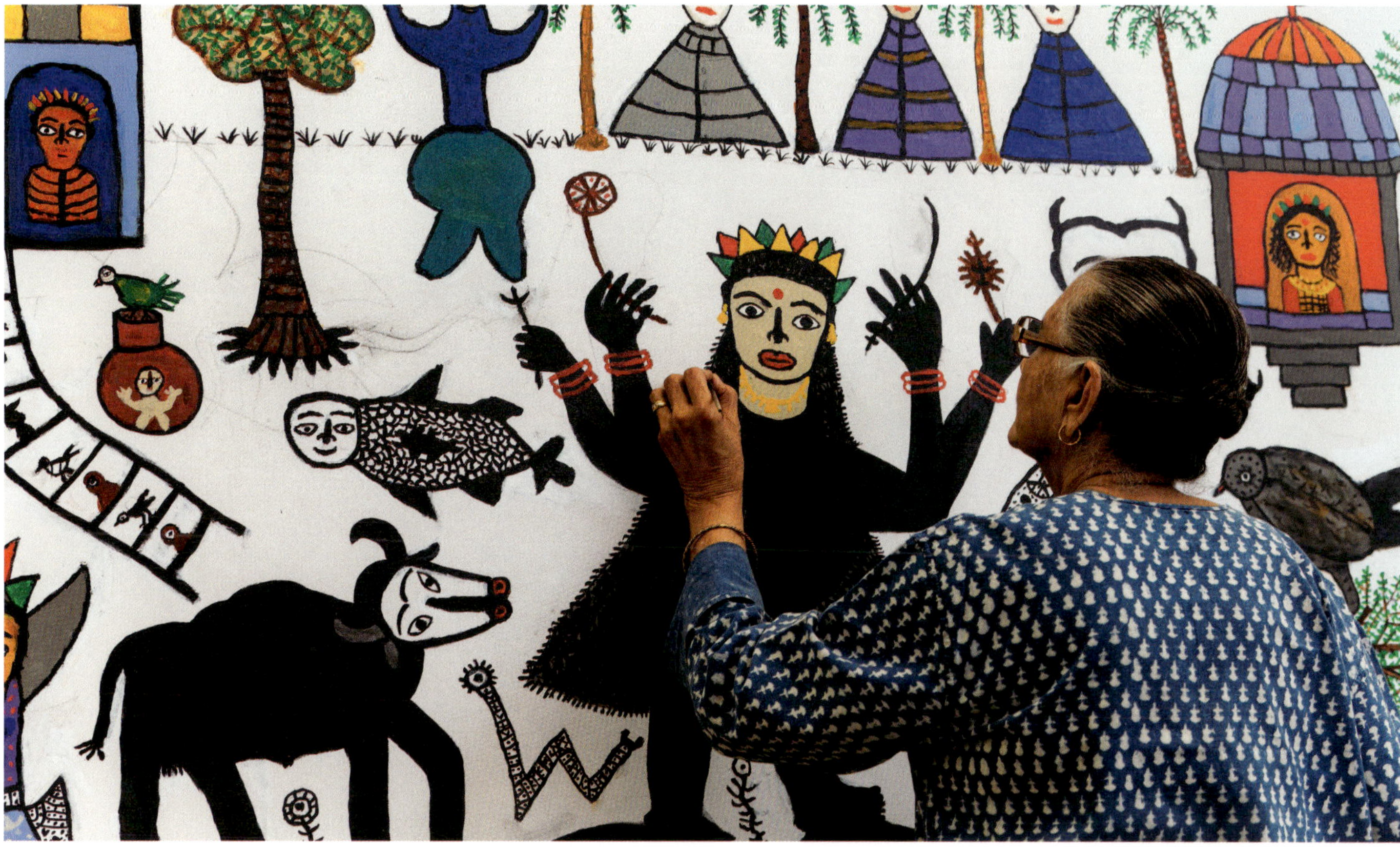

Madhvi Parekh at her studio in New Delhi
Photo by Sahiba Chawdhary. Courtesy of the Chanakya Foundation

greatest corpora of practice in the form of collaboration with the Chanakya School of Craft under the presiding leadership of Karishma Swali.

Madhvi Parekh: A Formless Language of Myth and Symbolism

Across India, storytelling is accompanied by the legends of deities and its immense lineage of symbolism. Various divinities intervene in our quotidian lives through stories of moral building, perseverance, and faith. Madhvi Parekh would draw deeply intricate forests in bold, rough lines but layered with metaphors that arose from her observations and the myths she was told as a child.

Madhvi Parekh is one of the most formidable painters in India, who has vivid imagery based on forms that can be drawn to just the inspiration in the folk, but that would be a futile exercise. Rather, she has scripted her vocabulary, marrying myth with life, drawing on her imagined pasts and relatively invoking her path of integrity by memories of childhood, discipline, and Gandhian values bestowed by her father. This simplification of the form and colour in the painting is a conversation Manu and Madhvi Parekh draw between themselves. Their domestic life is akin to this companionship in art as a form of rebellious conceptual living, with each taking turns in conversation and humour. Elements that are essential to South Asian cultural tenets — despite the diversity in language, religion, and form we see here — are easily recognisable.

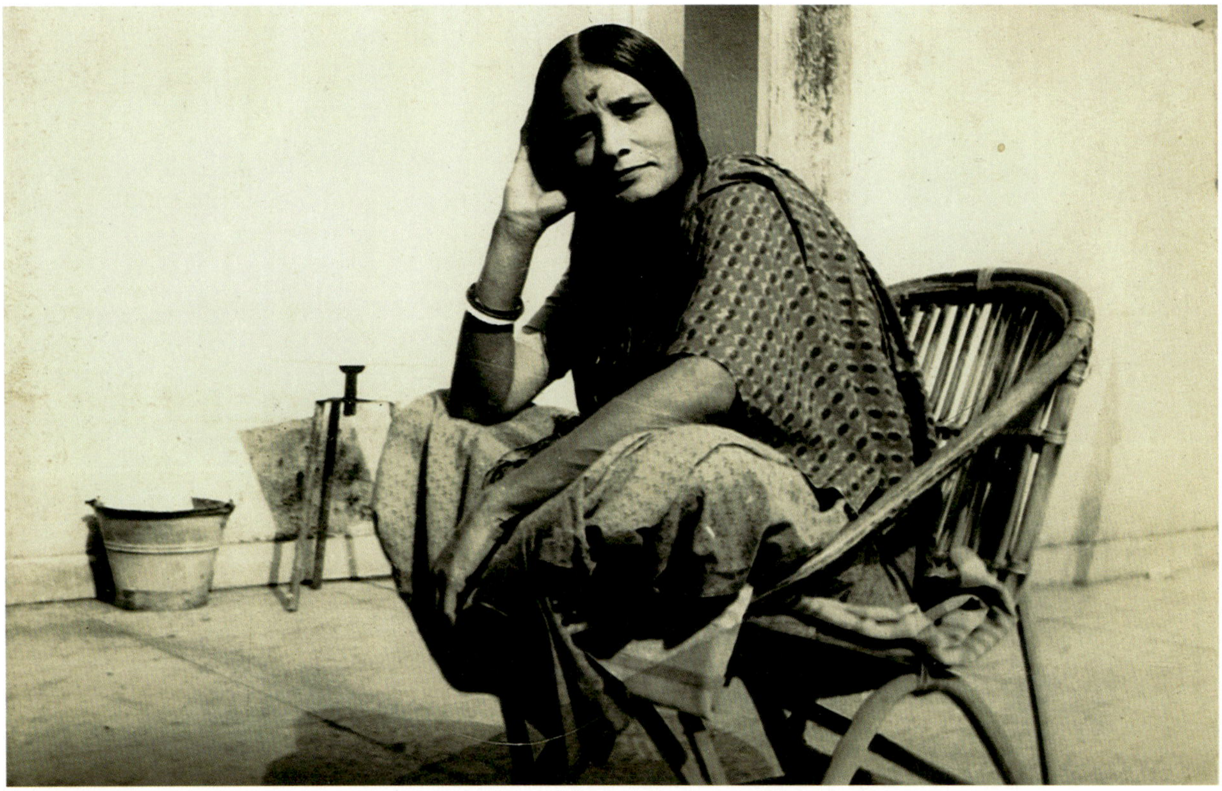

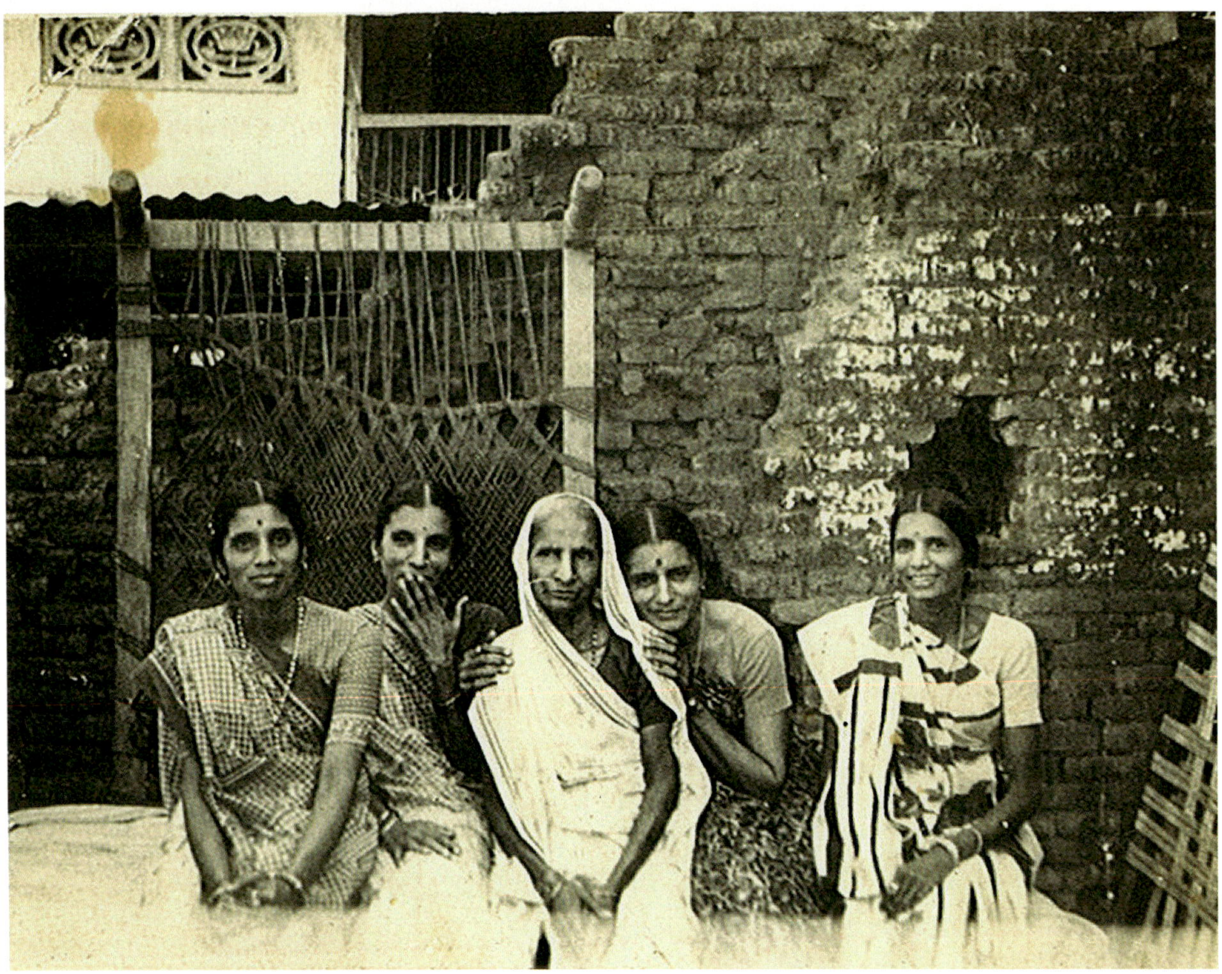

Trained in formal language by Manu Parekh in the early days, what arose from Madhvi's experiments with painting was a canvas that used a vocabulary entirely self-devised and one which captured her imagination and worldview. This was a world of ritual and belief where the human experience was not devoid of an animist presence. A part of our daily ritual of life, various birds and animals represent the mental and spiritual states of our minds. 'Rangoli', a traditional art form of drawing complex, intricate designs that mark prosperity at the doors of homes, was an activity most women took part in. Madhvi, drawing on those techniques, began envisioning a forest in symphony through her drawings.

Indian mythology is a long narration of syncretic beliefs and cultural assimilations of indigenous folk histories. Madhvi, in her *Last Supper* (2011), makes a bouquet of Christ with his apostles in a manner that would be depicted in an Eastern Church. The subject of Christ's *Last Supper* (1498), made iconic by Leonardo da Vinci (Italy), reappeared repeatedly in her practice after her return from Israel, where she made many renditions of the subject, much like her depiction of Kali. The colours she uses to depict them place them within the contours of the imagination and colour theory of the Indian subcontinent. We see these forms and colours re-emerge, magnified through the interdisciplinary works that give renewed dimension to the paintings of both Madhvi and Manu Parekh.

Nature, Myth, and the Sacred Feminine

> "The worship of the Great Goddess, the mother of all things, has been one of the most widespread religious expressions in human history. She is the Earth itself, the body of the world, the nourishing source of all life and the receiver of the dead. The symbolism of the Goddess, in myth and ritual, represents the whole mystery of the universe as a living organism."
> — Joseph Campbell, *The Power of Myth*.

Madhvi Parekh's depictions of Kali and the Mother Goddess bring alive a living culture of depicting deities with a visual vocabulary that retains a vernacular imagination, much like the wall paintings of India, such as the Madhubani paintings.[3]

The worship of Kali, often seen as the 'Goddess of Destruction and War', became popular in Bengal and Bihar when the people were subjected to recurring famines after the 17th century. These were man-made famines that were caused by the forceful cultivation of cash crops such as indigo, cotton, jute, and opium, which generated large revenues for the British empire. Women facing the death of their progeny then saw a man-made disaster as the wrath of Goddess Kali, who was punishing them for their ungratefulness. In the villages, a 'snake goddess' called Manasa came to protect children from snake bites, and in Bihar Chhathi Maiya, the sister of the Sun, ensured the well-being of children.

Madhvi Parekh paints goddesses in unison with nature and its purity, driven by ingrained passion and emotion. Flying benevolent goddesses were common in Gujarat, with traditions of painting cloth backdrops for a ritual theatre worship, referring to the folk art form of 'Mata ni Pachedi.' So were village

< Madhvi Parekh in her Calcutta house
Courtesy of Manu Parekh and Madhvi Parekh

< Madhvi Parekh with her mother and sisters in a village in Gujarat. Courtesy of Manu Parekh and Madhvi Parekh

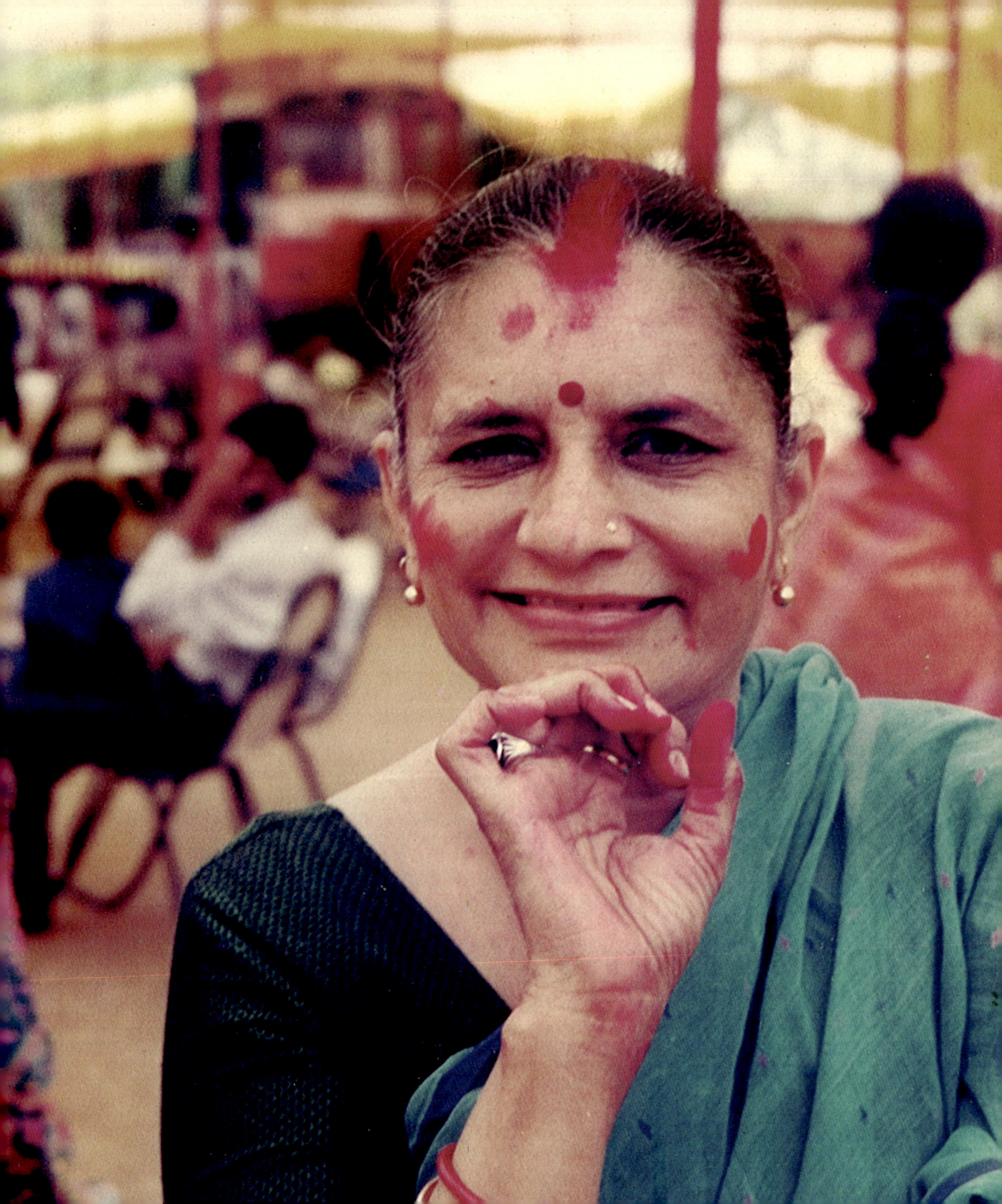

shrines that were rudimentary and decorated by bright contrasting colours: vermillion, turmeric and *multani* brown. Similarly, there are the animals who pose as wayfarers in our lives. In a time where we are desperately seeking an equilibrium with other life in our universe, elevating animals to hold an equal place reveals a deep philosophical approach to life. This perspective underpins a deep animist respect, where all life is essential and in rhythm with our own, as Madhvi conveys in her art. The icon-isation of the primal Mother Goddess is a mirror of the vision she holds for a world degraded by shrewdness, loss of innocence, and impure ailments. The expressionist forms of the goddess in Madhvi Parekh's depiction appear to be a relentless quest for the mysteries, as noted by Campbell, of the sustenance and retaining of the values that charge her brushes.

In *Cosmic Garden*, paper-mache is used to translate Madhvi Parekh's painted animal forms into sculptural presence — an act that echoes earlier traditions of material and collaborative innovation. Introduced to Indian craft practice in the 1970s by Pupul Jayakar as an accessible medium, paper-mache here becomes a vehicle for formal transformation. The sculptures, realised by Karishma Swali and the artisans of Chanakya, are composed of natural fibres such as raw linen, jute, silk, and cotton — materials that lend both texture and integrity to the works. This shift from two to three dimensions reflects a deliberate formal inquiry, one that requires not only technical finesse but also a deeper engagement with Madhvi's personal cosmology. Her sculptural language thus becomes a site of introspection — revisiting past associations with craft while creating them through the lens of lived experience and belief.

Re-Embroidering the Tapestry of Indian Crafts: Patronage and Artists

Originally established by Karishma Swali's father, Mr. Vinod Shah, in the early 1980s, Chanakya International, a textile and embroidery house, expanded under her leadership, fostering collaborations with luxury fashion brands like Dior, Gucci, Prada, and Valentino as well as other non-profit organisations to preserve and perpetuate India's diverse textile traditions. In 2016, recognising the imperative to formalise craft education and foster female autonomy, Karishma Swali established the Chanakya School of Craft. As a non-profit institution, the School is committed to sustaining cultural heritage while advancing new possibilities for women in the field. It offers training in regionally specific embroidery traditions — including *kantha* from Bengal, *ari* from Gujarat, and *chikankari* from Lucknow, among others — positioning these forms not merely as inherited techniques but as evolving artistic vocabularies.

Karishma Swali, the Creative Director of Chanakya International and the Chanakya School of Craft, has pioneered a holistic educational model that merges heritage craft with contemporary design. The school's pedagogical program focuses on training young women from the underserved communities of Mumbai in over 300 embroidery techniques. Through an 18-month curriculum, these artisans refine their skills before being integrated into professional ateliers, ensuring both economic empowerment and the continuity of traditional craftsmanship. Educational initiatives like the Chanakya School of Craft are

< Madhvi Parekh playing Sindoor Khela in Bengal after Durga Pooja in Calcutta. Courtesy of Manu Parekh and Madhvi Parekh

leading this shift by engaging students not only from traditional weaving communities but also from low-income backgrounds, particularly women from Bombay's informal settlements. The school offers a tangible path to economic independence, restoring dignity to textile craftsmanship and challenging systemic exclusion.

Through collaborations with Madhvi and Manu Parekh, she has facilitated a synthesis between their paintings and India's rich material traditions — *kantha*, *zardozi*, *chikankari*, and *kalamkari*. These embroidered works evoke the essence of the Parekhs' paintings into a tactile, dimensional experience, merging artistic vision with meticulous craftsmanship. The dialogue between Swali, the Parekhs', Paola Ugolini, and Maria Alicata culminated in the 2024 Venice exhibition *Cosmic Garden*. This project extends beyond mere visual translation — it is a meditation on materiality and storytelling.

Cosmic Garden: A Dialogue in Art & Life

South Asian artistic traditions, despite their diversity, share an underlying essence of accessibility and intra-level innovation. Whether in myth, language, or visual expression, there is an immediacy that allows audiences to engage without alienation. This is evident in the Parekhs' work, where recognisable symbols — temples, animals, flowers, infrastructure, deities, and ritualistic gestures — serve as entry points to ethnic narratives. Theirs is a language of art that speaks, listens, and, most importantly, maintains a conversation with the world.

However, what is a *Cosmic Garden*? How does one visualise it in a tangible space? The *Cosmic Garden* is both metaphor and material — a surreal landscape woven by many hands, many histories, and many artistic lineages. It is a space where the work of Madhvi and Manu Parekh gains new dimensionality, its formless undertones made manifest through the slow, deliberate process of embroidery. The artisans at Chanakya, under Karishma Swali's guidance, do not merely replicate the paintings; they reimagine them, layering stitch upon stitch to build forms that are at once monumental and poetic. The fragrance of this garden is not just metaphorical — it is the scent of collaboration, of skill passed through generations, of artistic traditions expanding into new realms and finding a new podium. It is a demonstration of the transformative power of art when placed in the hands of many, levied by a team, becoming something larger, something cosmic in its reach.

Cosmic Garden explores the nuanced convergence of painting, embroidery, and craft, positioning the evocative visual language of Madhvi and Manu Parekh in dialogue with material innovation. By collapsing distinctions between fine art and craft as well as material culture, this convergence underscores the potency of cross-disciplinary exchange — where tradition and experimentation coalesce to generate new paths replete with aesthetic possibilities. The fragrance of this garden comes from the sweet scent of collaboration between Karishma Swali and the women embroiderers who come to celebrate the iconic work of Manu and Madhvi Parekh in a monumental and poetic dimensionality.

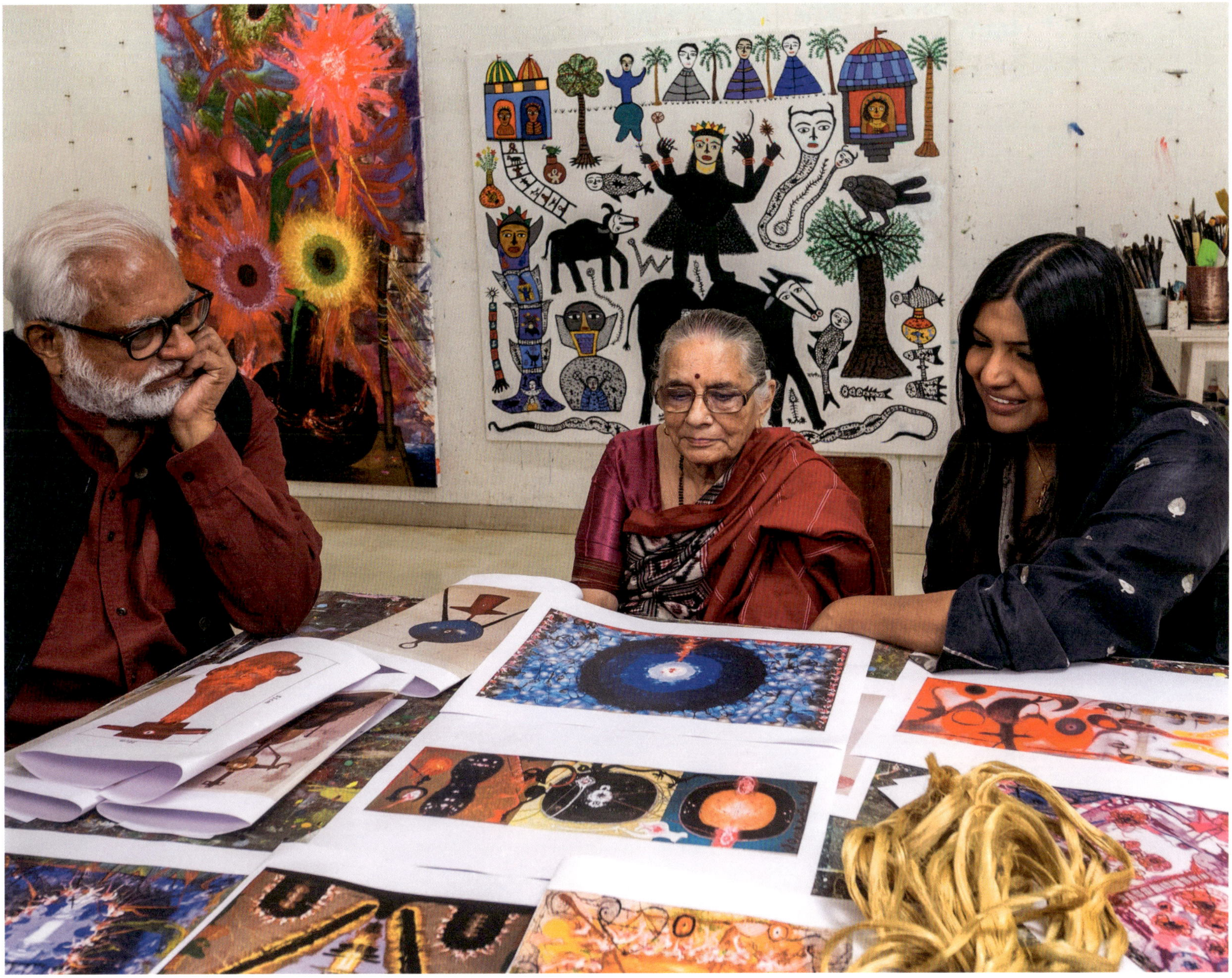

Karishma Swali, Manu Parekh, and Madhvi Parekh selecting
the works to be showcased at the exhibition
Photo by Sahiba Chawdhary. Courtesy of the Chanakya Foundation

Swali's collaboration with artists Manu Parekh and Madhvi Parekh materialised into a series of ambitious exhibitions, beginning with an exhibition at the Musée Rodin, Paris (2022) and followed by a presentation of 22 large, embroidered panels to supplement the Dior Fall 2023 show titled *Mul Mathi* at Snowball Studios, Mumbai. Extending the long-standing collaboration between Dior and Chanakya, Dior and Maria Grazia Chiuri lent two works originally created for the Dior show in 2022 to be part of the exhibition.

The collaboration reached new heights with *Cosmic Garden*, a collateral event at the Venice Biennale, which expanded the boundaries of craft by presenting large-scale interdisciplinary works and paper-mache sculptures derived from Madhvi Parekh's paintings. By bringing Madhvi Parekh's figures to life in sculpture, *Cosmic Garden* extends an invitation to engage with a more immersive narrative, one that urges us to look at craft as a living, evolving entity. Curated by Maria Alicata and Paolo Ugolini, this exhibition took an unconventional approach to presenting Indian art and craft on a global platform, introducing an audience unfamiliar with its rich symbolism, divinity, and history. India, often viewed through the dual lenses of economic ascendancy and spiritual mystique, is frequently reduced to simplistic stereotypes. This exhibition subverted such narratives by positioning embroidery as a conceptual and artistic medium. The scale and depth of this project demanded rigorous engagement, challenging any reductive reading of the works as decorative or exotic.

The relationship between Manu and Madhvi Parekh is as much a conceptual partnership as it is a domestic one. Their work reflects a shared ethos — an exploration of form through simplification, where folk narratives are transformed into contemporary compositions. Much like their paintings, their life is an ongoing dialogue, where art becomes an extension of conversation, humour, and mutual influence.

Cosmic Garden stands as an ode to the agency of the handmade — a celebration of the tactile act of making, where form and material become narrative. It honours the artist as both a steward and an innovator of cultural memory, sustaining ancestral lineages while articulating new, ever-evolving vocabularies of expression.

> Artist Madhvi Parekh at the Chanakya School of Craft
Photo by Vismay Mirgal. Courtesy of the Chanakya Foundation

> Artist Manu Parekh at the Chanakya School of Craft
Photo by Vismay Mirgal. Courtesy of the Chanakya Foundation

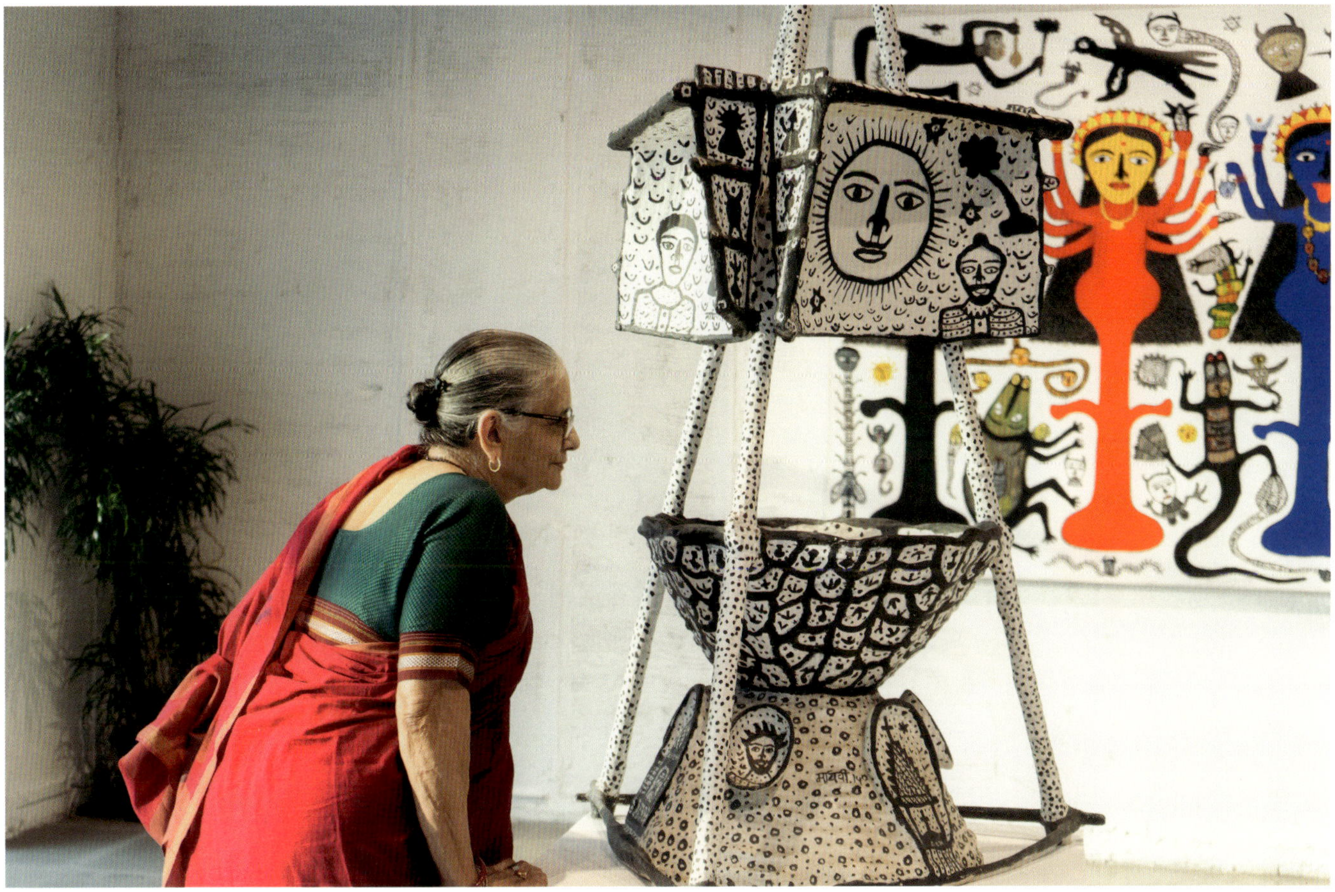

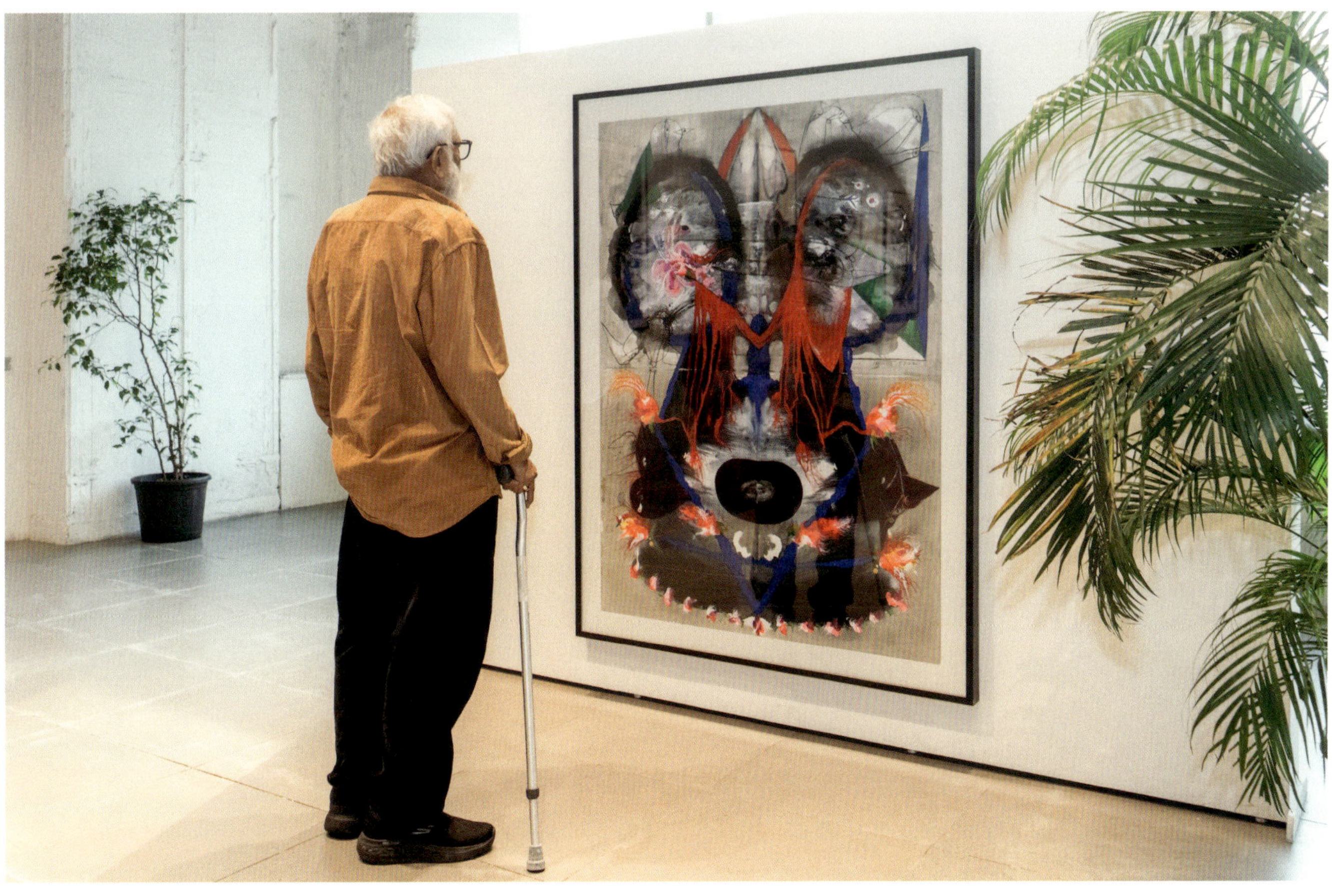

COSMIC GARDEN

Installation Views

60th International Art Exhibition – La Biennale di Venezia

> Images from the *Cosmic Garden* exhibition, a collateral event of the 60th International Art Exhibition – La Biennale di Venezia, showcasing the works of Madhvi Parekh, Manu Parekh, Karishma Swali, and the Chanakya Foundation, curated by Paola Ugolini and Maria Alicata. Photos by Daniele Zoico. Courtesy of the Chanakya Foundation.

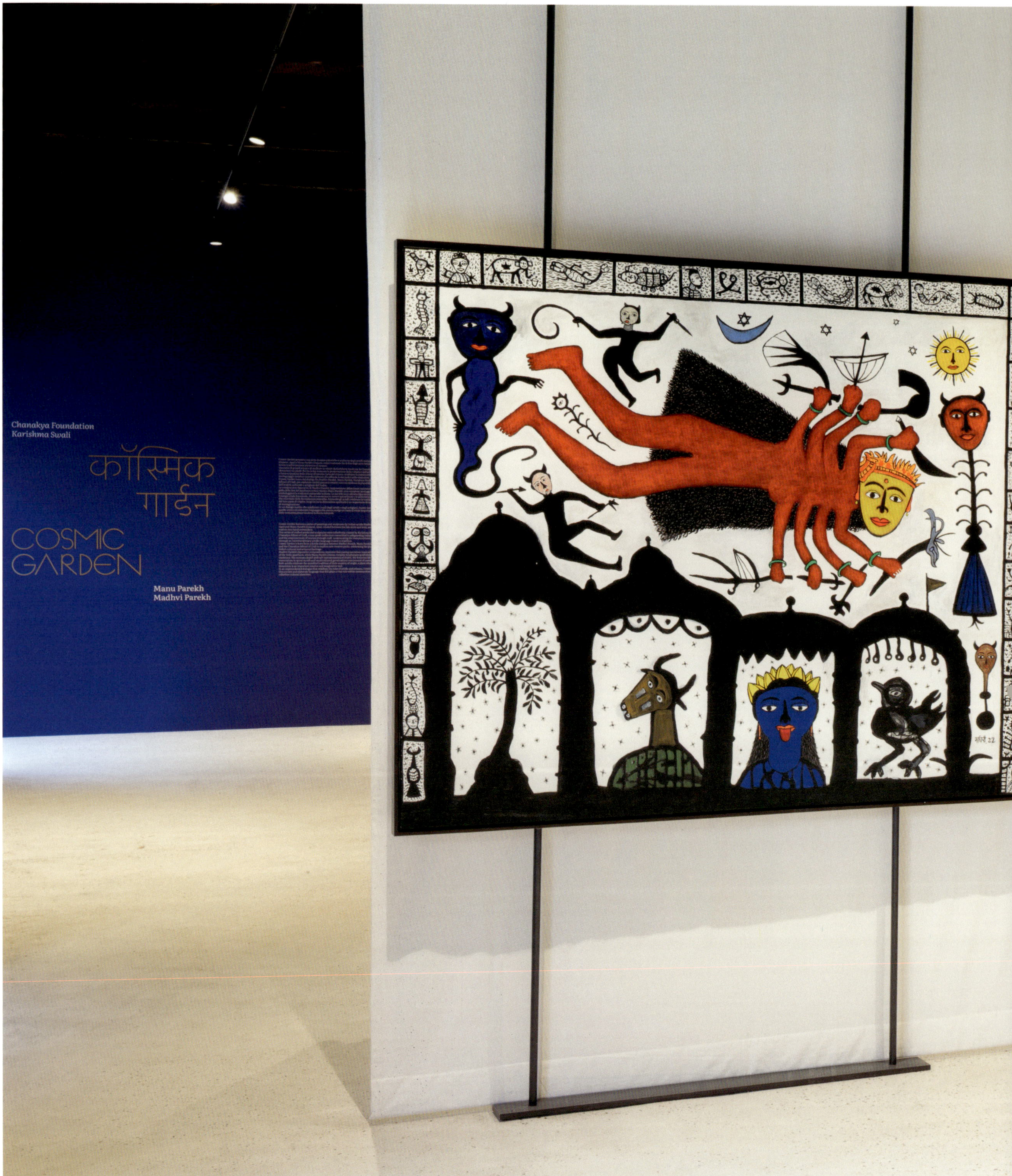
Chanakya Foundation
Karishma Swali
कॉस्मिक गार्डन
COSMIC GARDEN
Manu Parekh
Madhvi Parekh

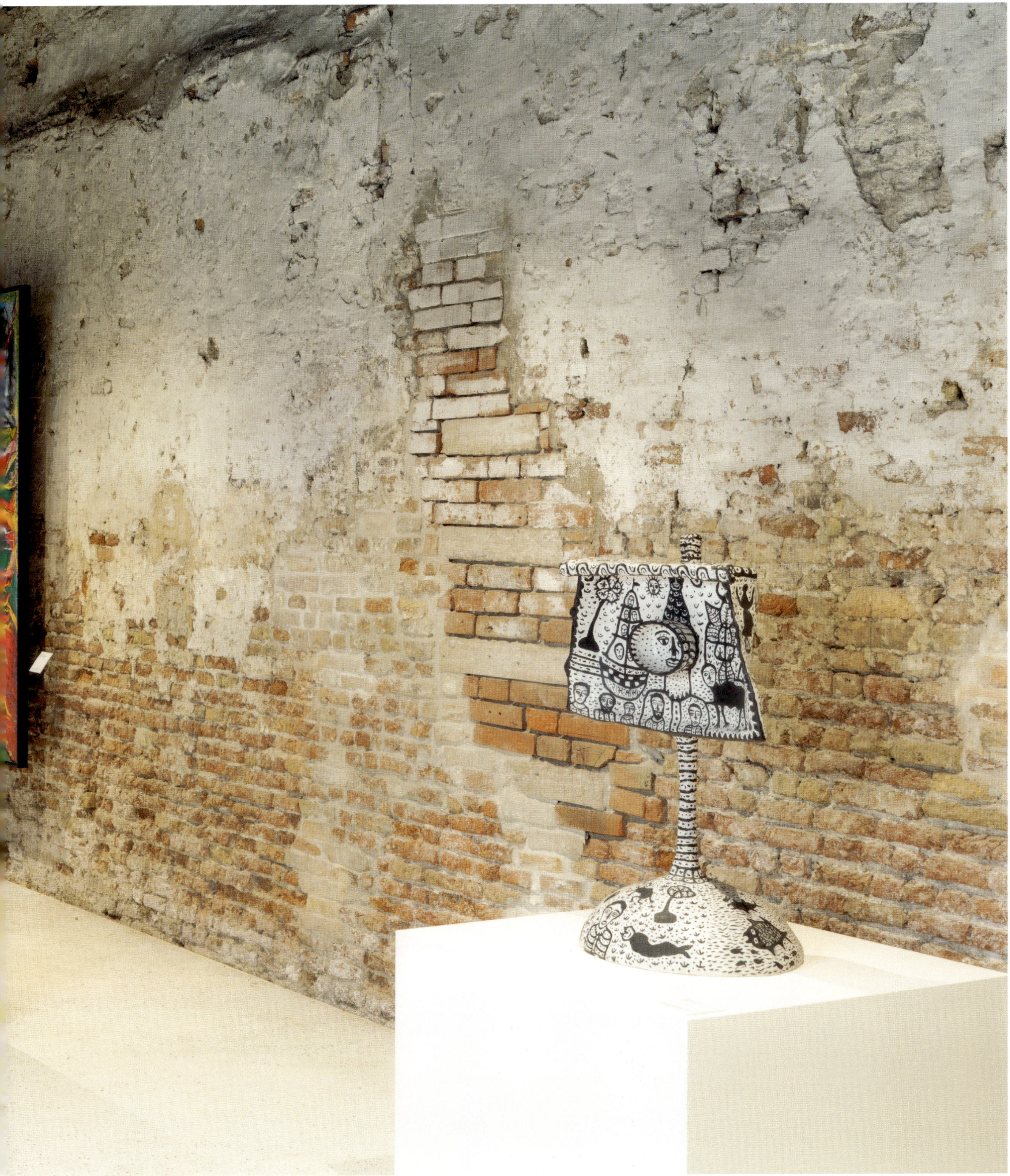

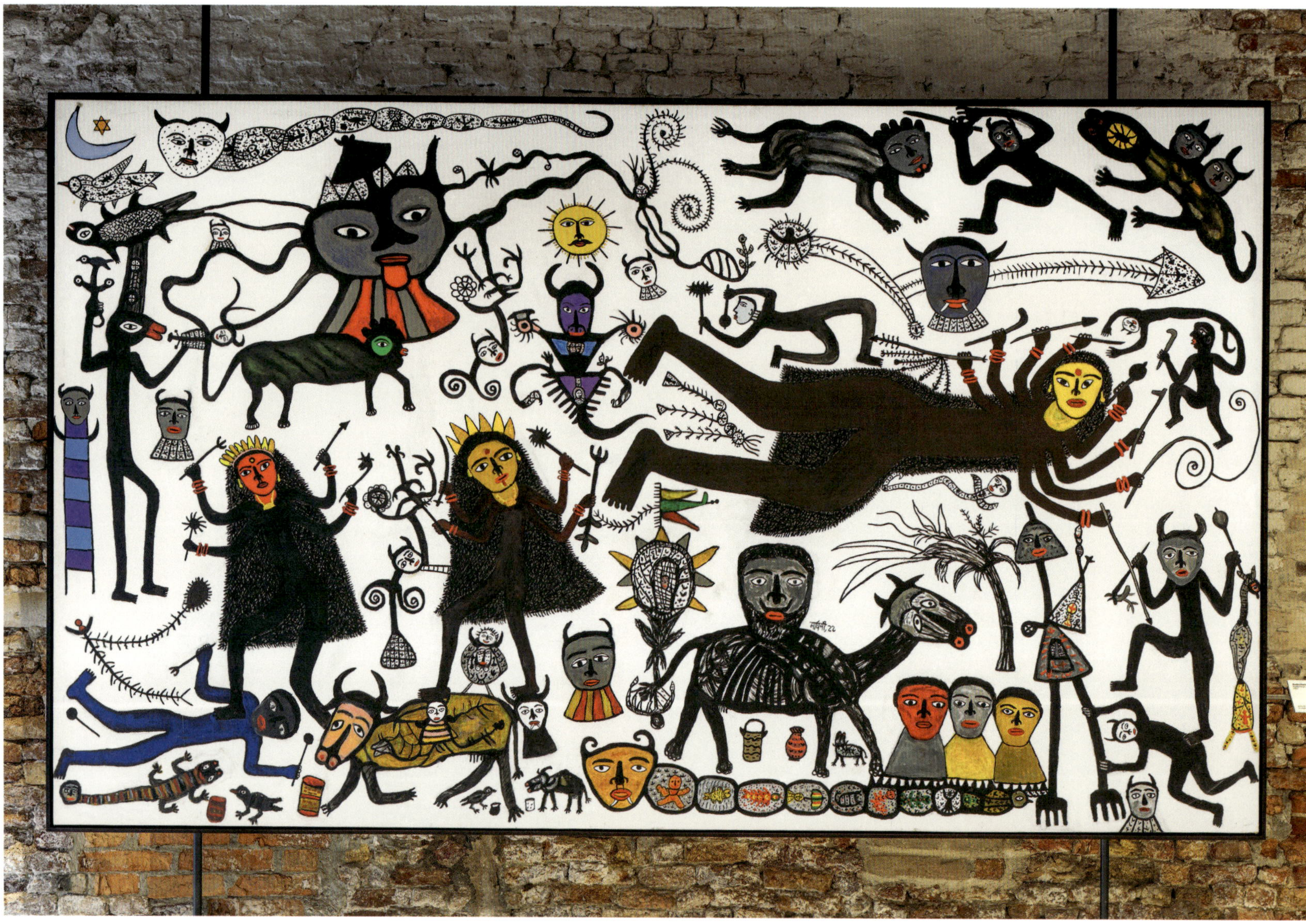

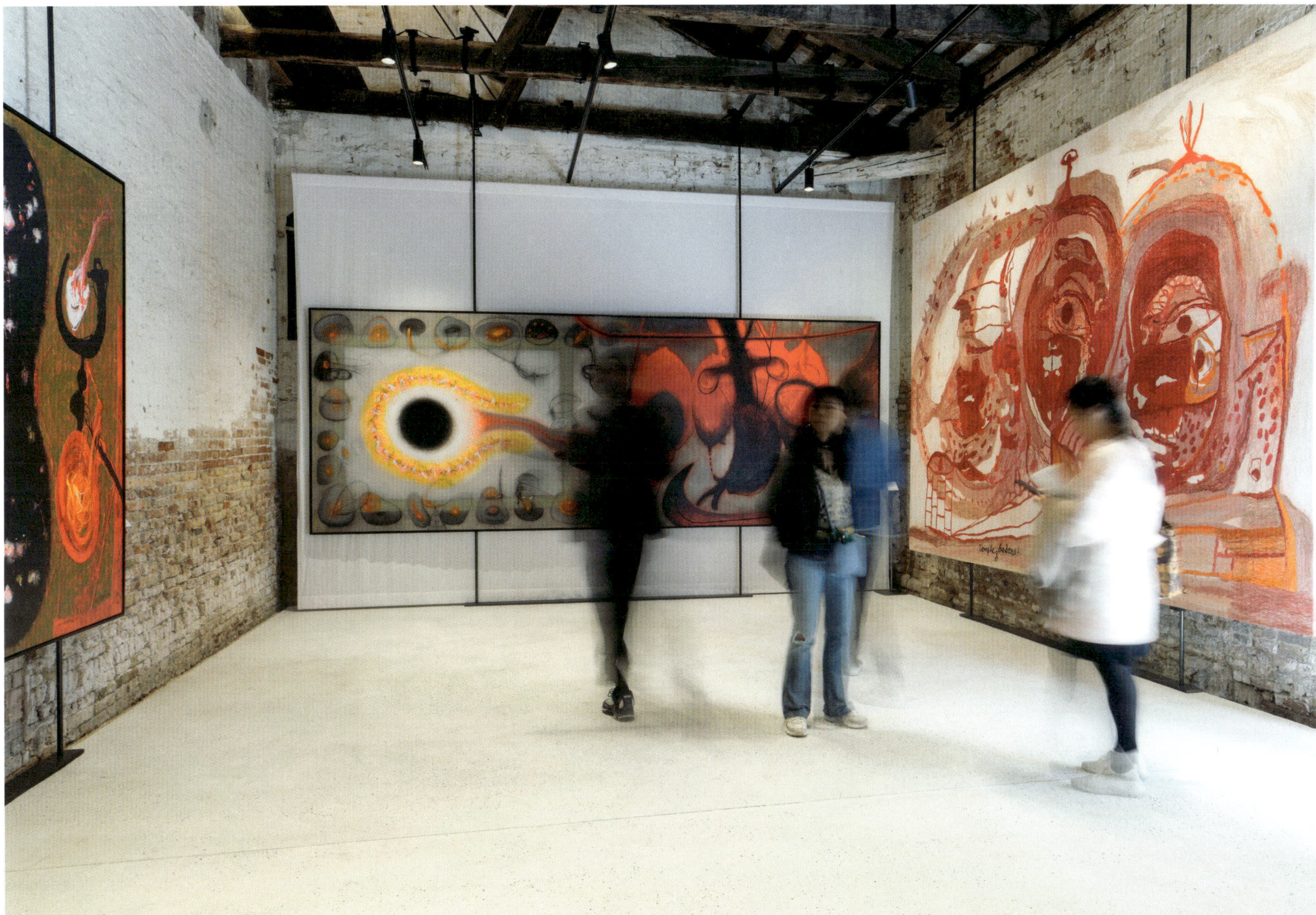

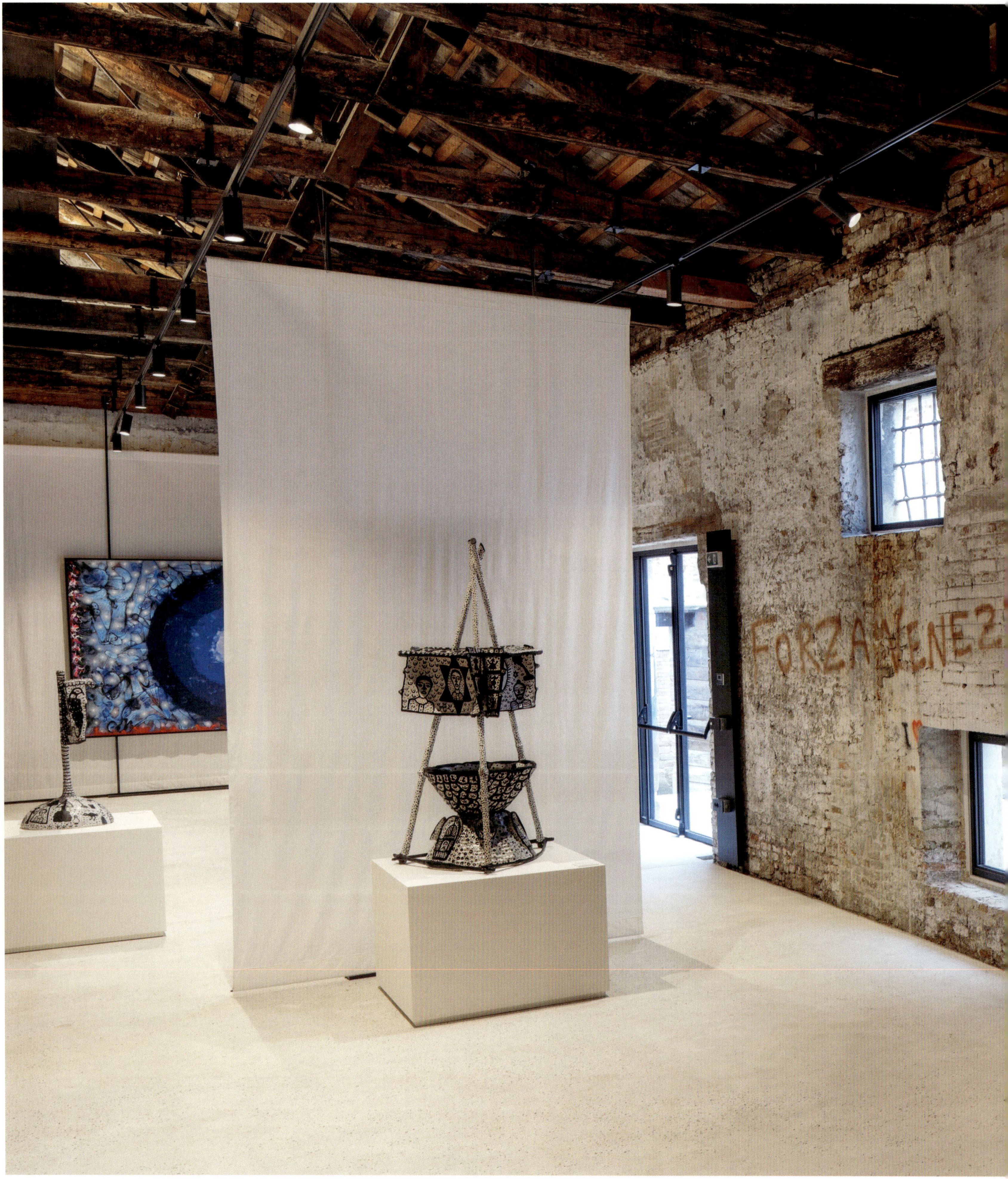

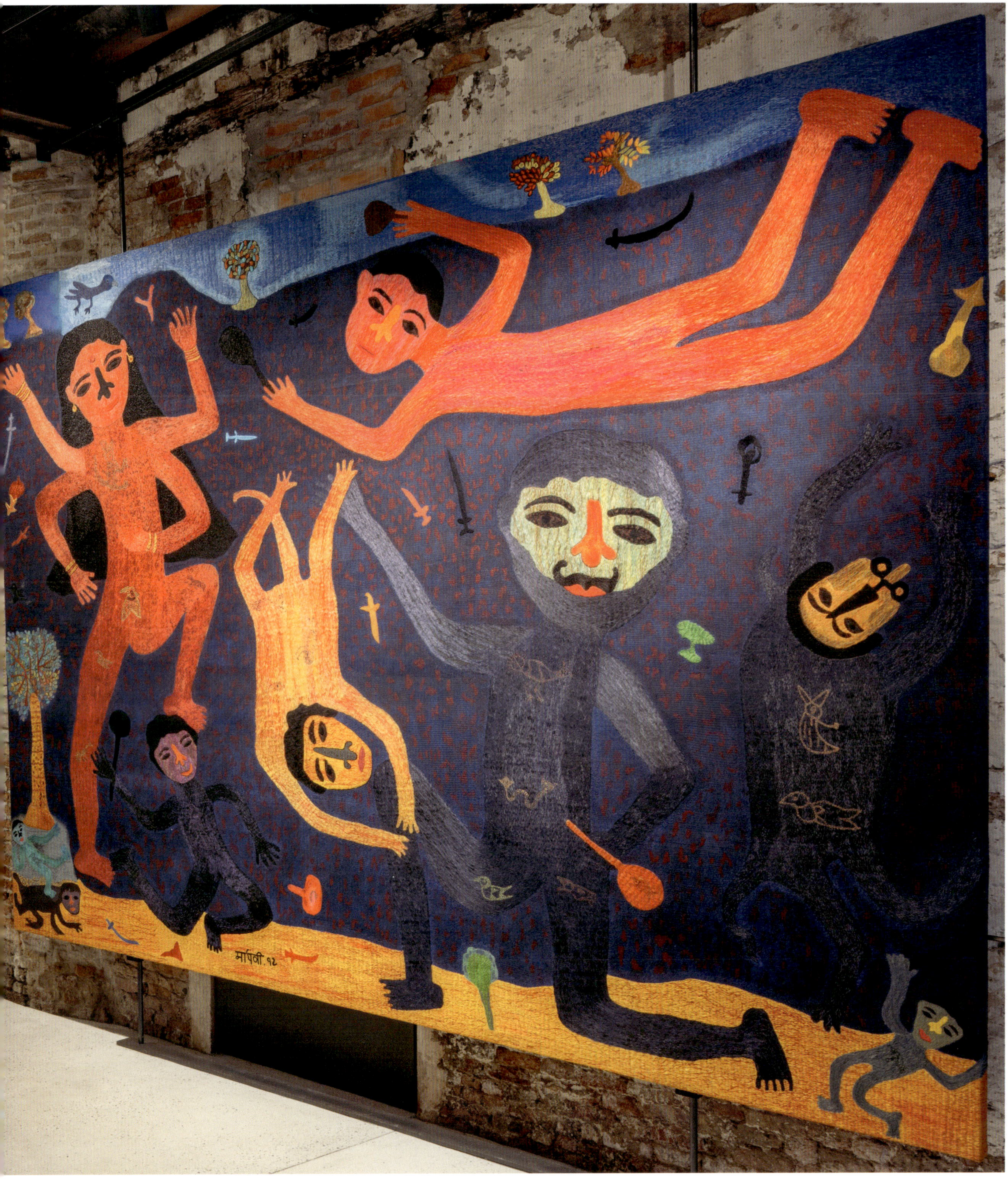
मार्पबी.१२

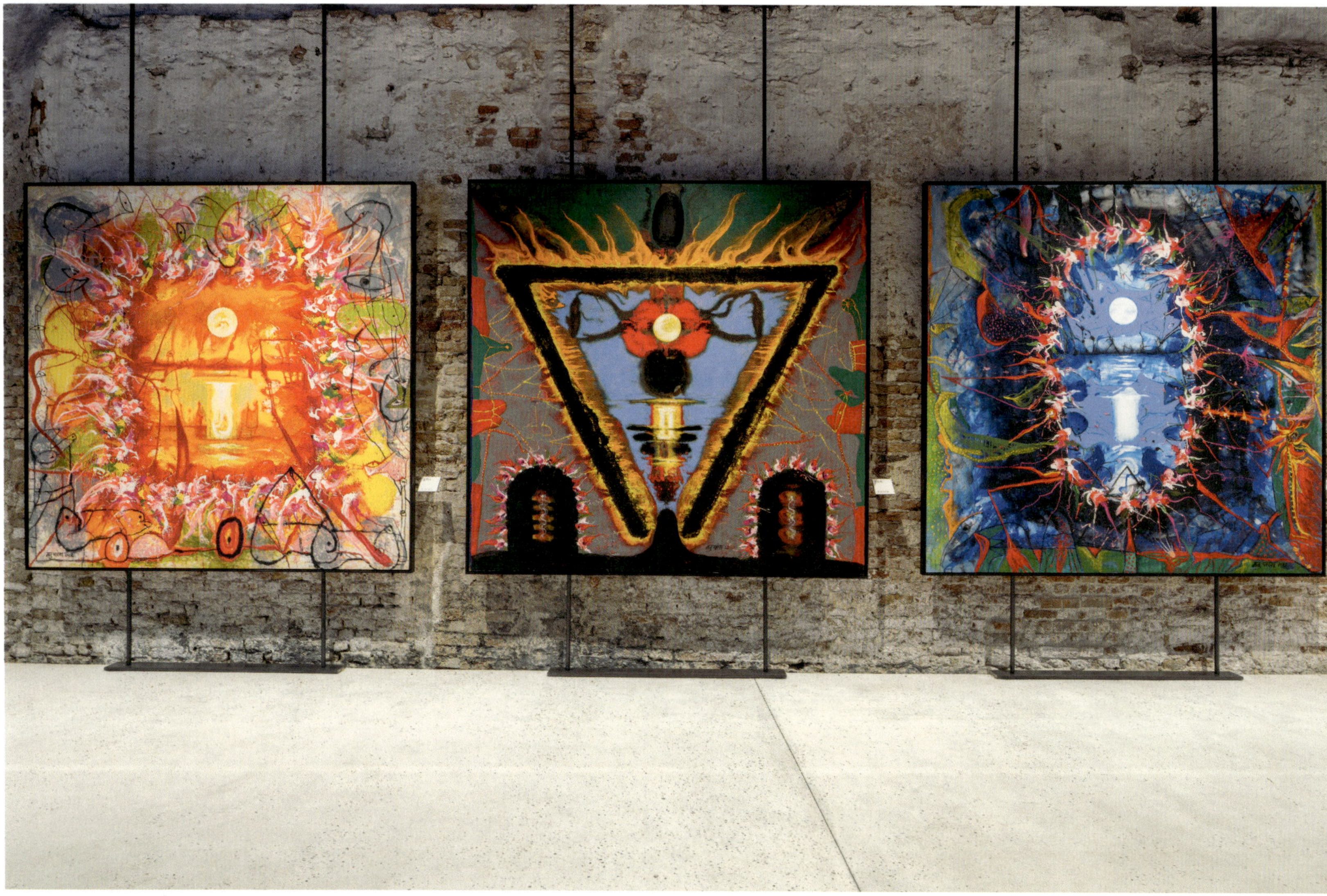

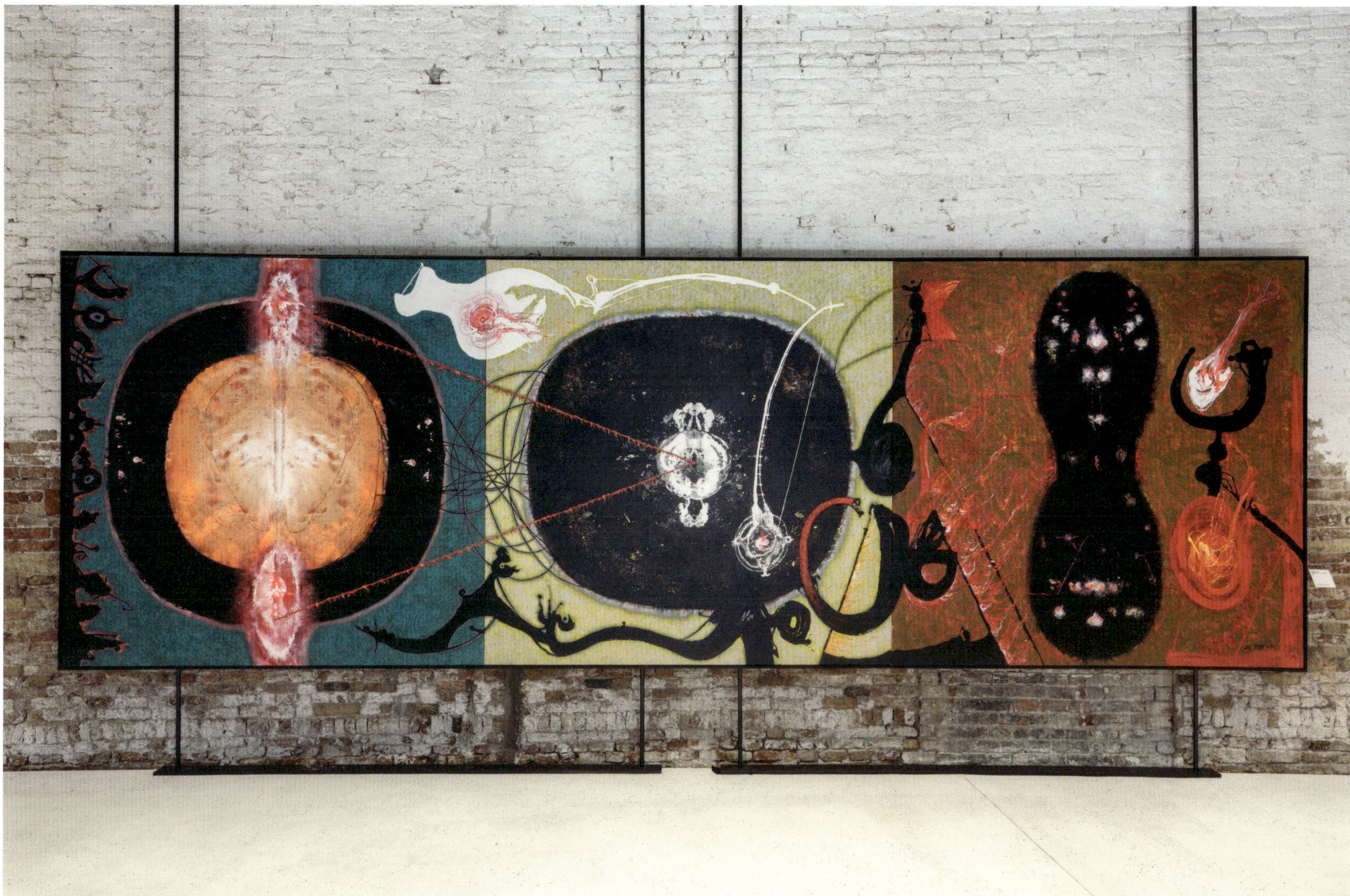

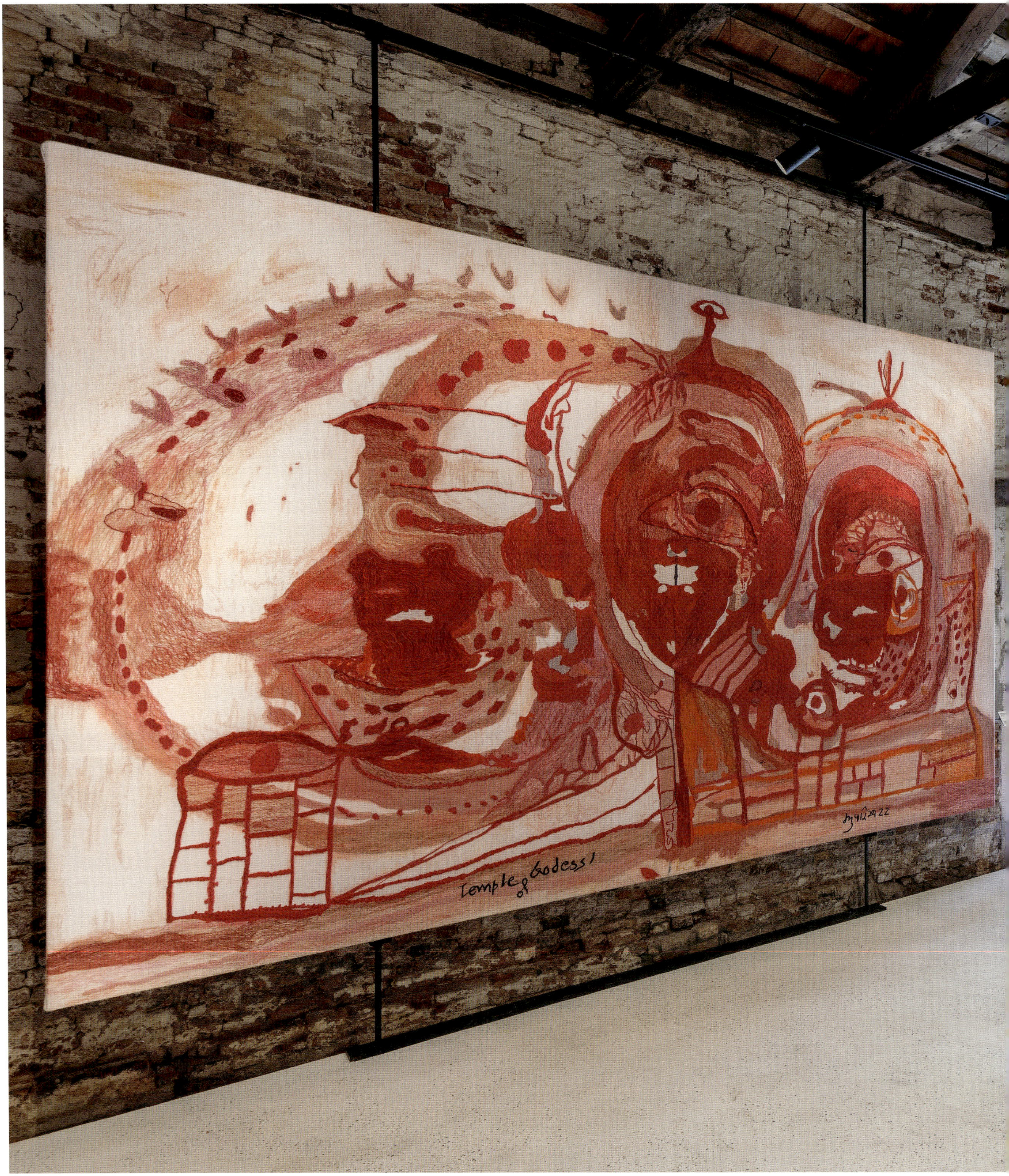
Temple of Godess

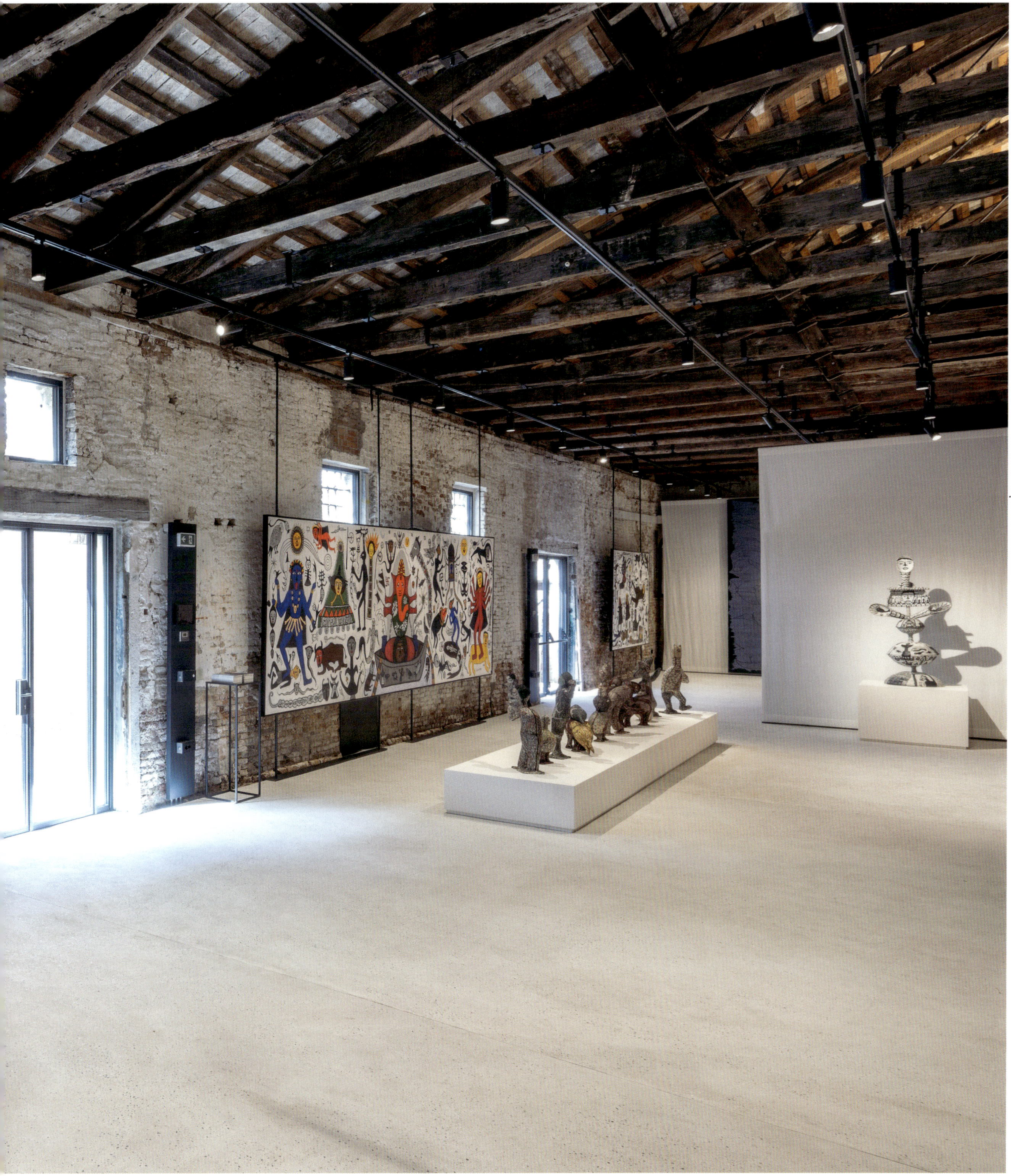

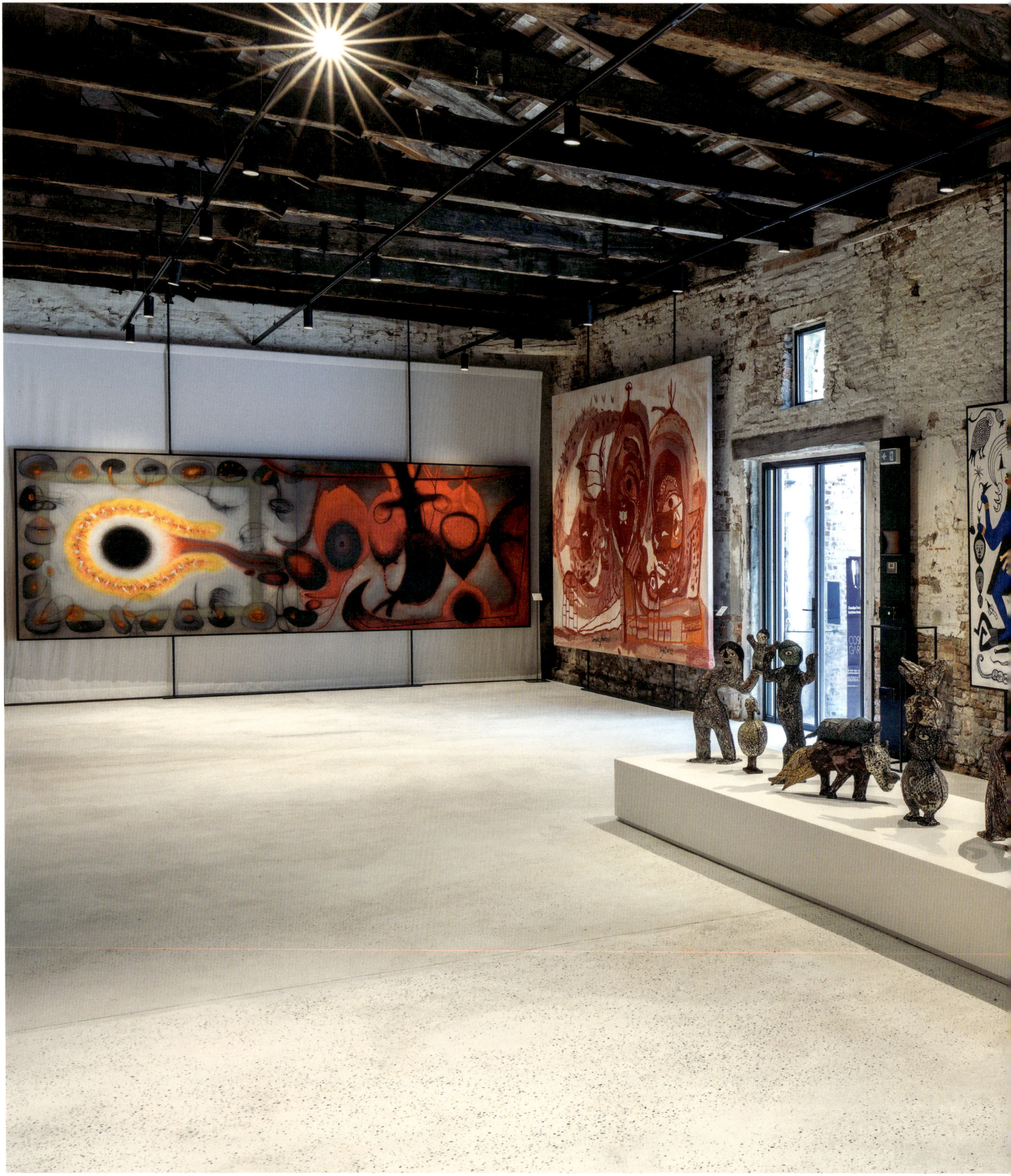

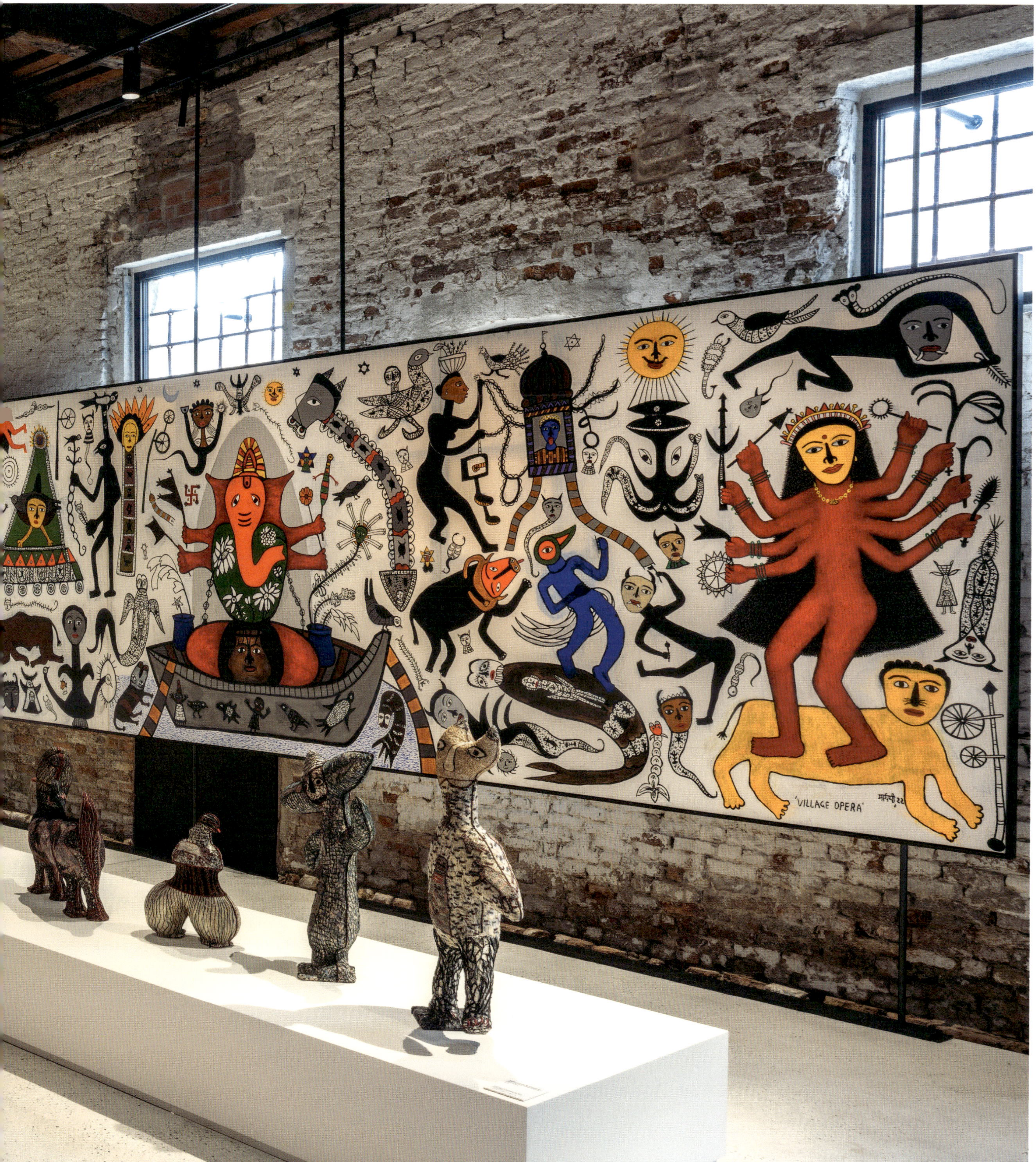
'VILLAGE OPERA'

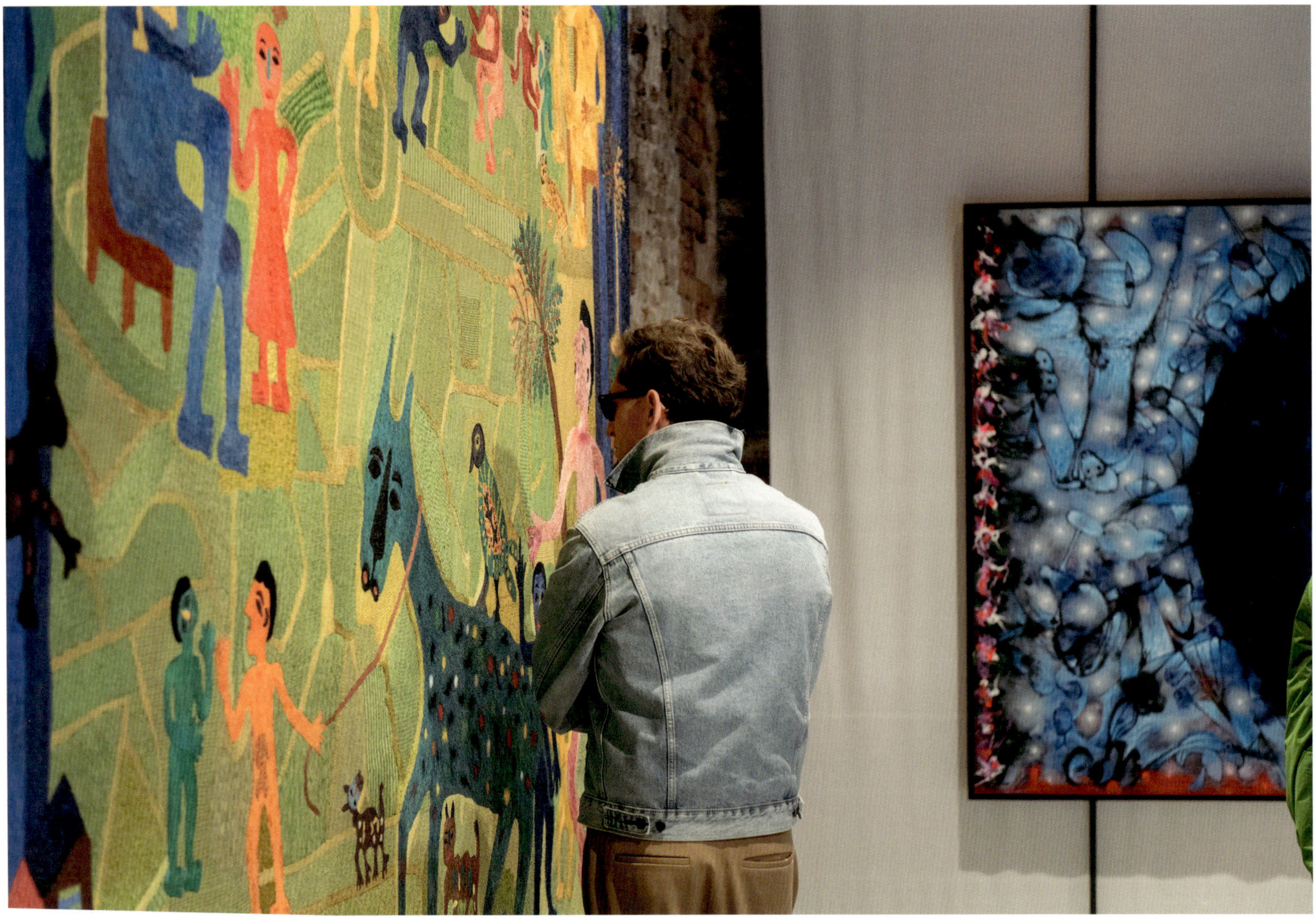

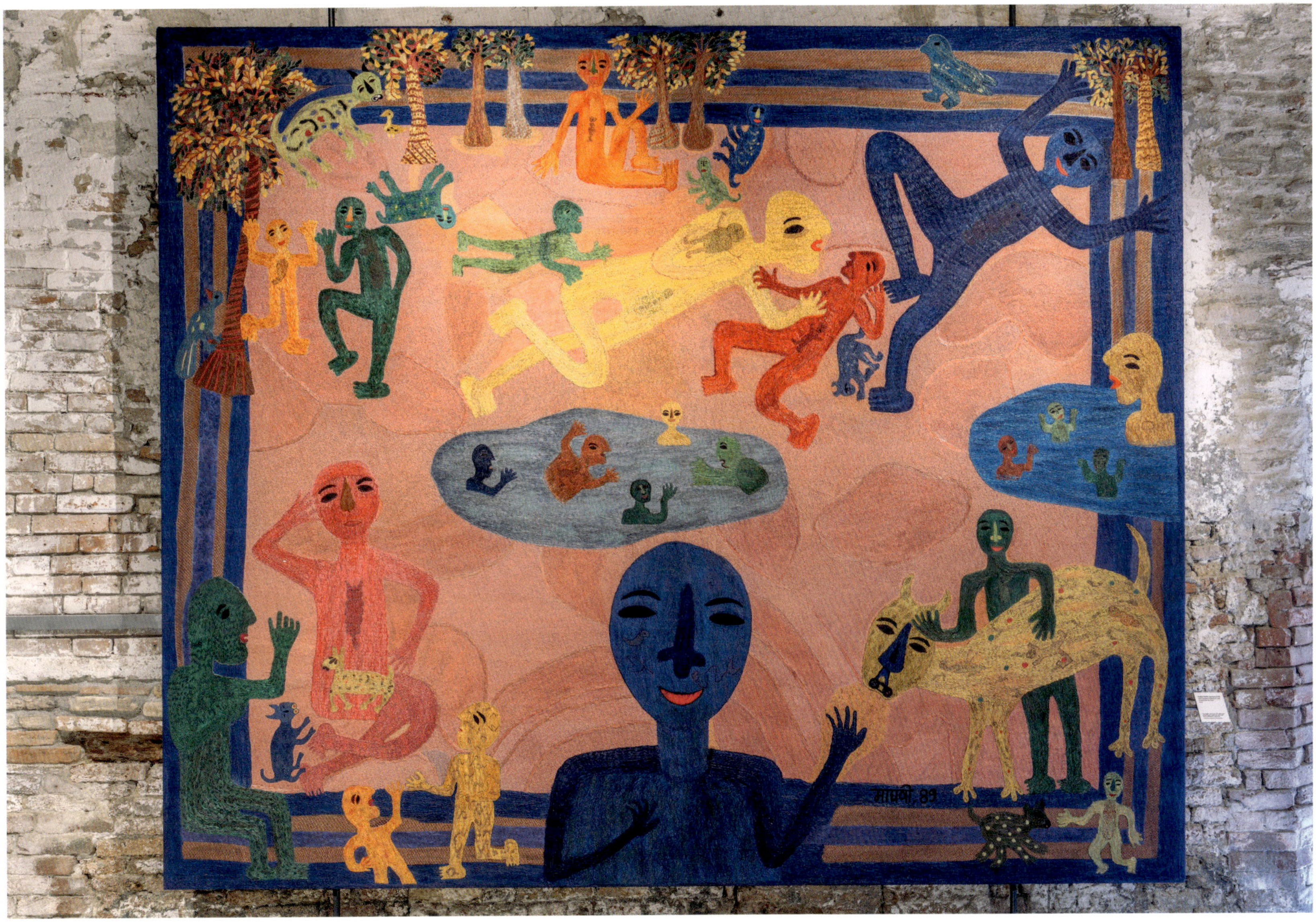

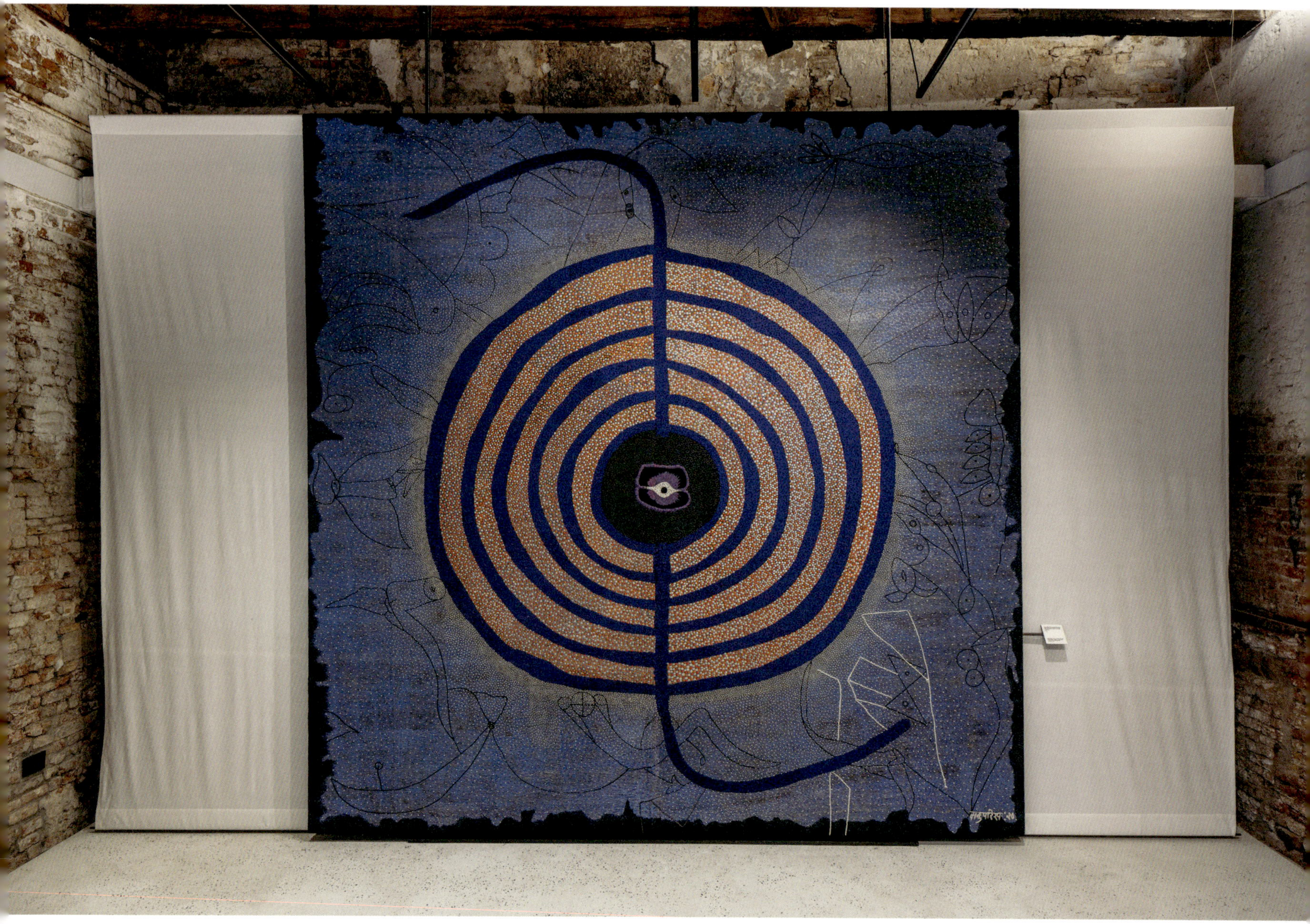

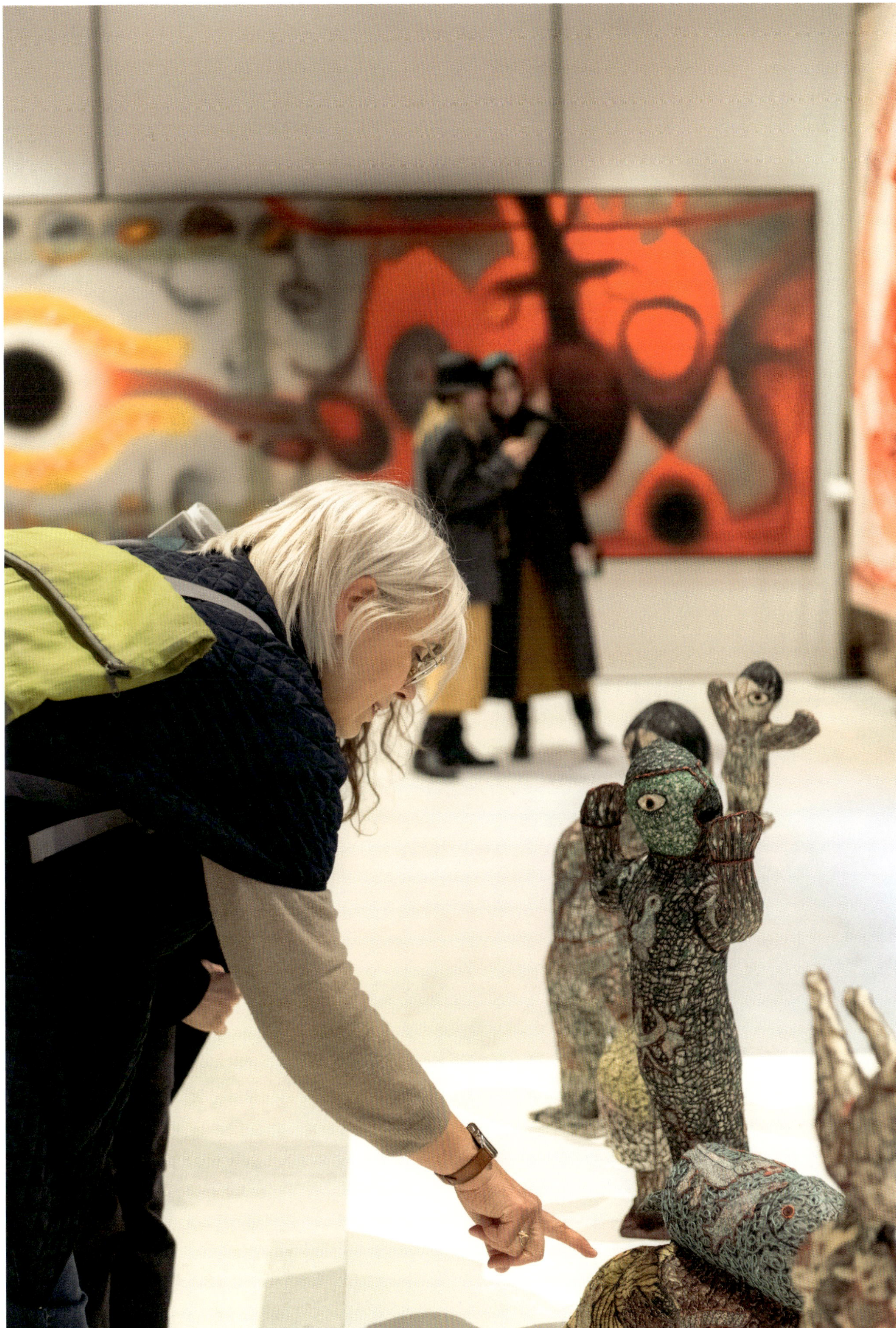

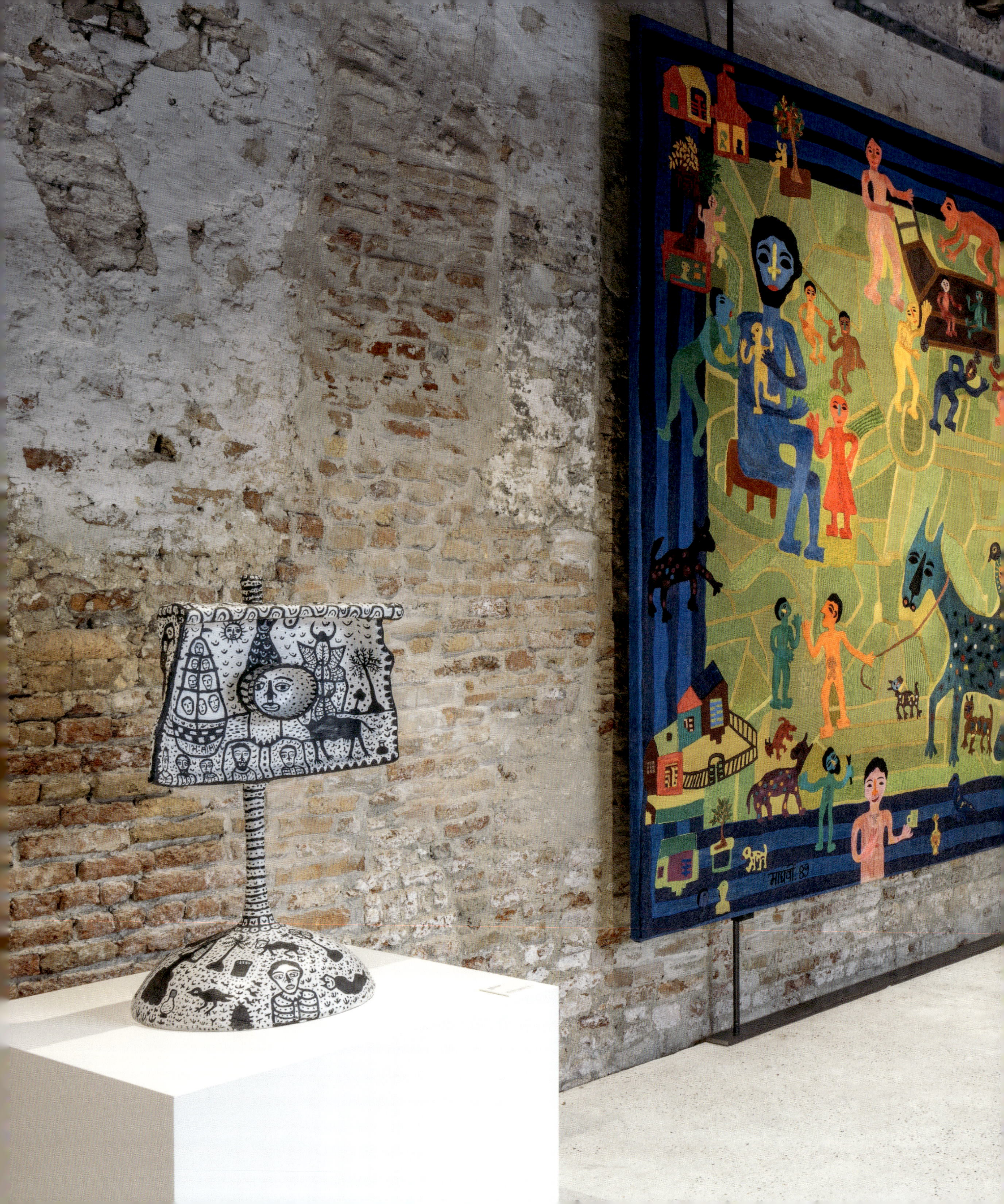

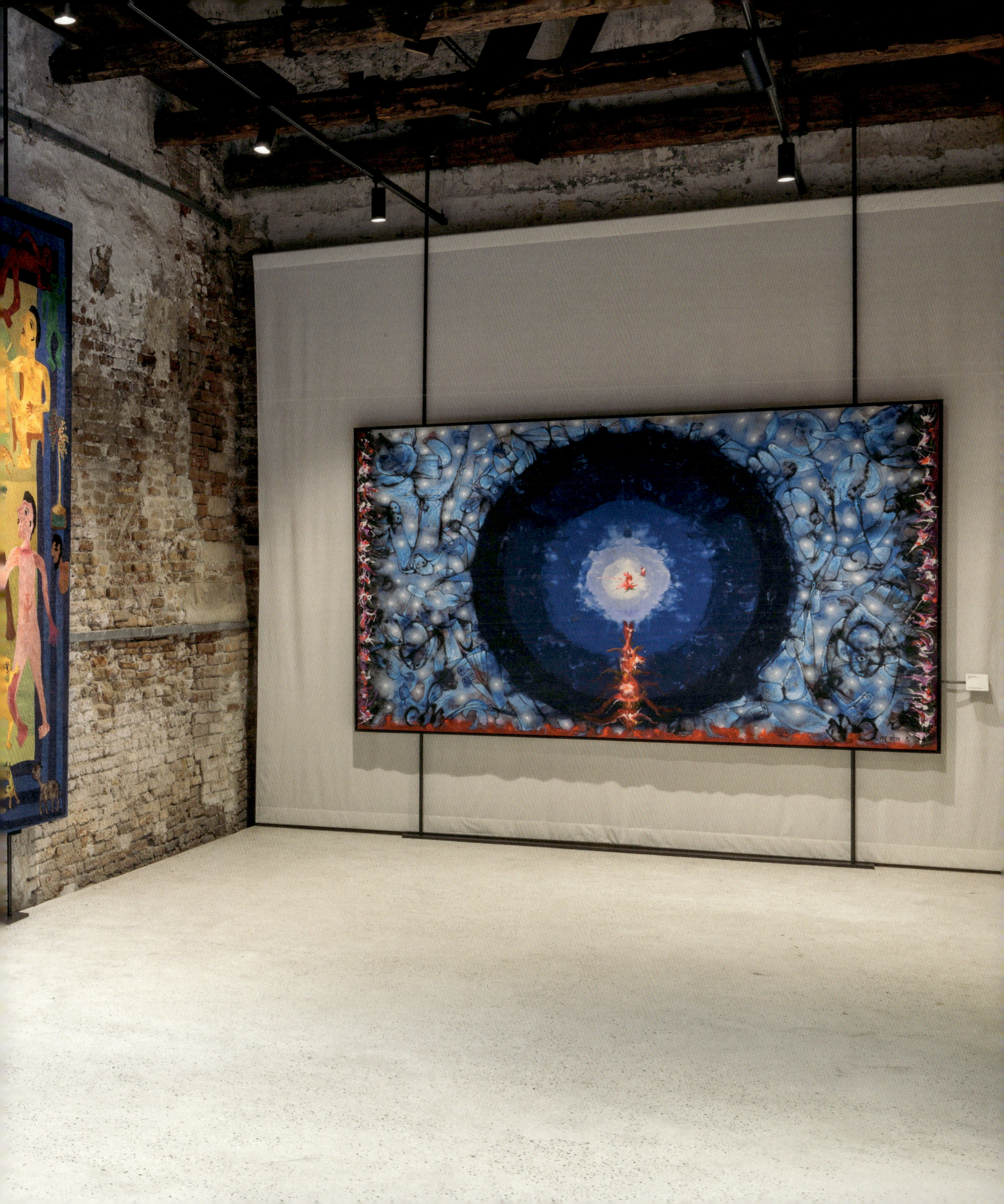

Crafted Sculptures

Madhvi Parekh, Karishma Swali,
and the Chanakya School of Craft

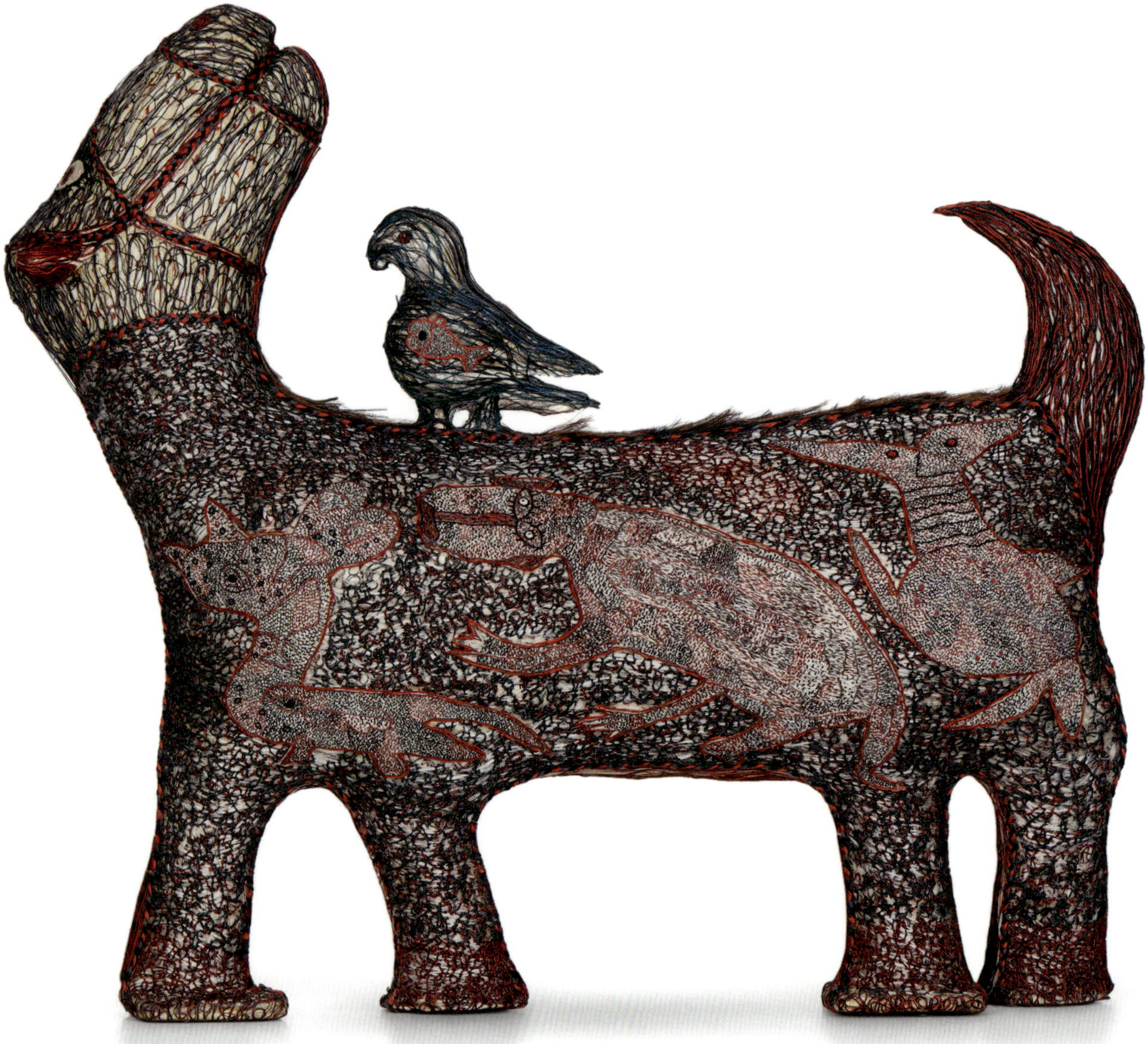

Madhvi Parekh, Karishma Swali, and the Chanakya School of Craft
Bird on Bull, 2023
Hand-sculpted paper-mache with organic jute, linen,
and cotton thread, 60 × 18 × 54 cm
Photo by Abner Fernandes. Courtesy of the Chanakya Foundation

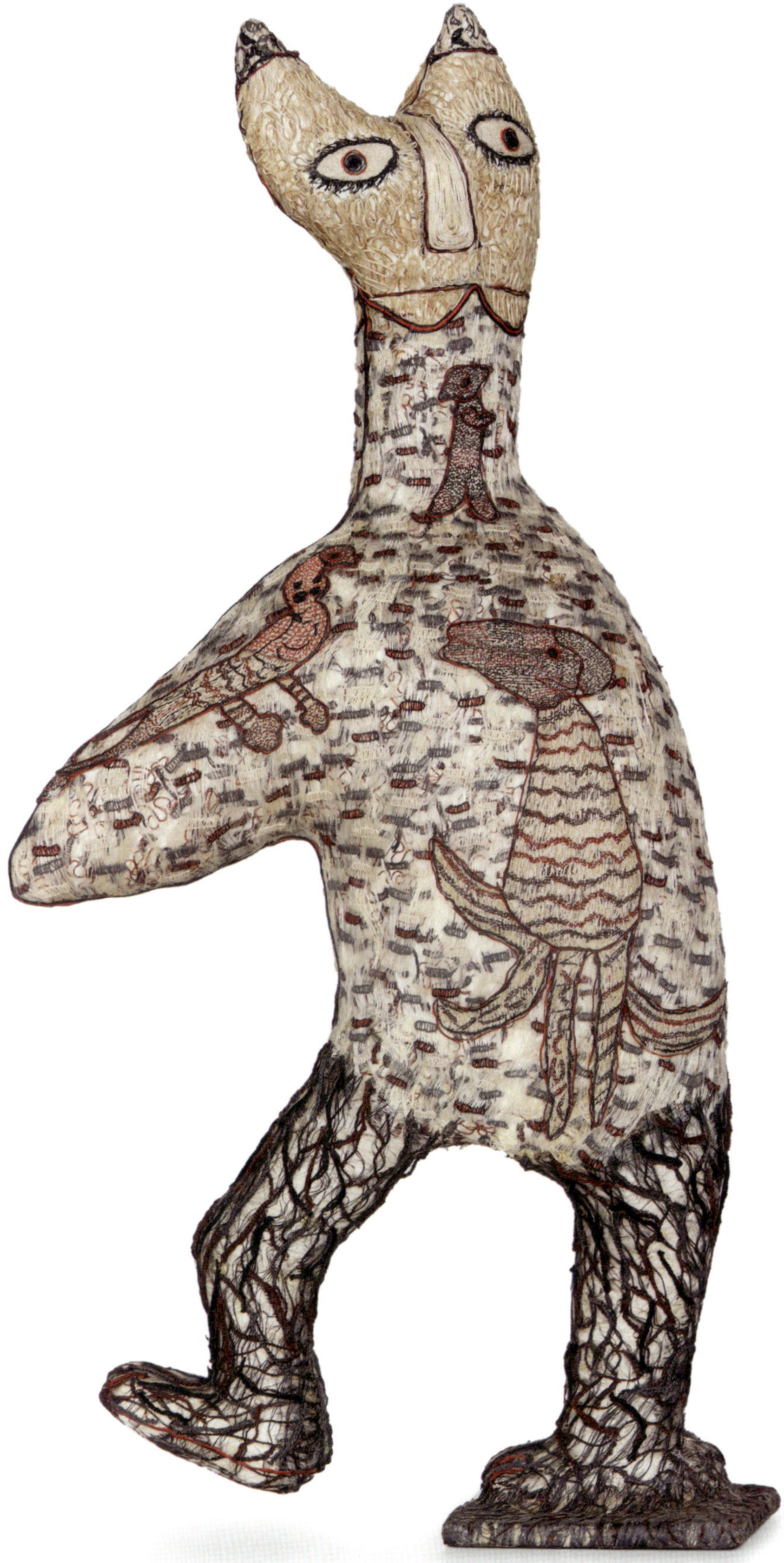

Madhvi Parekh, Karishma Swali, and the Chanakya School of Craft
Seeker, 2023
Hand-sculpted paper-mache with organic jute, linen,
and cotton thread, 40 × 18 × 80 cm
Photo by Abner Fernandes. Courtesy of the Chanakya Foundation

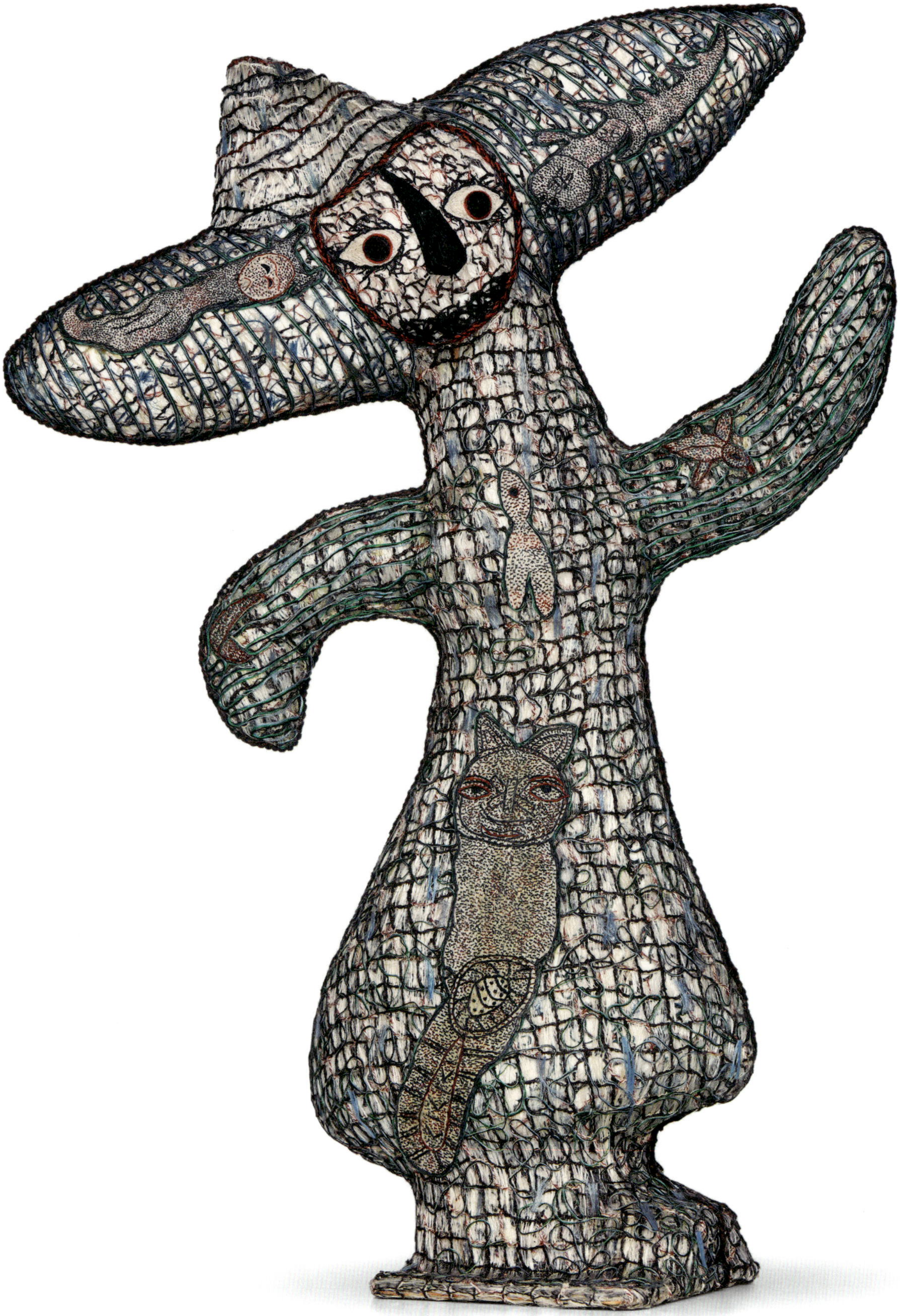

Madhvi Parekh, Karishma Swali, and the Chanakya School of Craft
Dancing Girl, 2023
Hand-sculpted paper-mache with organic jute, linen,
and cotton thread, 44 × 21 × 65 cm
Photo by Abner Fernandes. Courtesy of the Chanakya Foundation

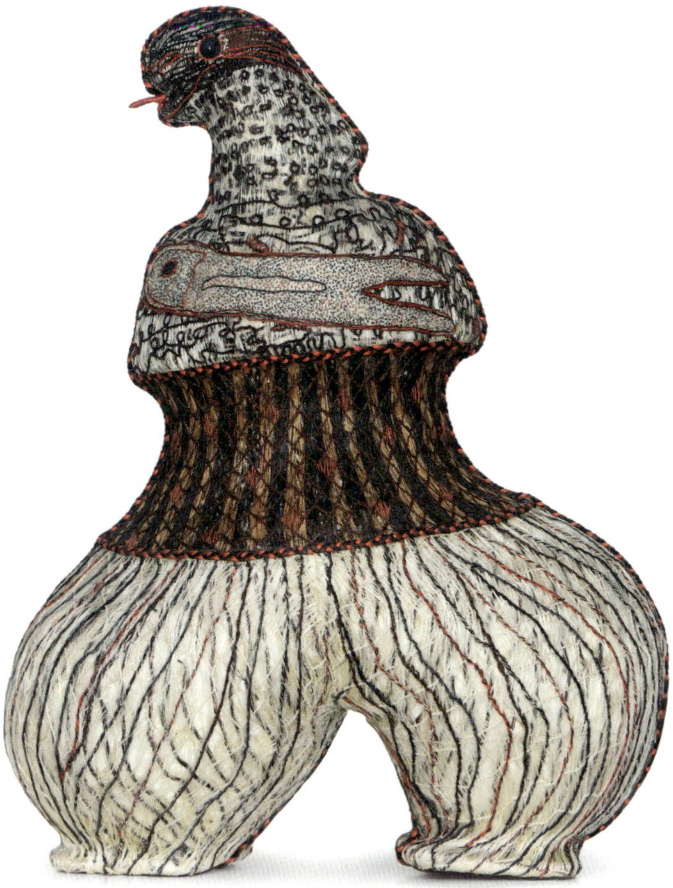

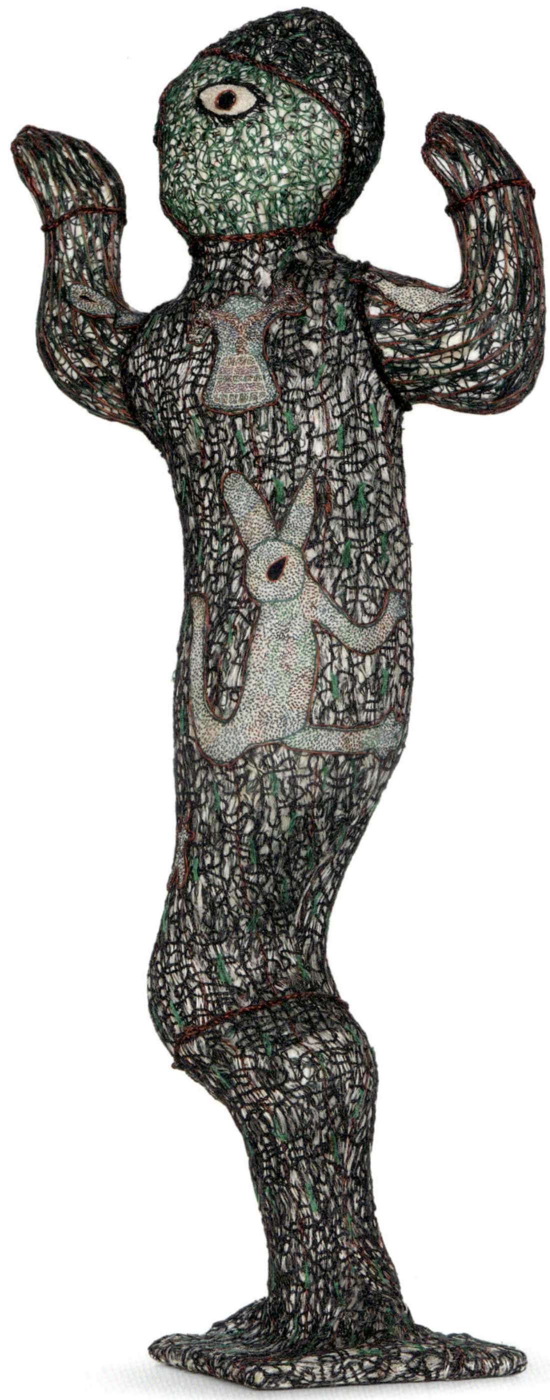

Madhvi Parekh, Karishma Swali and Chanakya School of Craft
Onlooker, 2023
Hand-sculpted paper mache with organic jute, linen
and cotton thread, 31 × 18 × 41 cm
Photo by Abner Fernandes. Courtesy of the Chanakya Foundation

Madhvi Parekh, Karishma Swali and Chanakya School of Craft
Figure with Raised Arms, 2023
Hand-sculpted paper mache with organic jute, linen
and cotton thread, 33 × 23 × 73 cm
Photo Abner Fernandes. Courtesy of the Chanakya Foundation

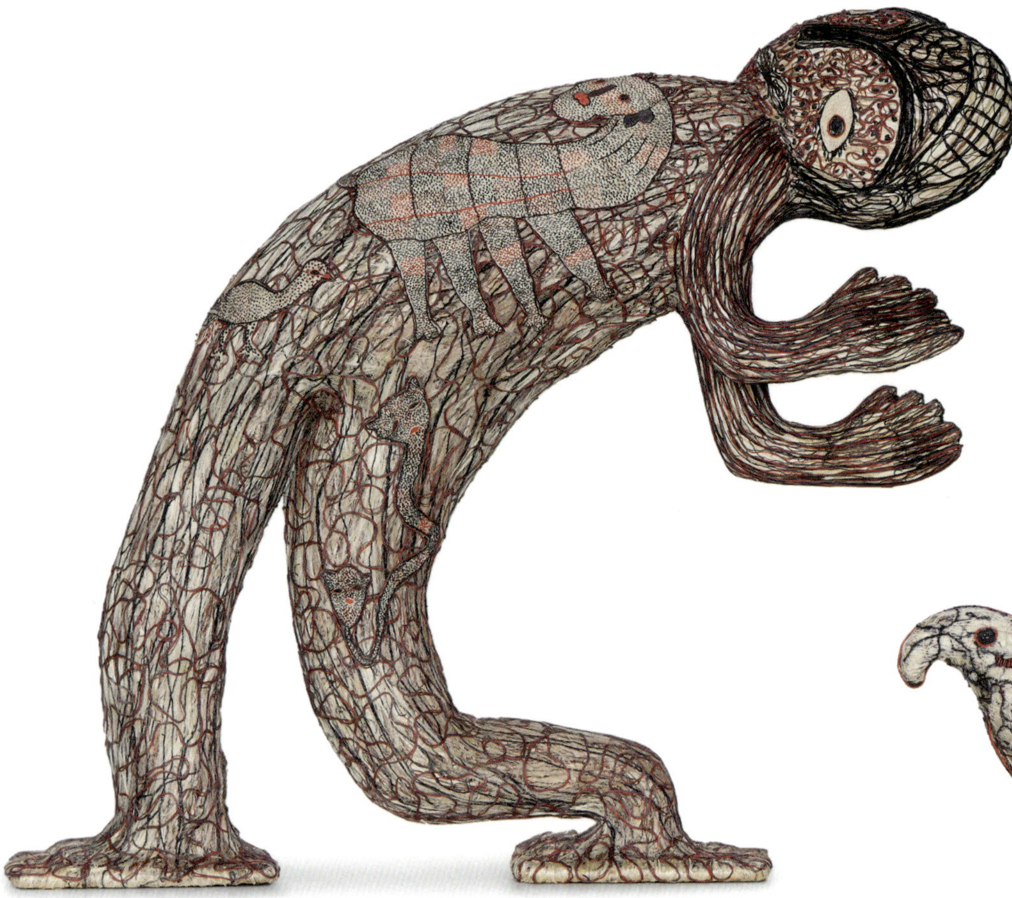

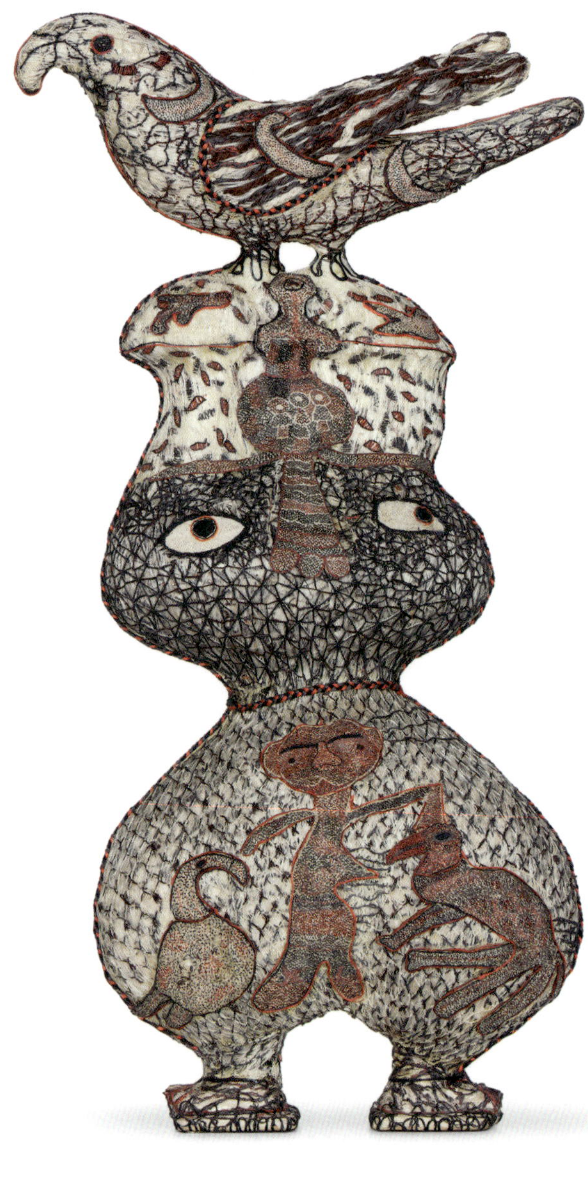

Madhvi Parekh, Karishma Swali, and the Chanakya School of Craft
Man with Flute, 2023
Hand-sculpted paper-mache with organic jute, linen, and cotton thread, 62 × 16 × 53 cm
Photo by Abner Fernandes. Courtesy of the Chanakya Foundation

Madhvi Parekh, Karishma Swali, and the Chanakya School of Craft
Friends in the Village, 2023
Hand-sculpted paper-mache with organic jute, linen, and cotton thread, 36 × 17 × 74 cm
Photo by Abner Fernandes. Courtesy of the Chanakya Foundation

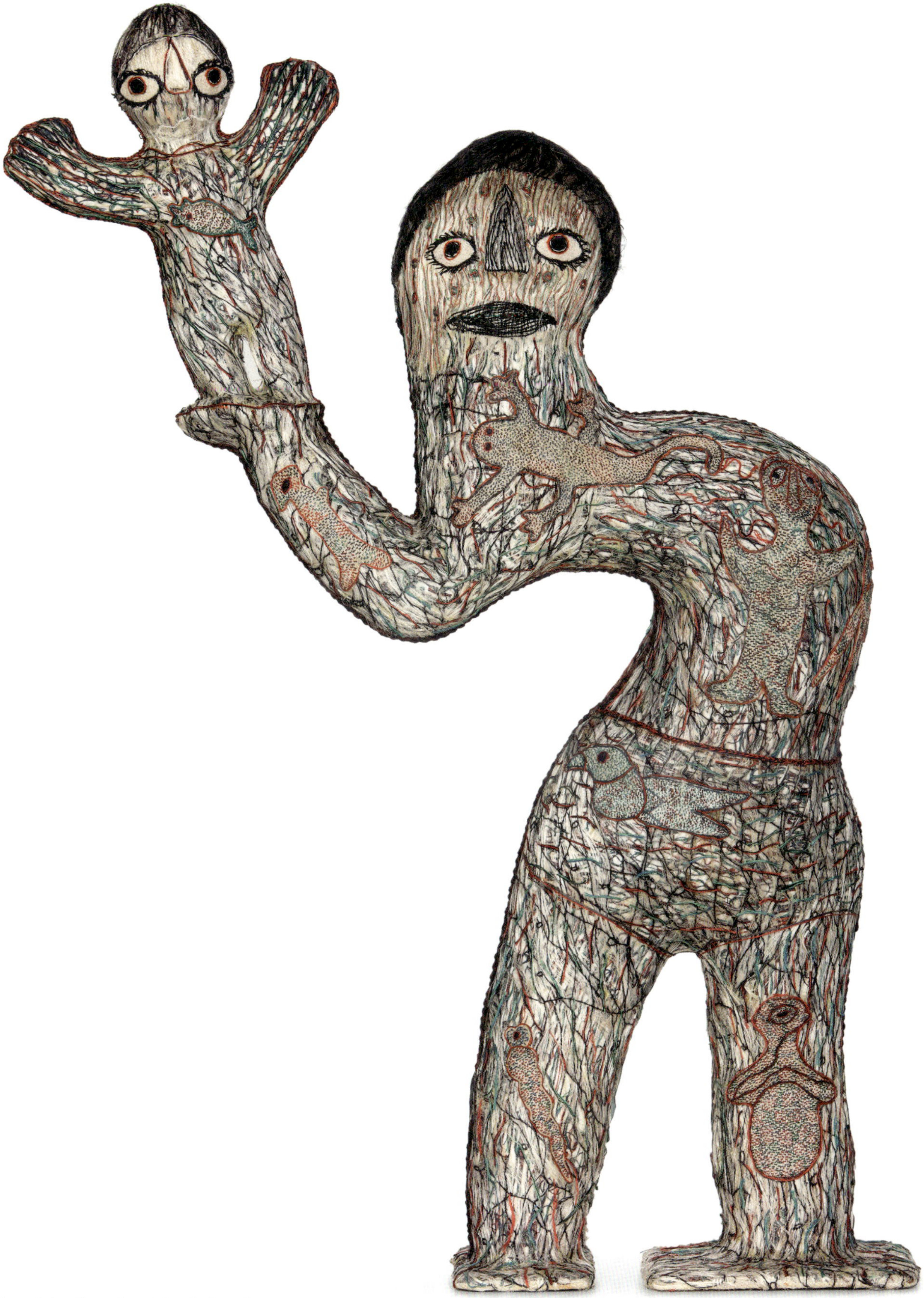

Madhvi Parekh, Karishma Swal, and the Chanakya School of Craft
Father & Son, 2023
Hand-sculpted paper-mache with organic jute, linen,
and cotton thread, 55 × 18 × 76 cm
Photo by Abner Fernandes. Courtesy of the Chanakya Foundation

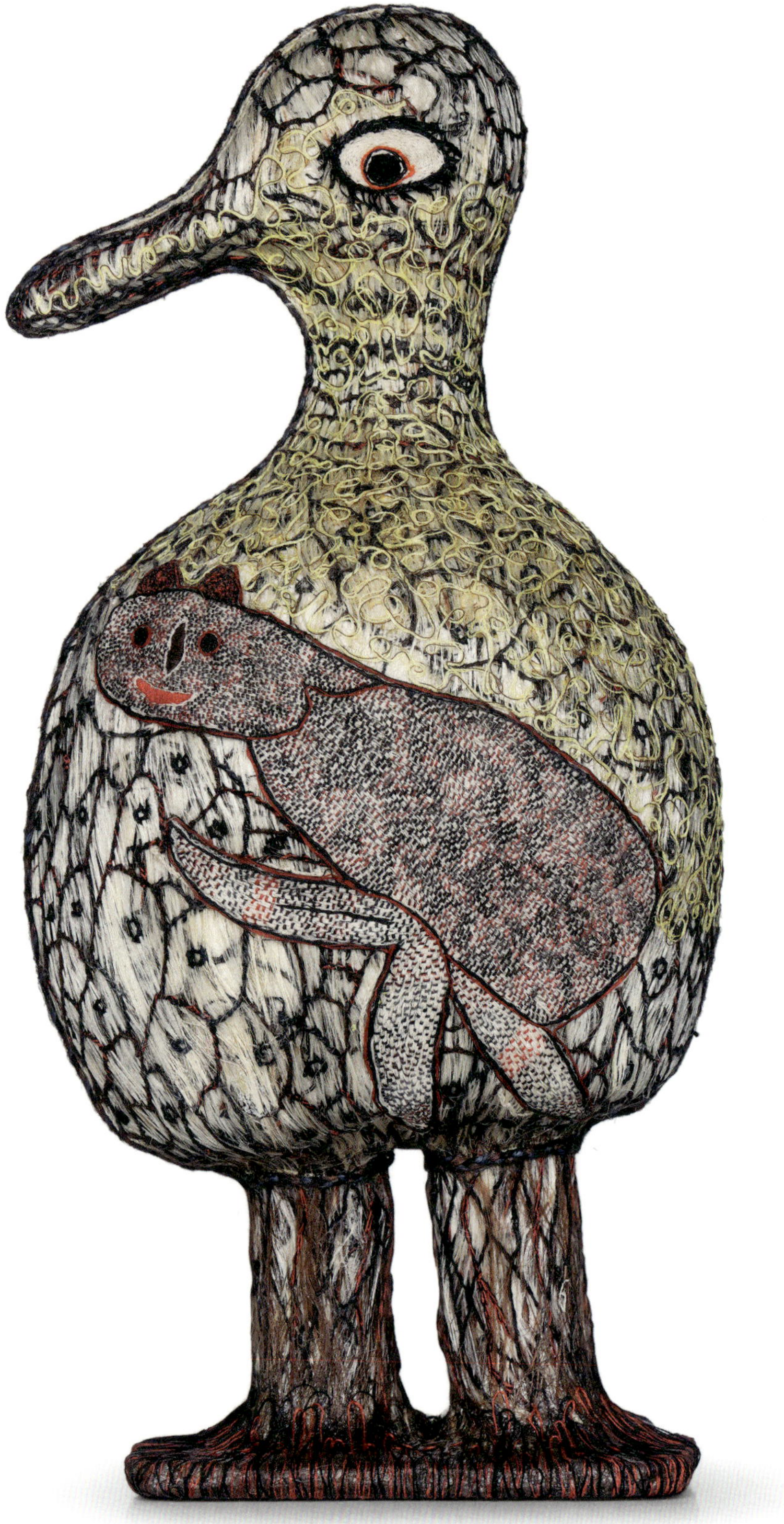

Madhvi Parekh, Karishma Swali, and the Chanakya School of Craft
Looking Bird, 2023
Hand-sculpted paper-mache with organic jute, linen,
and cotton thread, 19 × 17 × 41 cm
Photo by Abner Fernandes. Courtesy of the Chanakya Foundation

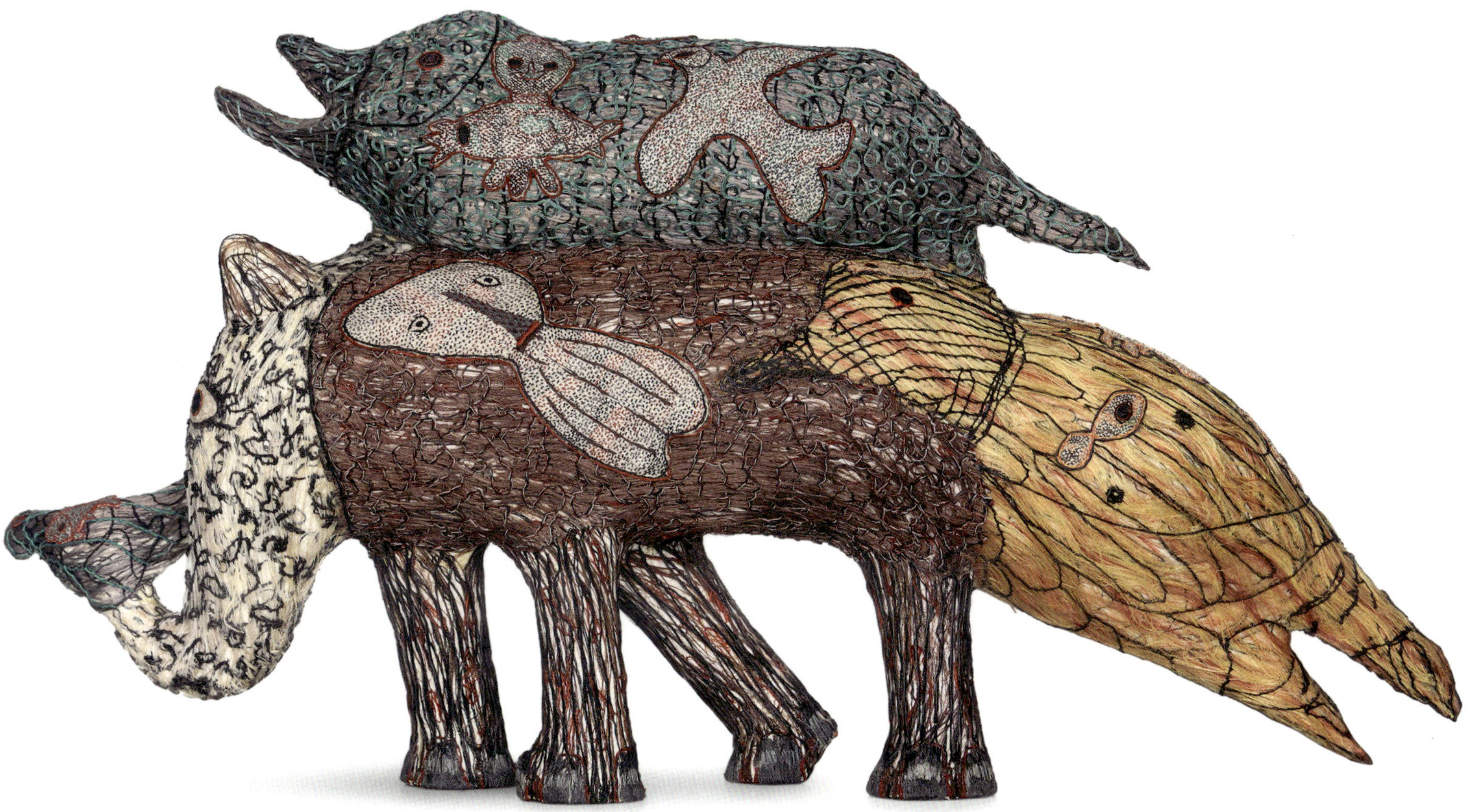

Madhvi Parekh, Karishma Swali, and the Chanakya School of Craft
Resting Figures, 2023
Hand-sculpted paper-mache with organic jute, linen,
and cotton thread, 33 × 23 × 73 cm
Photo by Abner Fernandes. Courtesy of the Chanakya Foundation

Biographies

Authors

Maria Alicata, an art historian and curator, holds a Ph.D. in contemporary art history. Her research focuses on intermedia and performative practices, including artists' cinema, as well as the archive within contemporary art and the history of exhibitions. She has worked with both private and public institutions, including Fondazione Adriano Olivetti, MACRO in Rome, and Fondazione Baruchello.

Maria Alicata's curatorial practice is rooted in interdisciplinarity, spanning exhibitions and public art projects across Italy and internationally. She has collaborated with institutions such as Le Consortium in Dijon, CNEAI - Centre National Édition Art Image, La Biennale di Venezia, and MAXXI in Rome. In 2023, she co-curated the solo exhibition *Maria Lai: Woven Writings* at Es Baluard Museum in Palma de Mallorca. She is an adjunct professor at La Sapienza University of Rome.

Dr. Ritu Sethi is the editor of *Global InCH*, a journal dedicated to living heritage, and oversees the Asia InCH Encyclopaedia, a comprehensive resource on the heritage arts, textiles, and crafts of India and the broader South Asian region. Her research explores the intersections of culture, history, and craftsmanship, focusing on textiles, arts, and crafts and their contemporary continuities in design, fashion, and everyday life. She has authored several key publications, including *Handmade for the 21st Century: Traditional Indian Textiles* (UNESCO), *Embroidering Futures: Repurposing the Kantha* (India Foundation for the Arts), and *Designers Meet Artisans: A Practical Guide* (UNESCO, translated into Spanish and French). Her work also includes *Painters, Poets, Performers: The Patuas of Bengal* (IFA) and *Kasuti Embroideries* (forthcoming), along with numerous essays on the cultural histories of hand-making, sustainability, and policy in both national and international publications. Dr. Sethi serves on advisory committees in India, Japan, Sri Lanka, the UK, and Argentina, most recently as a member of the editorial board for UNESCO's State of the Education Report, focusing on culture and arts education. She is the founder-trustee of the Craft Revival Trust, India, and Director of the League of Artisans, UK.

Sumesh Sharma is a Mumbai-based curator focusing on alternate art histories, socioeconomics, and cultural politics. His work engages with immigrant cultures, vernacular modernism, and Black consciousness. He curated Dak'Art 2016 and presently works on an extensive research project on aesthetics and its new philosophical bearings that emerge from India and Africa. In January 2023 he curated Mind's Cupboards, a retrospective of the artist Lalitha Lajmi at the National Gallery of Modern Art, Mumbai, Something Else, Cairo, in November 2023; and a trans-generational collaborative public art project in Paris on the contexts of immigration and against the continuous racialisation of social dialogue by the right wing. He curated Manu Parekh's retrospective exhibition *60 Years of Selected Works* at the National Gallery of Modern Art, Mumbai, in 2018. He co-founded the Clark House Initiative in 2010 with Zasha Colah. He is currently the Artistic Director of Strangers House, Mumbai.

Paola Ugolini's curatorial practice is distinguished by her focus on female artists and the dynamic intersections of Video Art, Body Art, Performance, and Feminist theory. Her exhibitions have been featured in prominent institutions worldwide, including the Museum of Modern Art (MoMA) and MoMA PS1 in New York; the Galleria Nazionale d'Arte Moderna, MAXXI, and MACRO in Rome; and Museo 900 in Florence. She currently serves as a curator at the In Between Art Film Foundation in Rome.

Paola Ugolini's expertise extends to academia, where she has held visiting professorships in Curatorial Practice and Gender Studies at Roma Tre University, John Cabot University, NABA Academy, Brera Academy of Fine Arts, and Rome Fine Art Academy. Since May 2021, she has also been a visiting professor at the master's program in Art Management, Communication, and Cultural Politics at IUAV University in Venice. Her recent publication, Artists and *Feminism in Italy: A Non-Hegemonic Way to Look at Art History*, released in 2022 by Christian Marinotti Editore, offers a critical exploration of feminist perspectives within Italian art history.

Artists

Madhvi Parekh (b. 1942, Gujarat, India; lives and works in New Delhi) is a self-taught artist whose practice navigates the confluence of personal memory, mythology, and the enduring traditions of Indian folk art. Her compositions are rich with dreamlike figures, spiritual abstractions, and symbolic narratives that evoke the dichotomies of male and female, real and surreal. Drawing from the visual lexicon of her childhood and the intricate craft traditions of Indian women, Madhvi Parekh transforms folk motifs into a deeply personal and universal storytelling medium.

Her artistic achievements have been widely recognised. In 1975, she received a Certificate of Merit at the Women's International Exhibition at the Rashtrapati Bhavan, New Delhi, and in 1979, she was honoured with the National Award by the Lalit Kala Akademi. Madhvi Parekh was also the subject of *Dwitiya*, a documentary film produced by the Ministry of External Affairs, Government of India, alongside her husband, artist Manu Parekh.

Madhvi Parekh's work has been exhibited globally, with notable shows in New York, London, Amsterdam, Seoul, and Hong Kong. Her pieces are part of prestigious collections, including the Metropolitan Museum of Art. In 2022, she was featured in the Frieze Masters London Spotlight on Women Artists of the 20th Century. A retrospective of her work, The Curious Seeker, debuted at DAG, New Delhi in 2017, before travelling to DAG, Mumbai in 2018 and DAG, New York in 2019. Most recently, in 2024, she collaborated with Karishma Swali and the Chanakya Foundation for Cosmic Garden, a Collateral Event of the 60th International Art Exhibition – La Biennale di Venezia. This interdisciplinary project reflects Parekh's enduring engagement with storytelling, craft, and the boundless possibilities of collective artistic dialogue.

Manu Parekh (b. 1939, Gujarat, India; lives and works in New Delhi) is a leading figure in contemporary Indian art, renowned for his instinctive and powerful works that explore the interplay of the tangible and the sensual — earth, fertility, and the human body. Deeply inspired by the modernist innovations of Paul Klee and Rabindranath Tagore, Parekh cultivated his artistic language under the mentorship of S.B. Palsikar at the J.J. School of Art. His early fascination with Gujarat's vernacular traditions, such as embroidery, informed his unique modernist expression, bridging the worlds of local craft and international art movements.

Manu Parekh's career was profoundly shaped by his work with the Weaver's Service Centre and the Handicrafts and Handlooms Export Corporation of India, guided by Indian cultural activist Pupul Jayakar. These roles enabled him to travel extensively across western, northern, and eastern India, deepening his engagement with vernacular art forms and renewing his artistic vocabulary. This synthesis of modernism and regional craft imbues his practice with a distinct vitality and cultural resonance.

Over the decades, Manu Parekh has exhibited widely, earning critical acclaim and numerous accolades. He was awarded the President of India's Silver Plaque and the All-India Fine Arts and Crafts Society Award in 1972, the National Award of the Lalit Kala Akademi in 1982, and the Padma Shri by the Government of India in 1992. In 2013, he received an honorary Doctorate in Literature from Rabindra Bharati University, Kolkata. Him and his wife, artist Madhvi Parekh, were the subjects of *Dwitiya*, a documentary film produced by the Ministry of External Affairs, Government of India. In 2024, he brought his dynamic vision to *Cosmic Garden*, a Collateral Event of the 60th International Art Exhibition – La Biennale di Venezia. Collaborating with Karishma Swali and the Chanakya Foundation, the project underscores his enduring ability to bridge artistic traditions with contemporary relevance, engaging deeply with themes of creation, transformation, and the human experience.

Karishma Swali has devoted her career to the preservation, revival, and contemporary reimagining of India's intangible cultural heritage. Immersed in art and craft from a young age, her work is profoundly shaped by the philosophies of Rabindranath Tagore and Jiddu Krishnamurti. Since 1998, she has led Chanakya International, a globally renowned textile house founded in 1984. In 2015, responding to the socio-economic and environmental challenges facing India's artisanal communities, Karishma Swali founded the Chanakya Foundation. This vision materialised further in 2016 with the establishment of the Chanakya School of Craft, a non-profit institution empowering women through craft education and cultural engagement, fostering autonomy and economic independence.

Over the past 25 years, Karishma Swali has shaped a distinct interdisciplinary language at the intersection of craft and contemporary art. Her practice is marked by collaborations with leading international artists, positioning artisanal knowledge as both medium and method in contemporary cultural discourse. In 2020, Swali and the graduated artisans of the Chanakya School of Craft collaborated with American feminist artist Judy Chicago to create 22 monumental hand-embroidered works, exhibited at the New Museum, New York. In 2021, she partnered with French contemporary artist Eva Jospin to produce Chambre de Soie (Silk Room), a 40-metre immersive installation. This was followed in 2023 by a collaboration with American visual artist Mickalene Thomas, resulting in large-scale, mixed-media portraits exhibited at the Brooklyn Museum. In 2024, Swali and the Chanakya Foundation co-presented Cosmic Garden — a collaboration with Indian artists Madhvi and Manu Parekh — as a collateral event at the 60th International Art Exhibition – La Biennale di Venezia. Most recently, in 2025, En Route, an artistic dialogue with Maria Grazia Chiuri, debuted at the Vatican Apostolic Library as part of its Jubilee Year celebrations.

She received the Grazia Millennial Award for Contemporary Craftsmanship in 2022 and was named to the BoF 500. In 2024, she was honoured with the Badass Art Woman Award (BAWA) for her pioneering work in education through craft. In the same year, she was conferred the Chevalier de l'Ordre national du Mérite. In 2025, she received the Officier dans l'Ordre des Arts et des Lettres from the Consul General of France in Mumbai, on behalf of the French government, and was also awarded the Cavaliere dell'Ordine della Stella d'Italia by the Consul General of Italy.

Chanakya Foundation & Chanakya School of Craft

In response to pressing social, economic, and environmental challenges, Karishma Swali founded the Chanakya Foundation in 2015, an initiative focused on cultural sustainability through education, skill development, and the preservation of India's rich cultural heritage. Building on this vision, the Chanakya School of Craft was established in 2016 as a non-profit institution to empower women by redefining traditional craftsmanship within a contemporary framework. The school honours and evolves India's intangible cultural heritage, offering women pathways to autonomy through the transformative power of craft.

The school's robust 18-month programme immerses students in over 300 hand-embroidery techniques, guided by a curriculum shaped by the legacies of historical women. The programme, structured into two semesters, culminates in an internship that provides hands-on experience in global craft-making traditions. Since its inception, the school has supported a diverse community of over 1,200 women from various socio-economic backgrounds. It also houses a dynamic cultural centre, featuring an artist residency and a 'living museum' that offers public access to live demonstrations of 20 schools of craft by 13th-generation master artisans. This fertile space serves as a hub of innovation, fostering a contemporary dialogue around the enduring relevance of craft.

The Chanakya Foundation and School of Craft reimagine the potential of craft practices, promoting equality, independence, and craft excellence. Their work stands as a testament to the transformative power of collaboration, innovation, and the intergenerational transmission of knowledge, shaping a sustainable future for craft and its practitioners.

Notes

Embroidery as Empowerment
Maria Alicata and Paola Ugolini

1 William Morris (1834–1896) was a British designer, craftsman, and writer. He was among the main founders of the Arts and Crafts movement; he is considered a forerunner of modern design and had a remarkable influence on the architecture and the architects of his time. He founded a design studio in partnership with the artist Edward Burne-Jones and the poet and artist Dante Gabriel Rossetti, which profoundly influenced the decoration of churches and homes in the twentieth century. He also made an important contribution to the regeneration of the traditional arts of weaving and the associated production methods. Moreover, he founded the Society for the Protection of Ancient Buildings (SPAB), which remains to this day a cornerstone for the conservation of historic properties in the United Kingdom.
2 Rozsika Parker, *The Subversive Stitch: Embroidery and the Making of the Feminine* (London: The Women's Press Ltd, 1984), p. 190.
3 Parker, op. cit., foreword and p. 10.
4 Colette, *Earthly Paradise* (London: Secker and Warburg, 1996), p. 205.
5 Margot Waddell is a Fellow of the British Psychoanalytical Society and a visiting lecturer at the Tavistock Clinic. She works in private clinical practice and was previously employed for many years in the NHS, as a child and adolescent psychotherapist in the Tavistock Clinic's Adolescent Department.
6 Margot Waddell, "The Containing Function of Art," in Rozsika Parker, op. cit., p. xix.
7 The Suffragettes were activists in the movement for female emancipation, established in the United Kingdom in 1869 with a view to obtaining the right to vote for women.
8 A. Kawrla, "The Question of Women and Craft, Pre- and Post-Independence India," in *De-/Anti-/Post-colonial Feminisms in Contemporary Art and Textile Crafts*, K. Deepwell, ed. (London: KT press, 2023), pp. 96–97.
9 Ibid.
10 Neelam Raina, "Women's Tacit, Uncoded Knowledge: Ownership and Value in Conflict Zones," in K. Deepwell (ed.), op. cit., p. 123.
11 Hinduism is the dominant religion of the Indian subcontinent and is thought to be the most ancient religion in the world. Its practitioners refer to it as Sanatama Dharma (the eternal law). In its modern form, this religion is composed of three great traditions: Shaivism, Vaishnavism, and Shaktism, whose followers considered Shiva, Vishnu, and Shakti (or Devi), respectively, to be the supreme deity.
12 *Kantha*, also spelled *kanta* or *qanta*, is a type of craft embroidery that is widespread in Bangladesh and in the Eastern regions of India, in particular in the Indian states of West Bengal, Tripura, and Odisha. *Sujani* is a type of embroidery that was first created in the village of Bahusura, in the Indian state of Bihar. It is said that *sujani* began around the 1920s and was practised only by Rajput women for personal use.
13 Traditional art forms that arose in Andhra Pradesh and Rajasthan more than 400 years ago, where the central figure is always surrounded by secondary figures.
14 Ganesha, son of Shiva and Parvati, is depicted as having an elephant's head with just a single tusk, a prominent belly, and four arms, as he straddles or is served by a mouse, his vehicle. He is the god of wisdom and acuity. The myth that recounts his creation has it that his mother, Parvati, created him so that he could keep guard while she bathed. So as not to be disturbed, she mixed a drop of her perspiration with clay and thus moulded the form of a baby, which she then instilled with life. Once animated, she required the child to protect the door of her bathroom and to stop anyone from entering. The child had beautiful features, and scrupulously obeyed his mother's orders, going so far as to prevent even his own father, Shiva, from entering. And so it was that Shiva, overwhelmed by rage as was his wont, threw himself on Ganesha, cutting his head clean off. In despair and fury, Parvati refused to make peace with Shiva. Shiva then gave the order to his underlings to place atop the little one the head of the first being that they came across as they headed northwards. The first creature they saw was an elephant, and so its head was duly position on the decapitated body of the unfortunate youngster. On seeing this strange configuration, everyone was horrified and repulsed by the child. Only his mother, Parvati, thanks to her infinite love, glimpsed beauty in him and ensured that whoever looked at him would see it, too. Thanks, then, to Parvati, the Divine Mother, Ganesha was adored by all and always succeeded in inspiring affection and sympathy.
15 Krutika Behrawala, "Modernist Flashback: Tour 60 Years of Manu Parekh's Art in a Mumbai Show," *Hindustan Times*, 2018, accessed 2 April, 2025, https://www.hindustantimes.com/mumbai-news/modernist-flashback-see-60-years-of-manu-parekh-s-artworks-in-a-mumbai-show/story-9UTUA06FfwEHcDzwrWHcvI.html.
16 Vasudeo S. Gaitonde (1924–2001) was a pioneering Indian abstract painter who revolutionised the art scene with his meditative, colour-driven canvases. Gaitonde studied at the Sir J. J. School of Art in Mumbai and was closely associated with the influential Bombay Progressive Artists' Group in the 1940s. "V. S. Gaitonde's Century: Celebrating a Master Abstractionist," accessed April 2, 2025, https:// dagworld.com/v-s-gaitonde-s-century-celebrating-a-masterabstractionist. html.

A Future Foretold: The Past, Present and Unfolding Future of Embroidery
Dr. Ritu Sethi

1 One of the principal Upanishads, the classical Sanskrit text Brihadaranyaka Upanishad, is one of the early Upanishadic scriptures of Hinduism and contains, among other subjects, a treatise on Atma (self), passages on metaphysics, ethics, and a yearning for knowledge. It is estimated to have been mainly composed in the 7th to 6th century BCE. Rolf Elberfeld, "Sensory Dimensions in Intercultural Perspective and the Problem of Modern Media and Technology," in *Technology and Cultural Values: On the Edge of the Third Millennium*, ed. Peter D. Hershock, Marietta Stepaniants, and Roger T. Ames (University of Hawaii Press, 2003), pp. 478–90, http://www.jstor.org/stable/j.ctvvn5ws.32.
2 On evidence of dye technology based on the unearthing of a fragment of madder dyed cotton, see Upinder Singh, *A History of Ancient and Early Medieval India: From the Stone Age to the 12th Century* (New Delhi: Pearson Longman, 2008), pp. 106–15.
3 E. B. Cowell, ed. *The Jātaka: or Stories of the Buddha's Former Births. Volume III, Book 6: Chanipāta No. 387 Sūci-Jātaka*, trans. H. T. Francis and R. A. Neil (Cambridge University Press, 1895; republished Pāli Text Society, 1969), accessed 24 December 2024, https://archive.org/details/cu31924072231073/page/n7/mode/2up.
4 Damodar Gupta, Kuttanimatam, ed. Tansukhram Manassukharam Tripathi (T. N. Roy, 1923).
5 Abu'l Hasan al-Mas'udi writings in his work *Meadows of Gold and Mines of Gems*.
6 Syed Nomanul Haq, "Gujarati Sandals in Baghdad: Decolonising history," *Herald Dawn*, November 2016, https://herald.dawn.com/news/1153594.
7 Accounts in Āʾīn-i Akbarī and later European traders recorded details on the *karkhanas* that were spread across the Empire including

embroidery ateliers in Agra, Delhi, Dacca, Burhanpur, Varanasi, and elsewhere.

8 See the court biography *The Jahāngīrnāma*.

9 These opulent textiles, presented to high-ranking officials and foreign emissaries, carried layered diplomatic messages, affirming Mughal supremacy.

10 The embroidery traditions adapted in Hindu and Muslim royal courts in their constellation mirrored the techniques but perhaps not the fabulous magnificence of the Mughal court at its peak. One instance being the Jaipur textile atelier set up during the rule of Maharaja Sawai Jai Singh II (1686–1743), the 29th Kachwaha ruler of Amber who later built the city of Jaipur and made it his capital.

11 By 1643, the English East India Company requested only 60 to 100 quilts annually, mainly for gifting rather than profit due to high costs. John Irwin, *Indian Textile Trade in the Seventeenth Century: Foreign Influences*, India Office Archives, Factory Records Miscellaneous, vol. XII, folio 99, p. 58.

12 Their production ceased in about 1650. Very fine pieces can be seen in museums across the globe.

13 *The Crystal Palace, and its contents: being an illustrated cyclopaedia of the Great Exhibition of the Industry of all Nations, 1851; embellished with upwards of five hundred engravings, with a copious analytical index* (London: W. M. Clark, 1851), p. 224. The 1851 *Great Exhibition of the works of Industry of all Nations* was inaugurated by Queen Victoria in London. Fifty nations and 39 British colonies participated with the Indian "territory" represented by the EIC. There were more than six million visitors to the exhibition.

14 Frank Cundall, ed., *Reminiscences of the Colonial and Indian Exhibition* (London: William Clowes & Sons, 1886), p. 9. The throne itself, of hammered gold, was formerly of Raja Ranjeet Singh, taken by the British at the capture of Lahore.

15 John Forbes Watson, *The Textile Manufactures and the Costumes of the People of India* (George Edward Eyre and William Spottiswoode, 1866), p. 2.

16 First five-year plan, Chapter 1.11: The Determinants of Economic Development, http://planningcommission.gov.in/plans/planrel/fiveyr/index1.html.

17 Chandaben, along with her husband, Kantisen Shroff, came to Kutch on behalf of the Rama Krishna Mission to see what could be done to alleviate the situation.

18 Feruzi Anjirbag, *Shrujan: Under the Embroidered Sky – Embroideries of the Ahirs of Kutch* (Shrujan Trust - Gujarat, 2011).

19 Set up in 1993, Judy Frater, an American anthropologist, textile specialist, and educationist has worked in Kutch for more than 40 years.

20 Sewa Lucknow grew from 31 embroiderers to more than 8000 women in 2015. Information based on conversation with Runa Banerjee, 2 June 2015.

21 Designer and Chairperson Dastkar. Established in 1981.

22 Sethi, Ritu, ed., *Designer Meets Artisan: A Practical Guide* (Craft Revival Trust, 2005), p. 46.

23 This number excludes the many professions associated with the trade. From block-makers and printers who print the patterns, the dry-cleaning community of washer-men and ironers, the tailors, the runners who connect the dots, the cloth merchants, and others.

24 Instituted by government the first national award to an embroiderer was given in 1965 to Shri Fyaz Khan for *chikan* embroidery and to Smt Maheshi Devi for Chamba Rumal embroidery.

25 The first festival was held in 1982 in the United Kingdom. Soon to be followed by others over the decade.

26 Activist and advocate of traditional weaving and handloom techniques Sally Holkar is best known as the revivalist of the Maheshwari saree. Known for her work at the Rehwa Society and the Women Weave Charitable Trust, Holkar's work has been focused on making handloom production more sustainable and accessible, with a specific focus on rural India.

27 Reema Nanavaty is the head of Self-Employed Women's Association of India (SEWA). Under her leadership, SEWA has grown to become the single largest union of informal sector workers in India.

Is Collaboration the Fragrance of the Cosmic Garden?
Sumesh Sharma

1 Latika and Balbir Singh Katt were sculptors and partners who worked extensively with stone, scrap metal, and bronze. They were based in the city of Banaras on the banks of the Ganges, where Balbir Singh Katt taught at the Banaras Hindu University. "Latika Katt," Jehangir Nicholson Art Foundation website, jnaf.org/artist/latika-katt/.

2 Bhakti movement: *bhakti*, in Hinduism, is a movement emphasising the mutual intense emotional attachment and love of a devotee toward a personal god and of the god for the devotee. "Bhakti," *Encyclopædia Britannica*, britannica.com/topic/bhakti.

3 Madhubani Paintings – Also known as Mithila or Maithil painting, Madhubani painting is a ritual and decorative art form primarily practised by women of the Madhubani region to make impermanent murals on the mud walls. Floor and wall paintings, known locally as *aipanas* and *bhitti chitras* respectively, were traditionally painted to mark occasions such as births, marriages, and religious events, while the more elaborate paintings, called *kohabars*, were reserved for marriage ceremonies. Since the 1960s and 1970s, the district town of Madhubani in northern Bihar has come to be considered a centre for the art form. "Madhubani Painting," MAP Academy website, 21 April 2022, mapacademy.io/article/madhubani-painting/.

17 Shiva (or Siva), one of the main Hindu deities. The figure of this many-sided god — the subject of an elaborate mythology and the embodiment of a sophisticated form of metaphysics — was fleshed out and consolidated with the Puranas, which are philosophical and religious texts transcribed between the third and twelfth century. This Shiva is the result of a gradual evolution in which the characteristics of the god ended up encompassing those of many other deities, such as Agni, god of fire, and Indra, god of the Vedic pantheon, as well as an enormous number of minor and local divinities associated with sex, death, and fertility. Over the course of time, as also occurred within the religious traditions, the figure of Shiva would take on different values and features, incarnating aspects and meanings that at times appeared contradictory. He is the calmest and most perfect of the ascetics (*mahāyogin*), but he is also the unbridled and sensual cosmic dancer (*naṭarāja*), the one who, naked, tempts the wives of the ascetics; he is the force that dissolves and destroys worlds, but also that which regenerates, preserves, and supports them; he is the parent who cuts the head off the child, but also he who dispenses happiness and spiritual well-being.

18 According to Indian mythology, Devas and Asuras are two classes of primordial beings generated by their shared progenitor Prajapati at the origin of the manifestation of the current universe. They are locked in an eternal battle with each other. In the most ancient Vedic texts, the term indicates "a being endowed with occult power," which could be benevolent or malevolent. Deva (devanāgarī: देव, Vedic Sanskrit: devá) is a Sanskrit term that, when used as an adjective, denotes what is divine or celestial, whereas when it is used as a noun (gendered male) it indicates a deity or a god. Only rarely is it used to signify a malevolent demon.

EXHIBITION

COSMIC GARDEN
Presented by the Chanakya Foundation

Manu Parekh, Madhvi Parekh,
Karishma Swali and Chanakya School of Craft

April 20, 2024— November 24, 2024
Salone Verde — Art & Social Club, Venice

Curatorial Team
Curators: Maria Alicata, Paola Ugolini
Assistant Curator: Giulia Mastropietro

Chanakya Foundation
Chairperson: Karishma Swali
Director of Atelier: Anisha Shetty
Vice President: Raja Ghanta
Senior Designers: Prashanth Naik, Daniel Mahimainathan
Senior Brand Manager: Ragini Vijay
Community Building Manager: Sunayan Shahani Vaidya
Associate Brand Manager: Srishti Roy

Master Artisans, Chanakya Ateliers
MD Badruddin, MD Firoz, MD Moniruddin, MD Sharif Khan, MD Taukir, Ashok Kumar Bera, Prafullo Dhara, Nazrul Khan, Abbas Uddin Koyal, Abdul Hanif Jamader, Samsuddin Mallick, Rashid Ali Naiya, Arup Patra, Shaikh Selim

Graduates, Chanakya School of Craft
Anita Auti, Veena Bavkar, Nilam Bhujbal, Gayatri Choube, Snehal Kasar, Ruksar Khan, Suvarna Mahale, Vaishali Mahadik, Rekha Phapale, Muskan Shaikh, Pramila Shitole, Sayali Shirke, Sayra Shaikh

Exhibition Design
Gerardo Cejas, Inmovimento Design

Production Partners
A Consulting SRL: Bianca Arrivabene, Mafalda Arrivabene, Benedetta Cazzaniga, Sue Ellen Pavin, Mascia Pavon
Graphic Design: Elisa Calore

Project Mediation
Giovanni Giacomo Paolin

Technical Partner
ILTI Luce (Nemo Group)

Press and Public Relations
Pickles PR: Rhiannon Pickles, Vanessa Saraceno, Shauna Serra

Internship Programme
Università Iuav di Venezia
Università Ca' Foscari

Interns
Ilaria Missiaggia, Gloria Radicchia, Alissia Lucini, Linda Pietrobelli, Maria Pia Testa, Ambra Zamengo, Carlotta Savio, Lorenzo Dell'Agnese, Francesca Gaspari, Federico Stocco, Elena Grandi, Serena Tomaino, Ana Maria Cernei, Lisamaria Bellini, Angelica Loss, Bhakti Böninger, Chiara Uliana, Francesco Cipollini, Elisa Arosti, Elena Barison, Sarah Boccia, Francesca Facchi, Gabriele Ferrario, Gaia Franzin, Alessia Leoni, Costanza Mazzucchelli, Mariachiara Nurra, Sara Pasquini, Sara Pellizzer, Sofia Saccenti, Francesca Strozzo

Photography
Hashim Badani
Sahiba Chawdhary
Abner Fernandes
Ryan Martis
Vismay Mirgal
Daniele Zoico / Danto Production

Videography
Raunaq Chopra
Daniele Zoico / Danto Production

With Grateful Acknowledgement to
Delphine Arnault
Maria Grazia Chiuri
Olivier Bialobos
Rachele Regini

With Special Thanks to
Cristina Baldacci (Università Ca' Foscari)
Maria Luisa Frisa (Università Iuav di Venezia)
Gabriele Monti (Università Iuav di Venezia)
Federico Palazzari (CEO, Nemo Lighting)

PUBLICATION

Patron and Principal Funder
Karishma Swali and the Chanakya Foundation

Edited by
Maria Alicata, Paola Ugolini

Project Management
Project Manager: Ragini Vijay
Assistant Project Manager: Srishti Roy
Translations: Gordon Fisher

Photography
Hashim Badani
Sahiba Chawdhary
Abner Fernandes
Ryan Martis
Daniele Zoico / Danto Production